IN SEARCH OF THE
SOUTH
POLE

KARI HERBERT & HUW LEWIS-JONES
INTRODUCTION BY SIR RANULPH FIENNES

IN SEARCH OF THE
SOUTH
POLE

CONWAY

Text © Kari Herbert and Huw Lewis-Jones, 2011
Volume © Conway, 2011

First published in Great Britain in 2011 by Conway,
an imprint of Anova Books Ltd
10 Southcombe Street
London W14 0RA
www.conwaypublishing.com
www.anovabooks.com

10 9 8 7 6 5 4 3 2 1

A catalogue record for this book is available from the British Library.

ISBN 9781844861378

Distributed in the U.S. and Canada by:
Sterling Publishing Co., Inc.
387 Park Avenue South
New York, NY 10016-8810

Edited by Christopher Westhorp
Designed by Nichola Smith and Georgina Hewitt
Printed and bound by L.E.G.O. s.p.a., Italy

Cover: Having unloaded some supplies, Captain Robert Falcon Scott, Edward Wilson and Teddy Evans make the long journey back across the pack-ice to *Terra Nova*, 9 January 1911.

Endpapers: A limited-edition centenary silkscreen print 'Polar Sky', which was created for this book by award-winning illustrator Andy Smith. Over the course of this project polar explorers, travellers, scientists and authors were asked to describe the South Pole in just five words. Their responses were combined with some phrases from books written during the 'heroic age' of exploration, and together these provided the inspiration for this skyscape of dreams and imagining.

Title page: A ground storm of blowing snow over the sea-ice of McMurdo Sound with Ross Island and Mount Erebus in the distance. Photograph by Ann Hawthorne.

Contents: 'Adventure tourists' practise on the Antarctic plateau in preparation for a 'last degree' trek to the South Pole. Photograph by Bryan and Cherry Alexander.

CONTENTS

PREFACE
FOOTPRINTS IN THE SNOW

It is not down in any map; true places never are.

HERMAN MELVILLE, 1851.

The South Pole is an imaginary spot in a highly unimaginable land-scape, a point somewhere piercing the two-mile-high surface of a variable ice-cap. The Pole is a mathematical conception, and its exploitation in the past half-century just shows what a trouble people can be led into by mathematicians.

DOUGLAS MCKENZIE, FROM *OPPOSITE POLES*, 1963.

After eight months they find the bodies. It is midday, 12 November 1912. They are 11 miles to the south of a stash of food, the means for continuing life. The top of a tent is just discernable, its sides covered by the drifting snow. Brushing some away, a flap of green canvas appears. Just nearby to windward, two pairs of ski sticks and a bamboo poke feebly through the carapace of ice, the remnants of the mast of a sledge. It takes some time, but eventually the tent is dug out and soon they can see outlines. There are three men inside.

On the floor cloth there is a small pile of letters. A chronometer, a flag, some socks, a few books. There is a lamp formed from a tin and some wick fashioned from the hair of a finnesko boot. It has been used to burn the little methylated spirit that remained before the light went out. Later, the tent poles are taken away, so the tent itself covers the bodies. And over them they build a cairn and erect a cross made out of a ski. By the time they finish it is almost midnight. The sun dips low above the South Pole, the Great Ice Barrier is almost in shadow. The sky blazes in sheets of iridescent cloud.

Beneath a sleeping bag they had found a green wallet, and within it a small brown diary. On its cover were simple instructions. The finder was to read what was inside and then bring it home. Spoken in hushed tones, this is the

Right: An Adélie penguin and sledges leave their tracks in the snow, photographed by Herbert Ponting, 8 December 1911.

first time the terrible tragedy that befell Captain Scott and his companions is read. It is the moment that news of the South Pole truly begins its remarkable journey, as the 11 men of the search party gather together on the ice and listen to the story. It is also the first time that Amundsen's achievement is confirmed. Here is the proof, offered up by the men who had the misfortune to see his victory with their own eyes. Here it is, scribbled in pencil, for generations to follow. Here it is, written for the benefit of all mankind, a message from the dead.

The Geographic South Pole, or International Reference Pole, can be found at 90° South latitude – it is one of only two points where all the mathematical lines of longitude meet. The Antarctic ice sheet on which men stand today moves about 30 feet (9 metres) each year. American geology teams resurvey the location annually and drive a metal pole topped with a bronze marker into the snow there to show its position, like a kind of birthday candle planted in the icing of some immense cake. There are other poles, too, both real and imagined. The Celestial Ephemeris Pole, the spin axis of the Earth, is somewhere about 30 feet (9 metres) away, wobbling invisibly in a circle during the year, compelled by the inner core of the Earth, the pull of the Moon and the motion of the tides – astrophysicists are still searching for all its secrets. A Ceremonial South Pole squats about 100 feet (30 metres) away; it has no scientific purpose, but all the flags of the Antarctic Treaty nations fly there in a half circle around a reflective silver ball on a

Below: Captain Robert Falcon Scott (centre) and his men outside the hut at Cape Evans, a group shot taken by Herbert Ponting on 13 April 1911.

striped barber's pole – here photographs are made and visitors create their own chapters of personal history. The Magnetic South Pole is an ever-wandering spot where a compass needle spins wildly around, unable to dictate a direction. Once in a great while it actually flips with its northern counterpart. At present the Magnetic South Pole is almost 2,000 miles (3,200 kilometres) away, hovering in the frigid seas off the coast of the Antarctic continent. Yet, there is just one South Pole that, like a siren song, drew men for over a century to death and to glory.

This is a world that offers no welcome. There are places on this frozen continent where your footprints will outlive you. Man is only a visitor here. Although the South Pole is now a workplace too, it is, of course, not at all like any *other* place. It is a landscape of the imagination, a region of heart's desire. It is a place where ambitions can run riot; where energy, and vanity, can freeze in an instant; and where the best-laid plans surrender to a turn in the weather. It is a place from which some never return. Their dreams escape into the wild.

In 1912, the western world is watching, waiting, hoping – hearts and minds are focussed on one desolate spot at the very end of the Earth, as two expeditions endeavour to be the first to conquer the South Pole. When the news is finally announced that the South Pole has been conquered by Roald Amundsen and his Norwegian team, Scott and his companions are still struggling north in a bid to reach safety. Men call out in the wind, but soon they are too exhausted to speak. The blizzard envelops them and they are confined to their tent. Eventually, Scott is alone. All his companions have died. He knows that rescue is unlikely; he waits for death.

In time the storm passes and there is nothing but silence until later that year when the search party discovers their tent. The drama of Scott's demise is soon enshrined in polar legend, his failure glorified into a national achievement. Initially lionized by the public as a figure of selfless heroism, chivalry and scientific endeavour, Scott's reputation has gone on many journeys in the century after his death and our fascination with Antarctica is as acute as ever. However, this is a book not just about Scott and Amundsen, a subject that still has the power to reveal fierce loyalties and spark bitter debate; there are plenty of books covering that ground and a centenary year will no doubt yield many others. We hope to offer something different, with a broader outlook. We have covered some unfamiliar ground and found new voices and insights. There is, of course, much more to the South Pole than that first unfolding drama.

This is a visual history of a cultural phenomenon, a 'biography' of the South Pole itself. Examining a number of expeditions to Antarctica – alongside Amundsen's triumph and Scott's tragedy – the South Pole is revealed as an enduring cultural icon. A century on from the epics of the 'heroic age', we search for the ongoing value of polar achievement and consider why people are still drawn to this bleak and inhospitable blank on the map.

Top: A souvenir brochure from the Royal Command Performance of the film 'Scott of the Antarctic', released in 1948. Produced by Ealing Studios, and directed by Charles Frend, the actor John Mills played the lead role of the doomed explorer. The outdoor scenes were shot largely on location in Norway.
Bottom: Until the mid-1960s Captain Scott was still characterized as a 'famous fighter', courageous until the end – a hero for each new generation of boys, who read about his exploits in comics such as *Valiant*. Scott's reputation suffered in the decades that followed and it has only begun to recover in recent years.

Above: The British Antarctic Territory stamp set from 1973, showing a line of 'illustrious international polar explorers', from the pioneer navigator James Cook through to modern aviators Hubert Wilkins and Lincoln Ellsworth. The issuing of stamps was, for a long time, a central part of sovereignty in this remote land. The United Kingdom is one of seven sovereign states to have historically registered a claim here, extending from the coast to the South Pole itself.

This is a story about a continent of nothingness, which can, in its unique way, be a story about everything. Although Antarctica is countless millennia old, only recently did it feature on the horizon of humankind to become an object of international attention, ambition and obsession. On the South Pole's hundredth birthday, this book is a scrapbook of sorts, showing happiness and heartache, dreams and despair. Like many things, this is neither complete, nor is it definitive. We have been selective, and any errors and omissions are ours alone.

The polar plateau is a dull, empty and featureless place where dismay seeps into your skin. Yet, it is also somewhere that can lift your soul at the same time as it chills your blood. The home of deep crevasses and fierce winds; a world where men can easily become lost, yet also a place where others travel far to find themselves. The South Pole is fickle and capricious. Humans go there at their peril.

This is a land where heroes are made. An environment made for a man to test himself and to come closer to understanding the depths of his courage. For now Ernest Shackleton's star is resurgent, while Scott is cast as his opposite, indecisive and incompetent. Scott should indeed shoulder his share of the blame for the disaster that enveloped him and his companions, but he is not the villain that he has been made out to be. The scientific legacy of his expedition may yet prove the more lasting achievement.

Unfortunately, in recent decades the South Pole has also been an open page for bitter debate and recrimination. Reputations of heroes past have been uncharitably attacked and both success and failure distorted. Scott's expedition is reframed as foolhardy and calamitous. Small mistakes and human failings have been exaggerated to obscure virtues and real achievements. Hindsight makes for easy criticism. It was a storm of unprecedented severity that denied Scott and his men survival. Even the fact that he wrote beautifully under awful circumstances has been used against him – a clear sign, say Scott's detractors, of his cynicism and eye for posterity. This is surely too much.

Antarctica is an uncompromising place that can kill the very best. The South Pole offers a perfect stage for human dramas to be revised and re-enacted. No doubt there will be new villains, as well as reconfigured heroes. A problem, some say, is that those who retell the stories have never been to the Antarctic, organized a voyage of their own, experienced a southern winter and its cold, or led men on expedition. Cherry-Garrard once wrote that 'it is difficult for those who have never been to the Antarctic to write about it'. Yet, there exists an Antarctic far from the ice itself: the South Pole in the landscape of the mind, which is dreamed of, wished for and worried about; the dramatic terrain that is presented in lecture halls, celebrated in books, or flickers in televisual fantasies, alive with danger and adventure. This is the *Journey Nowhere*, the *Great White Everything*, the *Silent Nothing*. The art of exploration truly is in its storytelling; it is a creative activity, as much as a physical pursuit. It is not necessary to travel as far as the Antarctic to understand the appeal of these tales of endurance.

One hopes history will be kind to Scott, although that will depend on who writes it. We prefer our account to be fair and appreciative. By opening their diaries and sharing their words, the men who ventured south tell their own stories. We have also interviewed scores of seasoned travellers and polar scientists to get closer to the actual experience of being there. Between them our modern contributors have spent almost a century on the ice.

Left: Norwegian Roald Amundsen (right), the first man to reach the South Pole, is greeted in New York by admirers during his lecture tour of the United States. To Amundsen's right stands Sir Ernest Shackleton, another hero to many.

As part of his grand plan to cross to the South Pole and beyond, Shackleton sent 28 men to lay supply depots for him on the other side of the continent. Although 'The Boss' is revered today as the polar leader 'who never lost a man', his Ross Sea party was woefully under-equipped. Disaster struck on 6 May 1915 as a blizzard blew their ship, *Aurora*, out to sea and left ten men stranded on the shore. Impenetrable ice would prevent the ship from returning that season and the men were forced to over-winter. Nonetheless, believing that the lives of Shackleton and his team, who would be trekking across Antarctica, depended on the Ross Sea party laying what depots they could, the men set to with makeshift sledging equipment to ferry stores about, much of the provisions gathered from those left by Scott's fateful expedition. In the process one man collapsed from scurvy and another two were lost in a storm when travelling across the sea-ice in an effort to help their friends.

In search of the South Pole, these men had been forced into a desperate bid to cling onto life. Although frequently ignored in most of the positive accounts about Shackleton, this catastrophic failure is at the same time yet another epic of survival that can go down in the annals of this 'heroic age'. Seven men were finally rescued from Cape Evans by veteran navigator John King Davis in 1917. Even he was shocked by what he saw: 'Their great physical suffering went deeper than their appearance. Their speech was jerky, at times semi-hysterical, almost unintelligible … these events had rendered these hapless individuals as unlike ordinary human beings as any I have ever met. The Antarctic had given them the full treatment.'

Forty years later, another voice speaks from the ice. Paul Siple is the leader of a team of 18 men. A permanent base has just been built at the South Pole. It is the austral summer of 1957. His party has become the first to spend a winter here; the first men to see the sun set and then rise again at the very end of the Earth. 'We were like men who had been fired off in rockets to take up life on another planet', he described. 'We were in a lifeless, and almost featureless world. However snug and comfortable we might make ourselves, we could not escape from our isolation. We were now face to face with raw nature so grim and stark, that our lives could be snuffed out in a matter of minutes.' This is the real South Pole – a daily reality, a lived experience.

There is far more to be found here than just the story of Captain Scott's struggle. So, let us travel southwards, doubtful of a safe return, but hopeful of a homecoming. Come across the sea where the icebergs roll and the air grows 'wondrous cold', and take a step with us in search of the meaning of the Pole. We race across the polar plateau, to find a lone tent, or later perhaps a signpost and a flag, a ring of oil drums, or even a vast scientific station. Bewildered, perhaps, by this century of progress, we rejoin the explorers of the past in their struggle back to the coast. Away from the claws of the winter blizzard and the burning rays of the summer sun, the bodies of Scott and his men are entombed deep within the ice, inching slowly towards the sea.

St Ives, 2011.

Right: Captain Scott's ship *Terra Nova* framed in the distance from within a cavern in a stranded iceberg, 5 January 1911. The photographer Herbert Ponting was captivated by this grotto, writing that it was 'the most wonderful place imaginable'. On this occasion, the scientists Griffith Taylor and Charles Wright went with him to admire it, providing this now famous shot with its human scale.

INTRODUCTION
THIS ENDLESS HORIZON

SIR RANULPH FIENNES

I stood for the first time at the South Pole on 15 December 1980. I was exhausted, relieved, and perhaps a little confused by what I found there. Where brave Scott had struggled manfully, only to come across Norwegian tracks and then discover the outlines of a tent holding fast on the desert of ice around him, I found a large American scientific base, obscured that morning by a thick mist. It was a set piece of prefabricated huts, oil drums, woollen socks, and bearded men sustained by a fug of central heating and obscure scientific data. Having travelled for over 1,000 miles (1,600 kilometres) across this vast plateau from the coast in Queen Maud Land, we were pleased to be taken in. We ate with some of the scientists in their canteen and washed dishes in exchange. I was also given the task of refilling their ice cream machine.

Previous pages: The emperor penguin rookery on the edge of the Weddell Sea at Halley, photographed by Joan Myers.

Above: The British adventurer Sir Ranulph Fiennes, photographed by Mike Stroud during their epic crossing of the continent to the Ross Ice Shelf. The pair reached the South Pole on 16 January 1993, and in doing so Fiennes became the first man to have travelled overland to the South Pole twice.

We stayed for four days or so with our new friends at the South Pole, and had a game of cricket and a few laughs before continuing on our way. There was no time for celebration though as our journey was only half done, and we had a huge slog to complete before reaching our base on the far side of the continent. For Scott, the merest sign of a human presence here was a rude shock, a fatal blow perhaps with still some 800 miles (1,300 kilometres) of 'solid dragging' yet to face in the hope of reaching safety. 'Great God! This is an awful place', he despaired that night, writing in his journal as his companions cooked up a warm hoosh of pemmican and biscuit. He nibbled on some chocolate and they shared a cigarette. 'Now for the run home and a desperate struggle', he continued. 'I wonder if we can do it?'

Antarctica is the coldest, windiest, highest, driest, most isolated and least populated of the seven continents. Large swathes of the Moon's surface are better known. It's a place of superlatives, of extremes, of implausible difficulties and unanticipated delights. As a region that had tickled the fancy of cartographers for centuries, it is no surprise that it took time for the continent to surrender its secrets. The early Greeks speculated about the existence of a continent, later cartographers would fill their charts with fabulous landmasses and the words *Terra Australis Nondum Cognita*, 'Southern Land Not Yet Known', inked appealingly across the empty, white spaces.

By the eighteenth century some men of science even suggested a tropical paradise could be found beyond the endless watery horizons of the great Southern Ocean. It was Captain James Cook who finally enlightened the world, literally sailing through speculation to describe instead a terrifying and awesome region where ice-choked seas were rich in seals and whales. His reports, as fate would have it, would entice generations of men to risk their lives in trying their fortune. Maritime explorers and determined merchant adventurers came here from many nations. Their logs and published accounts are masterpieces both of daily detail and fanciful conjecture, yet they sing with the spirit of high confidence, adventure and endeavour, as they successively pushed back the boundaries of the known world. Theirs was the freedom of new things, the beckoning horizon. The gift they enjoyed was the opportunity to sail 'beyond the sunset'. Wanderers among the oceans of ice, these mariners were made 'strong in will to strive, to seek, to find, and not to yield'.

And with them would come those souls who were willing to act out their dreams in the daylight, to brave terrible odds in the name of national glory and geographical knowledge. These were the dangerous men whose ambitions drove them south towards the Pole itself, longing for this much sought-after prize; to make possible all that was uncertain. I was one of many who followed in their footsteps, emboldened by their example to test myself in this most merciless yet beautiful of environments. The legacy of their exploits remains to inspire and confound us. Huw and Kari have created a stylish tribute to the rich history of the Pole, and I commend their work to you wholeheartedly. Treasure this book. In these elegant writings we can hear voices from the Pole and we are able to travel alongside the heroes from the past. There are few who return from the Antarctic unmoved by what they have seen and experienced. Although remote, and out of reach of most, there is something of the South Pole in the hearts of all of us. It's that place to harbour desire and aspiration, a home for that something that calls out to us, urging the human spirit to meet the challenge and the freedom of the wilderness. Layers of hope and thwarted ambition pile up here like drifting snows.

Yet, it's also a place that is so sensually overwhelming it's actually rather difficult to describe. Generations of poets, journalists, artists and adventurers have all tried their damnedest to get to grips with it, to search for the essential soul of the South Pole itself. Some conclude that it's not worth the fuss – it is meaningless, beyond the concerns of rational men. Yet there are many, many more people who just cannot escape its pull, yet they too are often unable to describe exactly why that is. But, of one thing I am certain; this is a *marvellous* land. Although you might not think so when you're lying rigid in your tent waiting for a blizzard to blow itself out, unable to hear anything but the roar of a cruel storm. In time, the tempest recedes, the sky returns and there is nothing but silence once more. Then, when you are finally able to crawl from your sleeping bag and feel the warm sun on your face, and know that you're alive, you come to feel the real joy of this place. Words fail you and they seem at that moment unnecessary. Words, Antarctica reminds us, are not really what the world is made of. Sit and listen awhile. You can hear your heart beat. But don't sit for too long. Keep moving or you may lose some of your fingers and toes.

Antarctica, the last true wilderness, emerges as a symbol of our age and the South Pole is still at the heart of that vision. The continent is a pure evocation of the natural world in this time of great crisis. The way we reconcile our human failings here, and the temptations of abundant resources, may well determine the future of our planet. Yet it is no longer a place apart, to exist only in the mind's eye, or flickering like a mirage somewhere in our imaginations. The activities of man elsewhere may yet pose even greater threats to this world of snow, but for one brief moment emerging from your tent you forget these concerns to simply enjoy the present. This place is always changing, always moving, despite what may seem a deadening stillness. It's a region where history, poetry, science, life itself, all meet in a chaotic drift that can envelop, overwhelm, and inspire you. That is what the South Pole means to me. Each of us, of course, can search for our own Pole amid this endless horizon of ice and dreams.

Exmoor, 2011.

Below: A sighting compass used in the Antarctic by explorers Sir Ranulph Fiennes and Sir Wally Herbert.

CHAPTER 1
THE HIDDEN CONTINENT

The ice shelf is a region of unearthly desolation, a place of strange forebodings stirred by the loss of horizons into an endless encirclement of ice invading the explorer's mind. Man travels here on a surface of white silences, punctuated only by the whispering drift. Such an environment created a new type of explorer, forcing upon him a sterner discipline than anything his discoveries had previously demanded. Antarctica was to prove the most alien of all environments, ice the most intractable of man's opponents.

EDWIN MICKLEBURGH, *FROM BEYOND THE FROZEN SEA*, 1990.

Human beings are not meant to live in Antarctica. The interior of this vast, isolated and inhospitable continent supports no native flora or fauna on which to survive. Anyone who lands on the Antarctic's frozen shores must take all the prerequisites for survival: fuel, food, shelter and clothing.

For early explorers, reaching the continent was challenge enough. Even the most experienced navigators found themselves bewildered by the intensity of the sudden southern storms, treacherous seas, fog and, of course, the ice. If one was lucky enough to overcome such obstacles unscathed, the Antarctic, with its imposing coastline of towering ice-cliffs and sharp, rocky ridges, presented little comfort or reward. Even if a safe landing place could be found, a person's trials were just beginning. Physical discomfort was a given, as polar explorer Anthony Brandt recently recalls:

> The continent is a killer overall. The ice is riddled with crevasses. Its surface is in many places shaped by the wind into sastrugi, as they are known, ice ridges shaped like waves and as hard as steel, and as much as five feet tall. They slow surface movement to a crawl for men and machines alike. The cold and the weather are appalling. Temperatures in the winter regularly reach -70° Fahrenheit. Exposed skin freezes instantly. Eyes freeze shut. Breathing itself is painful. Toes cannot be saved.

Those unfortunate enough to die in this intensely cold, dry desert remain eternally frozen. A century after its death, one of Scott's huskies guards its late master's hut, snarling in perpetuity at any unwelcome visitors.

Yet this enigmatic place has drawn to it some of history's greatest explorers and scientists. Early visitors were stunned by the precariousness of life in such a place, recording in their journals, letters and published accounts the physical and mental misery of the Antarctic experience. 'Polar exploration', opened Apsley Cherry-Garrard in *The Worst Journey in the World*, 'is at once the cleanest and the most isolated way of having a bad time which has been devised.' Even so, many of these men came back time and time again. The motivation behind their return was as varied as their personalities and backgrounds – some of the crew loved being a part of an adventure, others saw such journeys simply as yet another job – but for the leaders of these early expeditions the thirst for the unknown was inextricably linked with their own yearning for fame and a burning nationalistic pride. Antarctica – a place with no immediately discernable wealth or treasures, as had first been imagined – became a canvas on which evocative human stories were painted; a stage for heroic deeds and sizeable egos. Some of the strongest characters were inevitably drawn to the search for the South Pole – a natural goal for an ambitious polar explorer, although in essence it was nothing more than a geographical fantasy, because the discoverer of the Pole could claim to have conquered the very heart of the Antarctic, and there was little more impressive and romantic than that.

Above: The inhospitable coastlines of Antarctica are fringed with glaciers that tumble into the sea, forming formidable ramparts that prevent access to the secrets of the southern continent. Photographed by Sebastian Copeland in February 2006.

Ice Sublime

Stephen J. Pyne, 2011.

The ice was a shock. It's not simply that, as a desert dweller, I find snow exotic. It was the immensity and solitariness of it – its fusion of the simple and the huge – that stunned. The impression it made, perhaps oddly, was aesthetic. The Ice posed for me, as it does for everyone, a challenge in meaning, how to make something out of a scene that is close to nothing. Although I went as a historian, and had to attach myself to scientific parties, I turned to art to interpret Ice into significance.

There were two journeys. One was geographic, from outside in. Like Dante's underworld, Antarctica is a series of concentric rings. Each increases the proportion of ice to air, sea, and earth. The icebergs, the pack ice, the ice shelves, the glaciers, the ice sheets – to trek inward is to move further and further in a realm informed by ice and progressively by ice alone. The ice increases, everything else diminishes. A complex Earth shrinks to a single mineral. The ice not only reduces the world, it reduces itself. It becomes more and more simple, shedding the strata and shearing which gives it texture and history. At the source regions of East Antarctica even snow-flakes disaggregate into diamond dust. The classic journey inland is a journey to the source, but here the source obliterates rather than enlightens.

Right: An explorer skiing amongst the ice on 14 January 1915, shortly before *Endurance* was beset. 'Great pressure ridges thrown up 15 to 20 feet high bear evidence of the terrific force and pressure of the ice in these latitudes', wrote photographer Frank Hurley in his diary.

The second trek is mental. The only descriptive language beyond pidgin traveller is scientific, and certainly when I went, on a space-available basis through the United States Antarctic Program, the only justification was scientific inquiry. Yet the language and conceptual idiom of science broke down as a device to convey meaning at a landscape level or to evoke the eerie emptiness of the scene. The essence of experimental science is reductionism; but the Ice did that on its own, and was already reduced. The language of crystal structure conveyed nothing about the effect of the Ice on the imagination, much less on the sense of self. Robert Scott was right; by itself the pole is 'an awful place'. What began with science would have to end with art.

I can recall exactly the moment of epiphany. I had joined a small party of geologists in the Transantarctic Mountains. We rode snowmobiles from a remote camp to an outcrop near the Evans Neve. The geologists, geochemists mostly, hacked away at the exposed rock for samples. I turned and noticed that wind had scoured away the base of the small nunatak so that a slight depression resulted. It was enough to shift perspective from level ice-plain to one in which it was possible to see ice and sky as bands. There was a stray stone to one side and a comparably sized cloud above. It was a composed scene, not as Romantic landscapists would paint it, but perhaps as a Modern minimalist would. At that instant the problem, for me, became clear. I would use science to make the trek inward, but I would look to aesthetics to arrange it into meaning. The Ice was nature as Modernist and artist.

The initial shock turned from dread to awe. It was not a humane scene, or even a habitable one, but it harked back to the original meaning of sublime as an alloy of terror and transcendence. That vision has never left me.

TERRA AUSTRALIS INCOGNITA

Before the South Pole could be reached, the question to be answered was what exactly lay at the southern ends of the Earth? The idea of Terra Australis Incognita – an unknown continent that existed in the southern hemisphere – was first introduced by Aristotle, who reasoned that a southern landmass must exist to 'balance' the known lands in the northern hemisphere. It seemed a sensible proposal. So much so, in fact, that between the fifteenth and eighteenth centuries this fabled land was depicted on many European maps, even though such a continent remained undiscovered.

Portuguese explorers Bartolomeu Dias and Vasco da Gama had sailed around the southernmost tip of Africa in 1488 and Ferdinand Magellan had proved in the 1520s that South America was not connected to a southern continent by entering the Pacific Ocean from the east. As lands to the south became drawn in sharper focus, curiosity grew as to what lay at the very ends of the Earth.

Naturally there were high hopes that a large, temperate, southern continent existed, for therein lay the possibility of undiscovered riches. The promise of a southern paradise was reinforced by the dreams of such outspoken men as the Royal Society's Dr Alexander Dalrymple, who believed that James Cook would discover an El Dorado inhabited by 'hospitable, ingenious and civil peoples'. 'The scraps from this table', Dalrymple declared in the *Quarterly Review* in 1818, 'would be sufficient to maintain the power, domination and sovereignty of Britain.'

Below: A seventeenth-century Dutch map – *Hemispherius ab Aeqinoctiali Linea, Poli Antarctici –* that shows a landmass labelled 'Ter Australis incognita'.

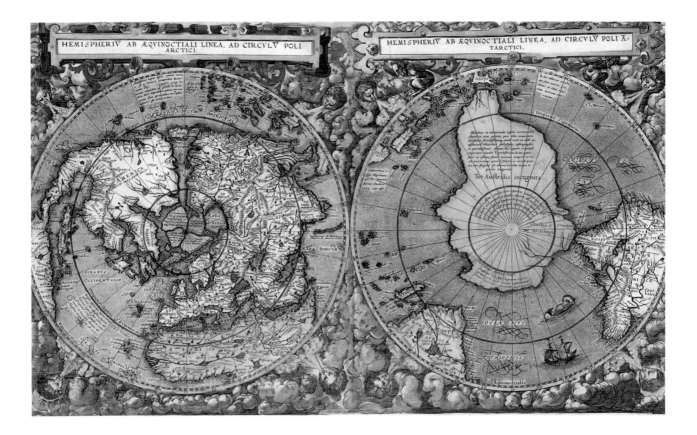

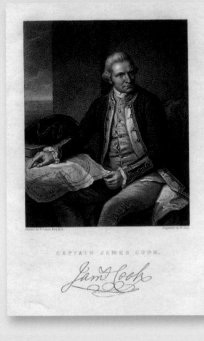

CAPTAIN JAMES COOK.

Above: Captain James Cook gestures to his chart of the Southern Ocean, in a popular engraving published in London by Fisher, Son & Co. It was based on an original portrait painting by Nathaniel Dance in 1776 that was commissioned by the naturalist Sir Joseph Banks, president of the Royal Society from 1778 to 1820, who praised it as an excellent likeness.

FIRST TO THE ANTARCTIC CIRCLE

The Royal Navy's Cook was a natural choice as the potential discoverer of this unknown land. In his first expedition (1768–1771) he had circumnavigated and mapped the coastline of New Zealand, claimed Possession Island for Britain and had become the first recorded European to encounter eastern Australia. Described by the writer Fanny Burney as 'the most moderate, humane and gentle circumnavigator who ever went upon discoveries', Cook was then commissioned by Britain's Admiralty and the Royal Society in 1772 to proceed as far south towards the South Pole as possible and thereby to investigate whether a south polar continent existed.

On 17 January 1773, Cook's ship, HMS *Resolution*, reputedly became the first to cross the Antarctic Circle. Later that day, Cook wrote: '... an immense Feild [sic] composed of different kinds of Ice such as High Hills or Islands, smaller pieces packed close together and what Greenland Men properly call feild ice, a piece of this kind of such extend that I could see no end to it, lay to the south east of us.' Just 300 miles (500 kilometres) away to the east, hidden in cloud, loomed a part of Antarctica that would later be named Enderby Land.

The following year, while sailing in waters off the opposite side of the continent, Cook again nudged his way south, this time to a latitude of 71° 10´S before he encountered impenetrable ice. Disappointed, but conscious of the welfare of his men, Cook wrote in his journal:

> I will not say it was impossible anywhere to get farther to the south, but the attempting it would have been a dangerous and rash enterprise, and what I believe no man in my situation would have thought of. It was indeed my opinion, as well as the opinion of most onboard, that this ice extended quite to the Pole or perhaps joins some land to which it has been fixed from creation .... I, who had ambition not only to go farther than anyone had done before, but as far as it was possible for man to go, was not sorry at meeting this interruption as it in some measure relieved us, at least shortened the dangers and hardships inseparable with the Navigation of the South Polar Rigions.

Even if there was a continent beyond Cook's reach, he could not believe that it was the land of riches being dreamed of back in Britain. Supposing a continent existed at all, Cook thought it 'must lay within the Polar Circle where the Sea is so pestered with ice, that the land is thereby inaccessible [sic]'.

Cook had crossed into the hydrological phenomenon known as the Antarctic Convergence, where the frigid current that flows around Antarctica meets and mixes with the warmer waters of the southern Atlantic, Pacific and Indian oceans. On crossing the boundary, one is confronted with a sudden drop in temperature, turbulent seas, impenetrable fog and ice, and frequent cyclonic polar storms. Below the convergence, the winter pack-ice can extend over an area of nearly eight million square miles (twenty million square kilometres), melting and splitting in the summer to more

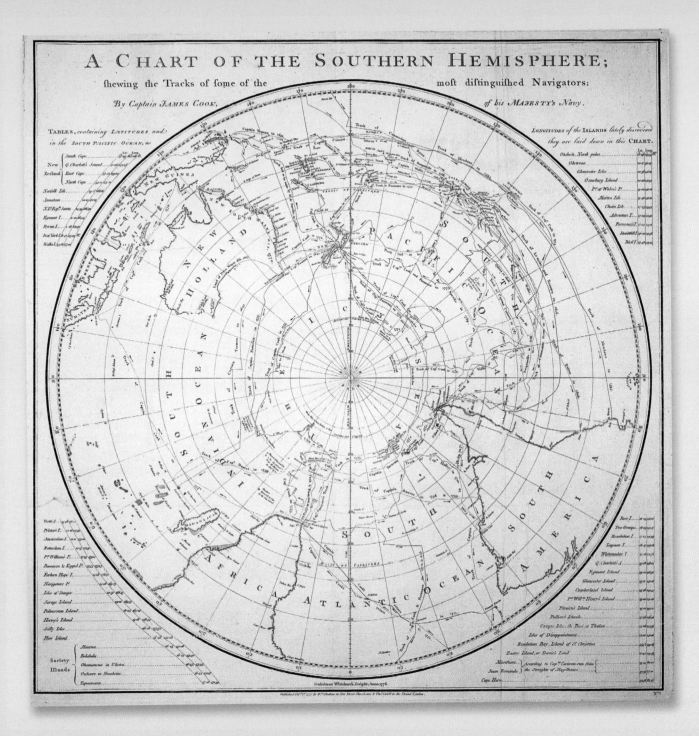

Above: A chart from Captain James Cook's *A Voyage to the South Pole*, published in London in 1777, which tracks the voyages of other explorers and navigators in the southern hemisphere, such as Tasman, Furneaux and Halley.

than one and a half million square miles (four million square kilometres) of ice that cling stubbornly to the frozen coastline. Sailing into this unfamiliar, unpredictable place was a challenge even for one of the greatest navigators in history:

> The risk one runs in exploreing a coast in these unknown and Icy Seas, is so very great, that I can be bold to say, that no man will ever venture farther than I have done and that the lands which may lie to the South will never be explored. Thick fog, snow storms, Intense cold and every other thing that can render

Everlasting Snow

JAMES COOK, SECOND VOYAGE OF EXPLORATION, 1772–1775.

Sunday, 3 January 1773

… We were now about 1½° or 2° of mean of Longitude to the West of the Meridian of Cape Circumcision and at the going down of the sun 4°45′ of Latitude to the Southward of it, the Weather was so clear, that Land even of a Moderate height might have been seen 15 Leagues, so that there could be no land betwixt us and the Latitude of 48°. In short … I am so fully of opinion that there is none that I shall not go in search of it, being now determined to make the best of my way to the East in the Latitude of 60° or upwards, and am only sorry that in searching after those imaginary Lands, I have spent so much time, which will become the more valuable as the season advanceth.

Monday, 4 January 1773

First and middle parts strong gales attended with a thick Fogg Sleet and Snow, all the Rigging covered with Ice and the air excessive cold, the Crew however stand it tolerable well, each being cloathed with a fearnought Jacket, a pair of Trowsers of the same and a large Cap made of Canvas & Baize, these together with an additional glass of Brandy every Morning enables them to bear the Cold without Flinshing.

Friday, 24 November 1773

… made sail to the west, under double-reefed topsails and courses, with a strong gale at north attended with snow and sleet, which froze to the rigging as it fell, making the ropes like wires, and the sails like boards or plates of metal. The sheaves also were frozen so fast in the blocks, that it required our utmost efforts to get a topsail down and up; the cold so intense as hardly to be endured, the whole Sea in a manner covered with ice, a hard gale and a thick fog: under all these unfavourable circumstances it was natural for me to think of returning more to the North, seeing there was no probability of find land here nor a possibility of get[ting] farther to the South; and to

have proceeded to the east, in this latitude, must have been wrong, not only on account of the ice, but because we must have left a vast space of sea to the north unexplored; a space of 24° of latitude, in which a large tract of land might have lain. Whether such a supposition was well grounded, could only be determined by visiting those parts.

Sunday, 30 November 1773

At 4 oClock in the Morning we perceived the C[l]ouds over the horizon to the South to be of an unusual Snow white brightness which we knew denounced our approach to field ice …. In the situation we were in just the Southern half of our horizon was illuminated by the rays of light which were reflected from the Ice to a considerable height. Ninety Seven Ice hills were distinctly seen within the field, besides those on the outside and many of them were very large and looked like a ridge of Mountains rising one above another till they were lost in the clouds …. Such Mountains of Ice as these were, I believe, never seen in the Greenland Seas, as least not that I ever heard or read of, so that we cannot draw a comparison between the Ice here and there; it must be allowed that these prodigious Ice Mountains must add such additional weight to the Ice fields which inclose them as must make a great difference between the Navigating this Icy sea and that of Greenland. I will not say it was impossible any where to get farther to the South, but the attempting it would have been a dangerous and rash enterprise and what I believe no man in my situation would have thought of. It was indeed my opinion as well as the opinion of most on board, that this Ice extended quite to the Pole or perhaps joins to some land, to which it had been fixed from the creation …. As we drew near this Ice some Penguins were heard but none seen and but few other birds or any other thing that could induce us to think any land was near; indeed if there was any land behind this Ice it could afford no better retreat for birds or any other animals than the Ice it self, with which it must have been fully covered. I who had Ambition not only to go farther than any one had done before, but as far as it was possible for man to go, was not sorry at meeting with this interruption as it in some measure relieved us, at least shortened the dangers and hardships inseparable with the Navigation of the South Polar Rigions; Sence therefore, we could not proceed an Inch farther to the South, no other reason need be assigned for my Tacking and Standing back to the north ….

Sunday, 6 February 1774

… I now came to a resolution to proceed to the North and to spend the insuing Winter within the Tropick, if I met with no employment before I came there I was now well satisfied no Continent was to be found in this Ocean but what must lie so far to the South as to be wholly inaccessible for Ice and if one should be found in the Southern Atlantick Ocean it would be necessary to have the whole Summer before us to explore it, on the other hand, if it proves that there is no land there, we undoubtedly might have reached the Cape of Good Hope by April and so have put an end to the expedition ….

Monday, 6 February 1775

We continued to steer to the South and SE till noon at which time we were in the Latitude of 58°15´, Longitude 21°34´ West and seeing neither land nor signs of any, I concluded that what we had seen, which I named Sandwich Land was either a group of Islands or else a point of the Continent, for I firmly believe there is a tract of land near the Pole, which is the Source of most of the ice which is spread over this vast Southern Ocean ... I mean a land of some considerable extent …. It is however true that the greatest part of this Southern Continent (supposeing there is one) must lay within the Polar Circile where the Sea is so pestered with ice, that the land is thereby inaccessible. The risk one runs in exploreing a coast in these unknown and Icy Seas, is so very great,

that I can be bold to say, that no man will ever venture farther than I have done and that the lands which may lie to the South will never be explored. Thick fogs, Snow storms, Intense Cold, and every other thing that can render Navigation dangerous, must be encountered; and these difficulties are greatly heightened, by the inexpressibly horrid aspect of the country; a country doomed by nature never once to feel the warmth of the sun's rays, but to lie buried in everlasting snow and ice …. After such an explanation as this the reader must not expect to find me much farther to the South. It is however not for want of inclination but other reasons. It would have been rashness in me to have risked all which had been done in the Voyage, in finding out and exploreing a Coast which when done would have answered no end whatever, or been of the least use either to Navigation or Geography or indeed any other Science …. These reasons induced me to alter the Course to East, with a very strong gale at North attended with exceeding heavy fall of Snow, the quantity which fell into our sails was so great that we were obliged every now and then to throw the Ship up in the Wind to shake it out of the Sails, otherways them nor the Ship could have supported the weight.

Above: Cook's vessel HMS *Resolution* depicted among the 'islands of ice' in January 1773, a detail from a popular engraving published in London in 1776.

Navigation dangerous one has to encounter, and these diffi- culties are greatly heightened by the inexpressible hor- rid aspect of the Country, a Country doomed by Nature never once to feel the warmth of the Sun's rays, but to lie for ever buried under everlasting snow and ice, whose horrible and savage aspect I have not words to describe.

Many of Cook's men shared his view of the frozen southern world. For George Forster, assistant naturalist and artist, icebergs were less objects of beauty than 'the wrecks of a shattered world', and Cook's repeated attempts to push farther south dismayed many of the crew.

Cook could not be certain that land did or did not exist beyond the farthest point south that they had been, but he eventually concluded: '... should anyone possess the resolution and for- titude to elucidate this point by pushing yet further south than I have done, I shall not envy him the fame of his discovery, but I make bold to declare that the world will derive no benefit from it.' Cook's words shattered the hopes of a nation bent on extending its empire, and it would be almost half a century before any man or ship journeyed beyond the region he had reached.

Cook's three-year journey was by no means unsuccessful. In January 1775 the *Resolution* had come within sight of the island of South Georgia, which would later become a significant land- mark in the history of Antarctic exploration. Cook regarded it as a spectacularly inhospitable place, where: 'Not a tree or a shrub was to be seen, no not even big enough to make a tooth-pick.' He named South Georgia's southern moun- tainous promontory Cape Disappointment, and concluded that the island was a desolate one of no value.

Back in England, Cook's account of the Southern Ocean inspired a new generation of artistic souls. Less than 20 years after Cook's death in 1779, a young poet called Samuel Taylor Coleridge produced in *The Rime of the Ancient Mariner* a piece of work that remains one of the most evocative pieces of polar verse ever written:

And now there came both mist and snow,
And it grew wondrous cold:
And ice, mast-high came floating by,
As green as emerald.

And through the drifts the snowy clifts
Did send a dismal sheen:
Nor shapes of men nor beasts we ken –
The ice was all between.

Cook's published descriptions of the lifeless cold of the far south also moved Percy Bysshe Shelley, who used the region as a backdrop to his heartfelt poem *Lines*, which was written following the death of his wife:

The cold earth slept below,
Above the cold sky shone;
And all around, with a chilling sound,
From caves of ice and fields of snow,
The breath of night like death did flow
Beneath the sinking moon.

Cook also inspired far more commercially minded men. According to the naval explorer, the only saving grace for this frigid outpost was the fact that the surrounding waters teemed with wildlife, such as blue, fin and humpback whales, and gentoo, macaroni and king penguins, which belly-flopped upon the island's beaches to mingle with vast, steaming colonies of seals. Unwittingly, this revelation, perhaps above all others resulting from Cook's expedition, was the one to have the most far-reaching effect. In the following decades, whalers, sealers and merchant adventurers, turned their fleets south, galvanized by the promise of rich bounty. By the time James Weddell arrived in those seas in 1822 he estimated that 'not less than 1 million 200 thousand seals' had been killed in South Georgia since the sealers first arrived. These animals, he noted grimly, 'are now almost extinct'. Driven less by a sense of adventure and more by the prospect of financial gain, sealers were for a time at the forefront of discoveries in the south as they pillaged each colony before searching for the next far-flung island, where the slaughter would continue.

THE MISTS CLEAR

Meanwhile, expeditions with more scientific and geographic purposes had also entered southern waters. Having been forced by severe storms to the far south of Cape Horn in February 1819, English merchant captain

Left: Accompanying Cook during his first voyage was the natural history and botanical artist Sydney Parkinson, who was employed by Joseph Banks. Parkinson's sketches were turned into paintings by a number of artists, including John Frederick Miller who produced 'Penguin, 1776', which was published in 1796 in Miller's book *Cimelia Physica*, illustrating 'rare and curious quadrupeds and birds'.

William Smith perceived what he believed to be a cluster of mountainous islands. After two failed attempts to land, Smith planted the Union Jack and claimed New South Britain for the King. Smith returned later that year to chart what is now known as the South Shetland Islands, as part of a privately funded expedition commanded by Irish-born naval officer Edward Bransfield. After claiming King George Island, Bransfield and Smith sailed south. On 30 January 1820 the pair sighted a long chain of islands extending to the far distance. 'The whole of these', runs the midshipman's log, 'formed a prospect the most gloomy that can be imagined, and the only cheer the sight afforded was that this might be the long sought southern continent as land was undoubtedly seen in latitude 64°S and trending to the eastward.' They had discovered Trinity Land, the northernmost tip of the Antarctic Peninsula, a narrow, spine-like archipelago that stretches northwards from the so-far elusive continent.

There is some debate over who was the first to sight the continent. As Smith and Bransfield approached the peninsula, Russian explorer Baron Thaddeus von Bellingshausen recorded the discovery of ice-cliffs in latitude 69° 21′S. The date was 28 January 1820. Bellingshausen could not be sure that the ice-cliffs were part of the continent, and because of this he was wary of claiming to have made a discovery. It is only in subsequent years that Bellingshausen's sighting has been accepted as having been the first, made just two days before that of Bransfield and Smith some 2,000 miles (3,200 kilometres) away.

Meanwhile, news of William Smith's discovery of the South Shetland Islands had spread quickly through the network of merchantmen in Europe and North America. Eager to make the most of this virgin territory before its resources were drained, American sealer Nathaniel Palmer left his home port of Stonington, in the New England region, aboard the sloop *Hero* and sailed in the company of five vessels towards the South Shetland Islands.

The promise of quick profits from as yet undiscovered, highly populated colonies of seals spurred some of the most successful journeys to the south. Yet, if you were a sealing or whaling captain, the attention that came with being a geographical pioneer was to be avoided at all costs. The locations of any newly discovered territories were guarded jealously. Logbooks and journals were burned so that no trace – of where the sealers had been or were heading to – could be found, other than the carcasses on the beaches. It is entirely possible that the Antarctic was sighted, maybe even landed upon, by sealers before the claims of Smith, Bransfield, Bellingshausen and Palmer were announced.

Right: Deception Island in the South Shetland Islands looms through the mists. A photograph taken in 2006 during a voyage to the Antarctic Peninsula by Michel Setboun.

THE FIRST GLORY-HUNTERS

However, an exceptional few could not resist the lure of celebrity. Among them was Benjamin Morrell, an American sealing captain who had a reputation among his peers for fantasy. His colourful narrative of his ten years of sea journeys from 1822 *(Narrative of Four Voyages to the South Seas and Pacific Oceans)*, includes a declaration that he, unlike other men, would remain undeterred by the great forces of nature on his search for the South Pole:

> Many enterprising navigators of the last and present centuries
> have made highly laudable, and some of them partially successful,
> attempts to penetrate the cloud of mystery which still hangs over
> the Antarctic Seas. But every one has stopped at a certain point,
> timidly shrinking from the farther prosecution of what they
> deemed an impracticable project. Some, it is said, have even been
> deterred by a superstitious notion that an attempt to reach the
> South Pole was a presumptuous intrusion on the awful confines of
> nature,   an unlawful and sacrilegious prying into the secrets of
> the great Creator; who, they contend, has guarded the 'ends of the
> earth' with an impassable bulwark of indissoluble ice; on which is
> written, 'Thus far shalt thou come, but no farther; and here shall
> thy proud course be stayed.' … I contend that genius, science, and
> energy combined can work miracles, and even remove mountains
> …. The day is not far distant when a visit to the South Pole will
> not be thought more of a miracle than to cause an egg to stand on
> its point.

After reaching a latitude of 70° 14′S, Morrell was forced to turn his ship due north because of low supplies and lack of suitable navigational equipment. It was a crushing disappointment, not least because the way before him appeared to be clear and unobstructed with ice, and he had already envisioned himself as winning the South Pole for the United States:

I felt myself compelled to abandon, for the present, the glorious attempt to make a bold advance directly to the south pole .... To the only free nation on earth should belong the glory of exploring a spot of the globe which is the *ne plus ultra* of latitude, where all the degrees of longitude are merged into a single point, and where the sun appears to revolve in a horizontal circle. But this splendid hope has since been lost in the gloom of disappointment! The vassals of some petty despot may one day place this precious jewel of discovery in the diadem of their royal master. Would to heaven it might be set among the stars of our national banner!

Morrell was not the only man to believe that conquering the South Pole was an opportunity for nation-building that was not to be missed. In an address delivered in the House of Representatives on 3 April 1836, Jeremiah N. Reynolds, a campaigner for an expedition, declared that:

Indeed, the enterprise, courage, and perseverance of American seamen, are, if not unrivalled, at least unsurpassed. What man can do, they have always felt ready to attempt … whether it be to grapple with an enemy on the deep … or pushing their adventurous barks into the high southern latitudes, to circle the globe within the Antarctic circle, and attain the pole itself; yea, to cast anchor on that point where all the meridians terminate, where our eagle and star-spangled banner may be unfurled and planted, and left to wave on the axis of the earth itself!

THE PIONEER

In Britain, too, there were those who urged their fellow countrymen to mount an expedition to the South Pole. Yet, except for an optimistic few, most people by now conceded that if a continent were to be found at all, it would not be a land of riches. Some, including the respected Norwegian Arctic explorer Fridtjof Nansen, believed that Terra Australis Incognita would be revealed as nothing more than a group of barren islands frozen in perpetuity to one another. One particularly eccentric notion was that of John Cleves Symmes, who believed that 'the earth is hollow, and habitable within; containing a number of solid concentrick spheres, one within the other; and that it is open at the poles 12 or 16 degrees ...'. His fanciful notion met with a mixed reception, and in time became a target for satirists.

On the whole, the scientific establishment refused to pass comment; nevertheless, the question of the extent and nature of an Antarctic continent, and what lay at the South Pole itself, was still unanswered, and therefore remained enough of a draw to justify a number of nineteenth-century scientific expeditions: French, British and American. Of these, James Clark Ross's British Royal Navy expedition of 1839–1843 was the most successful, because he pioneered an entry into a region of sea that now bears his name and opened the door to the inhospitable southern continent.

By the time he departed from England in 1839, Ross was already regarded as one of the finest polar explorers of his time. A combination of duty, curiosity and ambition pushed Ross forwards. He had already located the Magnetic North Pole, now his personal quest was to find its southern counterpart. Any further discoveries he might make on the way would be a bonus. But first he had to press through the countless challenges presented by the Antarctic Convergence, including barely navigable, swollen, ice-riddled seas. Ross, who was later to remark that it never ceased 'to be a source of wonder and gratitude' that his ships never sank, described the floundering of his vessels:

> ... amidst the heavy fragments of crushing bergs over which the ocean rolled in its mountainous waves, throwing huge masses one upon the other, and then again burying them beneath its foaming waters, dashing and grinding them together with fearful violence ... an ocean of rolling fragments of ice, hard as floating rocks of granite were dashed against them with so much violence that their masts quivered as if they would fall at every successive blow ....

Left: The discoverer of the Magnetic North Pole, Commander James Clark Ross, strikes a dashing pose in this 1834 oil painting by John Wildman. Shortly afterwards Ross was directing his energies towards the South.

Above: 'HMS "Erebus" passing through the chain of bergs, 1842', a dramatic scene captured in oils by Richard Beechey, and probably painted not long after James Clark Ross published his travel narrative in 1847. The perilous episode took place during the night of 12 March 1842 when *Erebus* collided with *Terror* in storm-swept seas and had her mast crippled, escaping disaster only by passing through a narrow channel between towering icebergs in an area that came to be known as the Ross Sea.

The southern polar region was a place of bewildering hostility. One can only imagine the profound surprise of Ross and his men when they sighted the smoking pinnacle of an active volcano and the immense Great Ice Barrier. His contemporary record read:

> As we approached the land under all studding-sails, we perceived a low white line, extending as far as the eye could see to the eastward. It presented an extraordinary appearance, and proved at length, as we drew nearer, to be a perpendicular cliff of ice, between 150 ft. and 200 ft. above the level of the sea, perfectly flat and level on the top, and without any fissures or promontories on its even seaward face. What was beyond it we could not imagine; for being much higher than our masthead, we could not see anything except the summit of a lofty range of mountains extending to the southward as far as the seventy-ninth degree of latitude.

Below: The smoking summit of Mount Erebus, the world's most southerly volcano, is seen for the first time by those aboard *Erebus* and *Terror* at a distance on 28 January 1841, a watercolour by John Edward Davis, second master aboard HMS *Terror* during Ross's Antarctic expedition.

The Great Ice Barrier (which now bears the name the Ross Ice Shelf) was, Ross noted, 'an obstruction of such a character as to leave no doubt upon my mind as to our future proceedings, for we might with equal chance of success try to sail through the cliffs of Dover, as to penetrate such a mass'. Sailing southwards along the coastline of what he named Victoria Land, Ross also named peaks of the vast mountain range after Lords of the Admiralty, and called the active volcano Mount Erebus and its dormant

companion Mount Terror, after his ships, before continuing for 200 miles (320 kilometres) along the vast ice shelf. No geographical feature like it had been seen before by man. Ross's discoveries, including that of Cape Adare and the sheltered McMurdo Sound, which would play a major role in later expeditions, made his expedition perhaps the most significant of his time.

Ross's one regret was that that he was unable to lay claim to the Magnetic South Pole. Trying to remain positive, he wrote to Prince Albert: '… although our hopes of complete attainment have been thus defeated, it is some satisfaction to have approached the [Magnetic South] Pole more nearly by some hundred miles than any of our predecessors ….' In his published account of the expedition he would continue:

> It was nevertheless painfully vexatious … to feel how nearly that chief object of our undertaking had been accomplished: and but few can understand the deep feelings of regret with which I felt myself compelled to abandon the perhaps too ambitious hope I had so long cherished of being permitted to plant the flag of my country on both the magnetic poles of our globe; but the obstacles

which presented themselves being of so insurmountable a character was some degree of consolation as it left no grounds for self-reproach ….

FRENCH DISCOVERIES

Meanwhile, French explorer Captain Dumont d'Urville's vessel *Astrolabe* was also encountering the other-worldly outer reaches of the elusive southern continent. Like those who were to follow, d'Urville found the prospect of this place disquieting:

> Austere and grandiose beyond words, while stirring the imagination, it filled us with an involuntary feeling of dread; nowhere else can man feel so strongly the sense of his own impotence …. Profound silence reigns over those icy plains and life is only represented by a few petrels, gliding soundlessly, or by whales whose loud, ominous spouting occasionally breaks its sad monotony.

Then the mood changed. On 19 January 1840, the hydrographer on d'Urville's *Astrolabe* called out from the rigging that there was 'an appearance of land'. As one of the midshipmen set down in his journal:

> There can be no further doubt that this is land; the sailors redouble their efforts and we enter into a labyrinth of icebergs we must get through to reach our goal. Never shall I forget the magical spectacle that then unfolded before our eyes! … We are in fact, sailing amidst gigantic ruins, which assume the most bizarre forms: here temples, palaces with shattered colonnades and magnificent arcades; further on, the minaret of a mosque, the pointed steeples of a Roman basilica, over there a vast citadel with many battlements; over these majestic ruins there reigns a deathly stillness, an eternal silence …..

At 10.50 p.m. d'Urville reported that the sun disappeared 'and showed up the raised contour of land in all its sharpness. Everyone had come together on to the deck to enjoy the magnificent spectacle'. Although unable to find a suitable place to land, nevertheless d'Urville wrote in his journal that 'joy reigned on board; henceforth the success of our enterprise was assured'. The following day a party of men made a landing and planted their flag. For d'Urville it was reward for being 'tormented almost nightly by dreams' about his efforts to discover the South Pole. Surprisingly, d'Urville's plans for a great oceanic journey had initially avoided the idea of exploring the south polar region; it was King Louis Philippe I's suggestion that the expedition should attempt to reach the South Pole, or at least beat Weddell's farthest south record of 74° 15´S, that had changed his plans. D'Urville noted that Napolcon Bonaparte had said that 'people like to be astonished' – a journey towards the South Pole would be astonishing enough. Now, claiming the land for France and naming it Terre Adélie (Adélie Land), after his wife, d'Urville happily wrote:

Our Landing

JULES-SÉBASTIEN-CÉSAR DUMONT D'URVILLE, *VOYAGE AU POLE SUD ET DANS L'OCEANIE*: VOL. VIII, 1844.

In the silence of the night, the huge masses of ice about us looked majestic, but also forbidding. … At midnight it was still dusk and we could easily read on the bridge. We judged that there was no more than half an hour of proper night. I took advantage of it to go below for a rest….

At four in the morning, I counted sixty bergs in the vicinity. … Before us, continually, we could see land, could follow its undulations: it had no obvious features, was smothered with snow, stretched from west to east, and seemed to slope gently towards the sea. But we could not make out a single peak nor find a dark spot to relieve its grey blandness. Therefore we had reason enough to doubt its existence. However, at midday all uncertainty vanished. A boat from *Zelée* came alongside, and announced that they had seen land yesterday. … Calm weather, unfortunately, prevented a positive confirmation. … Henceforth the success of our enterprise was assured; because the expedition could report, whatever else, the finding of a new country. … The two boats that were sent to find land did not return until half past ten, loaded with rock specimens that they had collected from the shore.

Here is an excerpt from the journal of M. Dubouzet (naturalist aboard the *Zelée*) recounting this interesting excursion. … 'It was almost nine o'clock when, to our inexpressible delight, we landed on the western promontory of the highest and farthest east of the islands. The *Astrolabe*'s boat had arrived a moment before us, and its crew were already climbing the rocky cliffs…. I sent one of the sailors to raise a tricouleur on this land which no human being before us had ever seen or trodden. … we took possession in the name of France, claiming too the nearby coast which we had been unable to reach on account of the ice. Our enthusiasm and our joy were increased by the fact that a new addition had been made to France's territories by dint of peaceful conquest. …

'We considered ourselves thereafter as being on French soil, and did so in the comfort that we had not involved our nation in war. The ceremony ended, as it should, with a toast. We consumed, to the glory of France, a bottle of its most noble wine …. Never was the wine of Bordeaux called upon to play a more worthy role; never was a bottle emptied so fittingly. Surrounded on all sides by eternal snow and ice, the cold was brisk, and this generous spirit was an excellent consolation against the temperature. All this took less time that it does to write it down. We then set to work, to see what this desolate land might yield of interest to natural history….'

Below: Captain Dumont d'Urville (1790–1842), a posthumous oil portrait from 1845 by Jerome Cartellier.

Above: In 1850 the adventurer and former
corsair turned marine artist, Ambroise Louis
Garneray captured this dramatic episode from
the voyage of d'Urville's *Astrolabe*, when in
February 1838 the crew had to free the ship
from the cold embrace of the ice.

Following the ancient and lovingly preserved English custom, we
took possession of it in the name of France … Our enthusiasm
and joy were boundless then because we felt we had just added a
province to France by this peaceful conquest … we did not dispos-
sess anyone, and as a result we regarded ourselves as being on
French territory. There will be at least one advantage; it will never
start a war against our country.

Officer Joseph-Fidéle-Eugéne Dobouzet wrote, 'We saluted our discovery
with a general hurrah … the echoes of these silent regions, for the first time
disturbed by human voices, repeated our cries and then returned to their
habitual silence.'

Some ten days later, to the immense surprise of the French, the *Astrolabe*
came across another vessel, the *Porpoise*, one of a four-strong squadron of
ships that formed the United States Exploring Expedition, commanded by
Charles Wilkes. Wilkes's venture was a wide-ranging, rambling affair – his
broad remit was to survey and explore the Pacific Ocean and the South
Seas, and, if possible, to better Weddell's farthest south. Although both
captains had seen one another, no signals or greetings were exchanged.

The *Astrolabe* continued north, while the *Porpoise* sailed west. On 19 January both expeditions claimed possession of the continent, although Wilkes changed his recorded date of discovery to 16 January in an attempt to lay sole claim. The coastlines that he laid down on his charts were later proved to be grossly inaccurate.

The reports of such journeys impressed a curious audience at home. The sublime desolation, the wild, unconquerable south, which had barred all but the bravest of men, was too good a subject to resist. In 1843, drawing on these voices from the south, James Croxall Palmer published *Thulia: A Tale of the Antarctic*, later reprinted as the *Antarctic Mariner's Song*:

> Among the palaces of snow,
> Where storms lay frozen into sleep,
> And silence brooded long ago,
> Over the stern, mysterious deep,
> We felt, with spirits hushed and awed,
> That nature was alone with God.
> Beyond the scope of aching sight,
> Lay, without limit, save the pole,
> A drifting waste of dismal white
> Whereon the sun could find no goal;
> For soon as he had reached the plain,
> The jaded orb arose again.

Despite the successes of these voyages, no major scientific expeditions followed for some time. It had become clear that Antarctica was no El Dorado, and the South Pole itself, fixed somewhere beyond the impenetrable ice, was just too difficult to reach. The attentions of the Admiralty and others were focussed instead on the north and the lure of a possible Northwest Passage. The vessels HMS *Erebus* and HMS *Terror*, having proved their steadfastness in icy conditions on Ross's expedition, were sent to the Arctic in 1845 under the command of Sir John Franklin. The disappearance of Franklin, his ships and his men, prompted the greatest search mission in polar history. With the world's best resources and explorers engaged in the north, Antarctica was forgotten; its vast, desolate coastline not yet drawn. And it would be another 50 years before human voices once again disturbed the Antarctic silence.

1

2

3

4

5

6

7

CHAPTER 2
DAWN OF THE HEROIC AGE

*The south polar lands are carefully shielded and fenced off by the
circumpolar pack. The regions beyond the outer edge are not to be
secured from the depths of mystery by a dash or assault. The fortifi-
cations are more firmly laid than ever a human mind suggested.
The prodigious depths of snow above, and the endless expanse of
ensnaring sea around are mostly impregnable to man. He who contemplates an attack on this heatless undersurface of the globe will
find many tempting allurements and many disheartening rebuffs.
Such has been our experience. The battle, however, should be fought,
though it promises to be the fiercest of all human engagements.
Science demands it, modern progress calls for it, for in this age
a blank upon our chart is a blur upon our prided enlightenment.*

Dr Frederick A. Cook, from *Through the First
Antarctic Night*, 1900.

On 18 February 1899 the *Southern Cross* pushed her way through the ice of
Robertson Bay and reached Cape Adare. It had been more than half a
century since a scientific expedition had made its way to Antarctica and its
leader, Norwegian-Australian Carsten Borchgrevink, was determined that
this expedition would exceed the achievements of James Clark Ross.

This part of the Antarctic was already familiar to Borchgrevink. Four years
earlier he had signed on as a seaman aboard the whaling ship *Antarctic*,
under the command of Norwegian entrepreneur Henryk Bull. Having
reached the coast of northern Victoria Land, Borchgrevink, along with six
companions, rowed towards a narrow pebble beach at Cape Adare and
made what the group believed to be the first landing on the Antarctic mainland. While ashore, Borchgrevink gathered a collection of rocks, seaweeds
and lichens, and carefully studied the foreshore. It was here that he
intended to establish a base, be the first to overwinter in the Antarctic and,
beating Ross, discover the Magnetic South Pole. The ambitious explorer
had then spent the next few years seeking support for that expedition.

Left: Studies of icebergs, as observed in the
Southern Ocean during the oceanographic
research voyage of HMS *Challenger*,
1872–1876.

Above: A rare photograph of Carsten Borchgrevink, most likely taken by William Colbeck in 1898. A brave and driven leader, Borchgrevink is an important yet often overlooked figure in Antarctic history and his expedition's tiny hut – the first building on the continent – of prefabricated pine still stands today, at Cape Adare in the Ross Sea region, preserved and protected by the Antarctic Heritage Trust.

However, in England he found that the reception to his appeals was lukewarm. Some disliked his blunt and abrupt manner, although, as geographer Hugh Robert Mill conceded, 'he had a dynamic quality and a set purpose to get out again to the unknown South that struck some of us as boding well for exploration'.

Indeed, Borchgrevink refused to give up until he had realized his ambition, and eventually his tenacity and enthusiasm paid dividends. Having obtained both the funds and the ship, renamed the *Southern Cross*, he needed, Borchgrevink must have been particularly satisfied when, at Cape Adare in 1899, his men were overawed by their first sight of the continent.

Since the expeditions of Ross and d'Urville, only a few ships had crossed the Antarctic Circle. Sir George Strong Nares had made a brief foray into Antarctic waters in *Challenger* during his round-the-world oceanographic research voyage; the rest had been whalers searching for new grounds. Although the distinction between the South Pole and Antarctica remained rather blurred, the motivation for explorers to head south was the possibility of being able to make important scientific discoveries. The expedition's physicist, Louis Bernacchi, declared:

> The exploration of the South Pole is … of capital importance to science. The geography of nearly 4,000,000 square miles surrounding the Pole is still a blank. The nature and extent of the Antarctic lands have still to be determined, and the interior penetrated … obviously the exploration of so large an unknown area means the advancement of our knowledge of many branches of science.

Camp Ridley, consisting of prefabricated huts and named after Borchgrevink's mother, was soon established at Cape Adare, but Borchgrevink's ten-strong wintering party was not blessed with much luck. After being hit by a succession of blizzards, on 24 July the huts were almost destroyed by fire after a candle was left burning in a bunk. Just over a month later three of the men almost died from asphyxiation by coal fumes. Another fell into a crevasse and only escaped by cutting toe-holds in the ice with a knife he was carrying. Less fortunate was the expedition's zoologist who died of unknown causes that October.

As yet, no one had experienced the long Antarctic winter, and as the darkness grew ever deeper the men began to long for even the briefest moment of sunlight. Bernacchi described this development:

> On May the 15th we saw the sun for the last time for 72 days; it not appearing again until the 29th of July.

> The long, long changeless night of winter was now upon us with no light but that of the moon and the weird Aurora Polaris. The landscape, bereft of the genial rays of the sun, lay as if frozen into sculptured stone. Gone the Great King of Light: the glorious god Helios, source of Life, and Light, and Heat.

Although Borchgrevink tried to keep the men occupied and distracted by assigning tasks, such as making observations, the isolation and the perpetual darkness was harder to endure than any of the men could have imagined. In particular, it became wearing to be confined with the same men telling the same stories. 'We were getting tired of each other's company', Borchgrevink later admitted, 'and began to know every line of each other's faces ... the darkness and the silence in this solitude weighs heavily on one's mind. The silence roars in the ears. It is centuries of heaped up solitude.' Thoughts of home flooded into quiet moments, sometimes in the most unexpected ways. In his journal Bernacchi recorded: 'The other day in turning over some old letters I came across a dried flower! A sweet scented carnation. Retained nearly all its subtle fragrance. I remember it was given to me on the day we left Melbourne. It was like a voice from another world.' But by midwinter, Borchgrevink had noted the change in spirits among his party:

> Such oppressive feelings is reigning within our four walls, that everyone looks as if he is half-dead. If one of us should try and start some fun [to] enlive[n] the rest, he would be suspected of an attempt to break down the discipline, and under such circumstances the safest thing is to keep as quiet as possible so as not to make the discomfort greater than it is.

Above: Among the intact items that can still be seen in the Borchgrevink team's hut at Cape Adare are food rations, such as tinned ox-tongue and pea soup. These metal containers are degrading slowly from the salty atmosphere and the summer humidity. The Symington company specialized in dehydrated food and was famous for products such as pea flour, which it had supplied to British troops in the Crimea.

A Spectacle of Chaos

LOUIS BERNACCHI, *TO THE SOUTH POLAR REGIONS*, 1901.

We were now in the open sea to the south, for not a particle of ice was visible in any direction. Large flocks of brown-backed petrels were seen, and numbers of whales of the finner type .... A sharp look-out was kept for land, and at 7 p.m. on the 15th of February it was sighted; but it was only a glimpse we caught of it through the dense canopy of clouds. Since noon the wind had increased steadily in force, until towards evening it was blowing a furious gale from the southeast and was accompanied by clouds of drifting snow. All that night and the following day the storm raged with full fury and the ship laboured heavily in the heavy seas. She lay to under half topsails, plunging fiercely into the seas and sometimes burying her whole bows beneath the waves, whilst ever and anon mighty green billows would pour over our decks and rush down into the cabins below. Our horizon was narrowly limited by the sheets of spray borne by the wind and the drifting snow, so we could see no land although we were not far from it.

The storm gradually abated towards the afternoon of the 17th, and we were able to stand in once more for the coast. The weather continued to improve and the dense mist cleared a little. At two o'clock in the afternoon land was again sighted distant some twenty-five miles, and we headed for a dark and high mass of rock which was evidently Cape Adare. It was a Cape of a very dark basaltic appearance, with scarcely any snow laying upon it, thus forming a strong contrast to the rest of the snow-covered coast. ... As we approached the coast it changed continually in aspect. Sometime dense clouds of mist would envelop it; at other times the clouds would roll up like a great curtain, disclosing to our eyes a long chain of snow-clad mountains, the peak of which tapered up one above the other like the tiers of an amphitheatre or those of the Great Pyramid of Cheops; but it was only a momentary vision, quickly disappearing, then all was again sombre, nothing but the heaving mass of waters,

the whistle of the wind in the cordage, and the blinding snow across our decks.

... As we drew closer, the coast assumed a most formidable aspect. The most striking features were the stillness and deadness and impassibility of the new world. Nothing around but ice and rock and water. No token of vitality anywhere; nothing to be seen on the steep sides of the excoriated hills. Igneous rocks and eternal ice constituted the landscape. Here and there enormous glaciers fell into the sea, the extremities of some many miles in width. Afterwards, when the mist had cleared away, we counted about a dozen of them around the Bay, rising out of the waters like great crystal walls. Approaching this sinister coast for the first time, on such a boisterous, cold and gloomy day, our decks covered with drift snow and frozen sea water, the rigging encased in ice, the heavens as black as death, was like approaching some unknown land of punishment, and struck into our hearts a feeling preciously akin to fear when calling to mind that there, on that terrible shore, we were to live isolated from all the world for many long months to come. It was a scene, terrible in its austerity, that can only be witnessed at that extremity of the globe; truly, a land of unsurpassed desolation.

... The Commander now decided to effect a landing and requested Mr. Fougner and me to accompany him ashore in a small canvas boat. We got into the frail craft and rowed her ashore, but it took nearly a quarter of an hour to reach the land, for, although the distance from the ship appeared small, it was actually great. The place of landing was a shelving beach, formed of gravel and pebbles; slight surf was breaking upon it and the boat had to be handled carefully so as to avoid capsizing.

Thus, after many months, we had attained our destination, notwithstanding the numerous obstacles with which our path had been beset.

After having hoisted up our boat out of reach of the

sea, we commenced an examination of the place. We had not walked many yards before we met the secluded and melancholy inhabitants of that South Polar land; these were the penguins scattered about it in groups of a hundred and more. They extended us but cold courtesy and gravely regarded us from a distance; but on our approaching closer they evinced more interest and commenced talking loquaciously together in their own particular vernacular. They had evidently discovered that there was something unusual about our appearance, and some were commissioned to investigate matters. These, with perfect sang-froid, slowly marched right up to our feet and ogled up at us in a most ludicrous fashion. Having finished this scrutiny, they returned to their fellows as sedately as they had come, and thenceforth took no more notice of us. What impressed us greatly was the general appearance of sadness prevailing amongst them; they seemed to be under the shadow of some great trouble. It is no small matter that will arouse them from their stolidity. …

The scene before us looked inexpressibly desolate. A more barren desert cannot be conceived, but one of immense interest from a geological point of view.

From the end of the Cape to the foot of the mountain-range beyond, a great waste of hollows and ridges lay before our eyes; ridges rising beyond ridges like ocean waves, whose tumult had been suddenly frozen into stone. Beds of snow and ice filled up some of these extensive hollows, which had been scooped out by glacier action.

Never before had I seen the evidences of volcanic and of glacier action laying side by side – the hobnobbing of extreme heat and extreme cold. Great

fire-scathed masses of rock rose out of the débris formed by the glaciers that had passed over the land. Vast convulsions must at one time have shaken the foundations of this land. But now silence and deep peace brooded over the scene that once had been so fearfully convulsed.

… When we had set out the weather was fine, but later on the sky became overcast, as dark ominous clouds rolled up from the north-east.

The prospects from where we were was extensive, but scarcely beautiful. Down at our feet lay the sea, almost free of ice-pack. Huge stranded icebergs, defying the power of the solar beams, were visible in various directions along the coast. Behind us lay the great Antarctic Land; snow peaks rising beyond one another until by distance they dwindled away to insignificancy. The silence and immobility of the scene was impressive; not the slightest animation or vitality anywhere. It was like a mental image of our globe in its primitive state – a spectacle of Chaos.

Above: The ice-edge in Neumayer Strait, a shot from the rich polar portfolio of Sebastian Copeland, 2006.

Although winter in the Antarctic was hard, the appearance of the aurora australis alleviated the feeling of melancholy. Bernacchi in particular was struck by the phenomenon.

> At 10 o'clock in the evening of June 3rd an exceedingly grand aurora was visible. It was a dazzling and incomparable spectacle …. At first it was of a fleece-like nebulous whiteness of a strange unearthly radiance.
>
> When at the zenith … the aurora attained its maximum intensity; great curtains of light would shake themselves across the sky with undulation motion in an especially striking manner; huge shafts of red and green light would shoot down towards the earth with a rapidity impossible for the eye to follow; palpitations of an unknown life. Once the streamers collected round a spot in the zenith and formed a luminous ring of a deep colour; a colour of celestial opulence impossible to define, and turn around in a small circle with a rapidity that was appalling; no sound whatever was perceptible. …
>
> It is impossible for one who has not seen it to even feebly understand its great beauty. How little we understand the nature of its origin. It appears as if Nature has reserved for those cold climates of the pole its most astonishing, soul-inspiring and baffling phenomenon.

With the return of the *Southern Cross* in January 1900, Borchgrevink and his men sailed towards the Ross Ice Shelf, landing at Possession Island, before setting out across the ice shelf to reach an estimated 78° 50′S – the closest any man had got to the South Pole up to that time. Borchgrevink sailed home satisfied with the large collection of botanical specimens he and his men had gathered and the advances that had been made, such as the new farthest south record and the first sledge journey on the surface of the ice barrier – but unknown to him another expedition had already found itself forced to overwinter in the Antarctic the previous year.

The Belgian expedition of 1897–1899, under the command of Lieutenant Adrien de Gerlache, had been trapped, its vessel *Belgica* frozen into the pack-ice of the Bellingshausen Sea to the west of the Antarctic Peninsula, since the end of February 1898. Among the ship's crew were two men, Dr Frederick Cook and Roald Amundsen, whose names would later become synonymous with the greatest polar discoveries – the attainment of the north and south poles (albeit the former's claim has since been discredited). The *Belgica* expedition, severely hampered by bad planning, found itself under-manned and under-provisioned. On the 21st, Cook observed: 'We are imprisoned in an endless sea of ice …. We have told all the tales, real and imaginative, to which we are equal. Time weighs heavily upon us as the darkness slowly advances.'

As Borchgrevink and his men discovered, overwintering in Antarctica was a great challenge to the health of body, mind and spirit. The suffering of

Gerlache's men was exacerbated by their poor diet, and had it not been for Dr Cook, who insisted that the men supplement their poor provisions with seal and penguin, many of the men would have perished. Poor physical health was one problem, but more worrying was the depression and even mental illness that several of the crew began to exhibit. Lieutenant Gerlache and Captain Lecointe wrote their wills and took to their beds, and even the ship's normally friendly cat Nansen became aggressive and withdrawn, eventually appearing to expire from misery. The strongest of the crew, Cook and Amundsen, took command and eventually the *Belgica* escaped from the ice on 14 March 1899. The expedition, which made some important scientific observations and geographical discoveries, including the Belgica Strait and its islands, had, crucially, illustrated to both Cook and Amundsen the impact of the darkness and prolonged stress upon the minds of men, and of the need for future expeditions to the south to have an adequate diet and to be prepared for the worst eventualities.

THE UNANSWERED QUESTION

Back in England, while Borchgrevink had been trying to raise support for his *Southern Cross* expedition, there were others strongly advocating the need for a British venture. On 27 November 1893 the academic John Murray, a leading authority on Antarctic matters, gave an influential address at the Royal Geographical Society (RGS). Murray challenged: 'Is the last great piece of maritime exploration on the surface of our earth to be undertaken by Britons, or is it to be left to those who may be destined to succeed or supplant us on the ocean? That is a question that this generation must answer.' There was, he insisted, a 'great extent of ignorance concerning all that obtains within the South Polar regions' – implying this was something that should be remedied. It was, he concluded, 'impossible to overestimate the value of Antarctic observations for the right understanding of the general meteorology of the globe'.

Murray's address met with an enthusiastic response from the Marquis of Lothian, who closed the meeting by saying:

> I should, too, like to say one word, which I think would appeal to
> many people, and that is, that the work of Antarctic research
> should be done by Englishmen. Looking at the map which hangs
> before me, it strikes me that almost every name in the south has
> been given by this country. I know that foreign countries are at this
> moment striving to inaugurate expeditions in order to discover
> what we ought to try and do ourselves. I should not like to see for-
> eign names upon that hemisphere where all civilized points are
> inhabited by our countrymen and belong to this country.
> Therefore, though I am not urging the work upon you from so
> high a level as that of science, still I think that our historical record
> in all parts of the world, which has been begun by Great Britain,
> should not [be allowed] to fall into the hands of others. We cannot
> expect to do all, but we should be first in the field.

Into the Night

Frederick A. Cook, 'Through the First Antarctic Night', 1900.

May 16. The long night began at 12 o'clock last night. We did not know this until the afternoon. At 4 o'clock Lecointe got an observation by two stars which placed us in latitude 71° 34' 30", longitude 9° 10'. According to a careful calculation from these figures the captain announces the melancholy news that there will be no more day – no more sun for seventy days, if our position remains about the same. If we drift north the night will be shorter, if south it will be longer. Shortly before noon the long prayed-for southerly wind came, sweeping from the pack the warm, black atmosphere, and replacing it with a sharp air and a clearing sky. Exactly at noon we saw a brightening in the north. We expected to see the sun by refraction, though we knew it was actually below the horizon, but we were disappointed. The cold whiteness of our earlier surroundings has now been succeeded by a colder blackness. Even the long, bright twilight, which gladdened our hearts on first entering the pack, has been reduced to but a fraction of its earlier glory; this now takes the place of our departed day.

May 17. … At about seven o'clock the captain went out to find two stars from which to obtain an observation for position. The sky was too hazy … but his eye rested upon an inexplicable speck of light in the west. He stood and looked at it for some moments. It did not change in position, but sparkled now and then like a star. The thing came suddenly, disappeared and again reappeared in exactly the same spot. It was so curious and assumed so much the nature of a surprise, that Lecointe came into the cabin and announced the news. We accused him of having had too early an eye-opener, but we went out quickly to see the mystery. … We looked for some time in the direction in which Lecointe pointed, but we saw only a gloomy waste of ice, lined in places by breaks in the pack from which oozed a black cloud of vapour. We were not sure that the captain's eyesight was not defective….

After we had stood on the snow-decked bridge for ten minutes, shivering and kicking about to keep our blood from freezing, we saw on a floe some distance westward a light like that of a torch. It flickered, rose and fell, as if carried by some moving object. We went forward to find if anybody was missing – for we could only explain the thing by imagining a man carrying a lantern. Everybody was found to be on board, and then the excitement ran high. Soon all hands were on deck and all seemed to think that the light was being moved towards us. Is it a human being? Is it perhaps some one from an unknown south polar race of people? For some minutes no one ventured out on the pack to meet the strange messenger. We were, indeed, not sufficiently dressed for this mission. Few had had breakfast; all were without mittens and hats, some without coats, and others without trousers. If it were a diplomatic visitor we were certainly in an uncomfortable and undignified uniform with which to receive him. Amundsen, who was the biggest, the strongest, the bravest, and generally the best dressed man for sudden emergencies, slipped into his *annorak*, jumped on his *ski* and skated rapidly over the gloomy blackness of the pack to the light. He lingered about the spot a bit, and then returned without company and without the light, looking somewhat sheepish. It proved to be a mass of phosphorescent snow which had been newly charged by sea algae, and was occasionally raised and brushed by the pressure of the ice.

May 20. It is the fifth day of the long night and it certainly seems long, very long, since we have felt the heat of the sun. … Since entering the pack our spirits have not improved. The quantity of food which we have consumed, individually and collectively, has steadily decreased and our relish for food has also slowly but steadily failed. There was a time when each man enjoyed some special dish and by distributing these favoured dishes at different times it was possible to have some one gastronomically happy every day. But now we are tired of everything. We despise all articles which come out of tin, and a general dislike is the normal air of the *Belgica*. … Everybody having a connection with the selection or preparation of the food, past or present, is heaped with some criticism.

… I do not mean to say that we are more discontented than other men in similar conditions. This part of the life of polar explorers is usually suppressed in the narratives. An almost monotonous discontent occurs in every expedition through the polar night. It is natural that this should be so, for when men are compelled to see one another's faces, encounter the few good and the many bad traits of character for weeks, months, and years, without any outer influence to direct the mind, they are apt to remember only the rough edges which rub up against their own bumps of misconduct. … The truth is, that we are at this moment as tired of each other's company as we are of the cold monotony of the black night and of the unpalatable sameness of our food. Now and then we experience affectionate moody spells and then we try to inspire each other with a sort of superficial effervescence of good cheer, but such moods are short-lived. Physically, mentally, and perhaps morally, then, we are depressed, and from my past experience in the arctic I know that this depression will increase with the advance of the night, and far into the increasing dawn of next summer.

The mental conditions have been indicated above. Physically we are steadily losing strength … and the muscles, which were hard earlier, are now soft, though not reduced in size. We are pale, and the skin is unusually oily. The hair grows rapidly, and the skin about the nails has a tendency to creep over them, seemingly to protect them from the cold. The heart action is failing in force and is decidedly irregular. Indeed, this organ responds to the slightest stimulation in an alarming manner. If we walk hurriedly around the ship the pulse rises to 110 beats, and if we continue for fifteen minutes it intermits, and there is also some difficulty of respiration. … The sun seems to supply an indescribable something which controls and steadies the heart. In its absence it goes like an engine without a governor.

Above: Frederick Cook, surgeon on the *Belgica* during her Antarctic voyage, published his account of their endeavours on his return to America. It was his skill and care for the men on board that played a major part in keeping them alive and healthy during the long polar winter. The multinational crew also included Roald Amundsen, who would later rise to global fame in his conquest of the South Pole. Cook would also become well known around the world, claiming to have reached the North Pole in April 1908, but his account was soon challenged and discredited. His Antarctic achievements are now too often overlooked.

May 27. The little dusk at midday is fading more and more … All have an abundance of work, but our ambition for regular occupation, particularly anything which requires prolonged mental concentration, is wanting; even the task of keeping up the log is too much. There is nothing new to write about, nothing to excite fresh interest. There are now no auroras, and no halos, everything on the frozen sea and over it is sleeping the long sleep of the frigid night.

By the mid-1890s a number of journeys were being planned in several different nations. The inspiration for these came, in part, from the Sixth International Geographical Congress held in London in July 1895, at which it had been proclaimed: 'Exploration of the Antarctic Regions is the greatest piece of geographical exploration still to be undertaken.' This statement ushered in a new era of Antarctic exploration, with Swedish, German, French, British and Scottish expeditions all heading south in the name of science and endeavour.

THE SWEDISH EXPEDITION

On 16 October 1901, using the same vessel, *Antarctic*, that Borchgrevink had once sailed with, Norwegian explorer and geologist Dr Otto Nordenskjöld left Gothenburg bound for the far south. Although the focus of his Swedish Antarctic Expedition was primarily scientific, the element of adventure was not lost on him and his men. As experienced Norwegian navigator and polar explorer Captain Carl Anton Larsen took the *Antarctic* beyond the South Shetland Islands and into the Orleans Strait, the sense of excitement was palpable. Nordenskjöld recorded in January 1902:

> We were now sailing a sea across which none had hitherto voyaged. The weather had changed as if by magic; it seemed as though the Antarctic world repented of the inhospitable way in which it had received us the previous day, or, maybe, it merely wished to entice us deeper into its interior in order the more surely to annihilate us. At all events, we pressed onward, seized by that almost feverish eagerness which can only be felt by an explorer who stands upon the threshold of the great unknown.

Nordenskjöld and five companions were put ashore at Snow Hill Island, off the coast of the Antarctic Peninsula, where they quickly erected a small magnetic observatory and a base in which to overwinter. From there, the six made several exploratory journeys using boat, husky- and man-hauled sledges, and eventually reached a portion of the eastern part of coast, which they named after King Oscar II of Norway and Sweden. 'We did not make much ado about choosing our camping-ground (October 18) but pitched our tent on the ice at the foot of a projecting, brown, weather-worn, rocky headland, torn by the frost into a mass of mighty blocks. The reader can easily imagine with what feelings I hurried forward to these rocks, the first spot trodden by human foot on the whole of the eastern coast of the mainland of West Antarctica.' It was not a comfortable place to camp, and after their provisions were devoured and the tent was torn to shreds by their dogs, they quickly headed back to base. They had covered an extraordinary 380 miles (610 kilometres) in 33 days.

The adventure was far from over for Nordenskjöld's party. After dropping Nordenskjöld off at Snow Hill Island, Larsen had returned to the Falkland Islands in the *Antarctic*, planning to return the following year to pick them up. Encountering impassable pack-ice, Larsen was finally forced to deposit

Le Petit Journal

SUPPLÉMENT ILLUSTRÉ

CHAQUE JOUR — SIX PAGES — 5 CENTIMES
5 Centimes
5 Centimes
ABONNEMENTS

Le Supplément illustré
CHAQUE SEMAINE 5 CENTIMES
L'AGRICULTURE MODERNE, 5 cent. — La Mode du Petit Journal, 10 cent.

Quatorzième année
DIMANCHE 6 DÉCEMBRE 1903
Numéro 681

DANS LES RÉGIONS ANTARCTIQUES
Le docteur Otto Nordenskjold retrouvé

Left: Adventures in the Antarctic and other far-flung places appealed to the general public in Europe and North America, which meant they were of particular significance to periodicals that specialized in sensational stories, such as the mass-market Parisian newspaper *Le Petit Journal*, which liked to feature an action-packed colour plate on its front page. Here, Nordenskjöld's rescue is featured in the 6 December 1903 issue.

a three-man rescue party at Hope Bay, along with a depot of supplies, in the hope that if the ship continued to be unable to reach Nordenskjöld and his men, the rescuers would be able to reach Snow Hill Island overland.

The *Antarctic* never made it to Snow Hill Island. Fierce storms blew her southwards until she neared Paulet Island. One afternoon, as the men sat down to a game of cards, the ship, as Nordenskjöld put it, 'began to tremble like an aspen leaf'. The ice was threatening to crush her. For nearly two weeks the crew tried to stem the leaks of the damaged ship, while Larsen made desperate attempts to get her closer to land. On 12 February 1903 the order was given to abandon ship. In a scene that would be repeated on Shackleton's *Endurance* voyage, the men watched as their ship fell victim to the ice. Scientist Carl Skottsberg recorded the moment in his journal:

We stand in a long row on the edge of the ice and cannot take our eyes off her … the pumps are still going, but the sound grows fainter and fainter … she is breathing her last. She sinks slowly deeper and deeper .... Now the name disappears from sight. Now the water is up to the rail, and with a rattle, the sea and bits of ice rush in over her deck. That sound I can never forget, however long I may live. Now the blue and yellow colours are drawn down into the deep. The mizzen-mast strikes against the edge of our floe and is snapped off; the main-mast strikes and breaks; the crow's nest rattles against the ice-edge, and the streamer, with the name *Antarctic* disappears in the waves. The bowsprit – the last mast-top – She is gone!

Just over two weeks later, the shipwrecked crew finally managed to cross the 25 miles (40 kilometres) of treacherous, constantly moving ice-pans to Paulet Island. With no way to communicate their predicament, they could only hope that the alarm would be raised when the *Antarctic* failed to return.

Meanwhile, Dr Gunnar Andersson, Lieutenant Duce and Seaman Toralf Grunden, the trio deposited at Hope Bay, had become lost attempting to reach Nordenskjöld's winter quarters, and had instead found themselves gazing over the frozen entrance of what is now known as the Crown Prince Gustav Channel. 'We stand silent and perplexed, and gaze at the new and wonderful scene,' wrote Andersson in his diary. 'Mile upon mile of snowy plain, such as we have never seen before, meets our eyes; one can actually imagine that a gigantic snow-clad city lies before us, with houses and palaces in thousands, and in hundreds of changing, irregular forms – towers and spires, and all the wonders of the world ... I have never before been able even to imagine such a picture of the sovereign dominion of ice, as the one offered by this landscape.' Nevertheless, they were not where they expected to be, and with their way blocked, they were forced to retreat to Hope Bay, imagining that *Antarctic* had already rescued Nordenskjöld's party and would return to pick them up.

By the time they were reunited with Nordenskjöld the following October, the three men had endured a full winter in a makeshift shelter and had then undertaken a remarkable journey through virgin territory to Snow Hill Island. Clearly marked by their ordeal, they were barely recognizable – as is evident from what Nordenskjöld wrote: 'Black as soot from head to toe; men with black clothes, black faces and high black caps, and with their eyes hidden by peculiar wooden frames ... my powers of guessing fail me, when I endeavour to imagine to what race of men these creatures belong.'

Meanwhile, on Paulet Island, Larsen and his companions had also weathered a hard winter. Like Andersson, Duce and Grunden, they had built a shelter from rocks and tarpaulin, and survived by hunting seal and penguin. Amazingly, they had managed to keep their spirits up, although at times it was terribly hard. Skottsberg wrote:

Many hundred dreams have been dreamed in our island but I do not know if they helped to brighten our existence. They grouped them-

selves around two objects – food and rescue. Why, we could dream through a whole dinner, from the soup to the dessert, and waken to be cruelly disappointed. How many times did one not see the relief vessel in our visions – sometimes as a large ship, sometimes as nothing but a little sloop? And we knew the persons on board, they spoke about our journey; took us in their arms; patted us on the back ....

Shortly after the group of three had begun their journey to rendezvous with Nordenskjöld, Larsen and five companions set out from Paulet Island in their small whaleboat to find succour. Remarkably, after a challenging journey, they made it to Snow Hill Island just as a joint Argentinian and Swedish mission arrived to rescue Nordenskjöld and his men.

SCIENCE BEFORE ADVENTURE

In January 1902, at the same time as Nordenskjöld had first recorded sailing into the unknown, German explorer Erich von Drygalski's expedition had also entered Antarctic waters aboard the *Gauss*. Drygalski, a professor of geography and geophysics at the University of Berlin, had experience in Greenland and was considered well versed in polar travel, but it was science rather than adventure that had drawn him to the south, and an attempt to reach the South Pole was simply not a part of his plans. Fame for its own sake was of no interest for him.

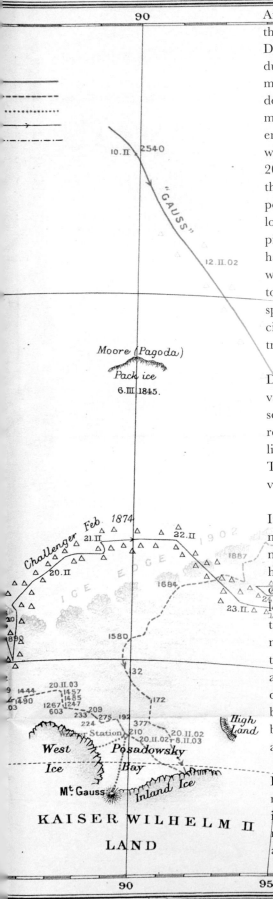

After the expedition had discovered and named Kaiser Wilhelm II Land, the ship attempted to sail between two ice-ridges, only to become trapped. Drygalski reminisced: 'Later, nobody recalled exactly what happened during the next hours but we all felt that we had become a toy of the elements. A snowstorm blew up, floes and 'bergs closed in ....' The men tried desperately to free the ship from the ice, but by 2 March Drygalski and his men had to accept defeat – 'our fate had been sealed: the trap we had entered had closed'. As with the *Belgica*, the expedition was forced to over-winter, but although the *Gauss* was frozen into ice with a thickness of nearly 20 feet (6 metres), the ship was comfortable and well provisioned. Unlike their Belgian counterparts, the men happily tucked into fresh seal and penguin meat – 'Their hearts and livers made a most delicious ragout ... we loved it better than our tinned food' – and they kept themselves fully occupied and entertained. Meteorologist Dr Friedrich Bidlingmaier wrote happily of their off-duty times: 'Sundays were beer-nights, Wednesdays were lecture-nights, but Saturday nights were best of all: on them we sat together behind a glass of grog, united in games or conversation. Clubs sprouted like mushrooms. There were several card-clubs, a gentleman's cigar-smoking-club, glee-clubs, a band composed of a harmonica, flute, triangle and two pot-lids for a cymbal.'

Drygalski's scientific programme was ambitious. Huts were built for obser-vations of meteorological, astronomical and magnetic phenomena. The sea floor was dredged through holes in the ice, the movements of birds were recorded and specimens of rocks were collected. In all 1,440 species of living organisms endemic to the Antarctic were recorded and described. The scientific results from the expedition would eventually fill 20 published volumes.

In addition, during one of the party's sledging journeys, a 1,000-foot (300-metre) solitary volcanic cone was discovered standing starkly in a monotonous plain of ice. They named it Gaussberg. Intrigued, Drygalski had the expedition's balloon filled with hydrogen and he rose to an altitude of about 1,600 feet (490 metres): 'The view was so extensive that it was like looking into infinity', he recorded. 'It was so warm up there I could even take off my gloves ... the sight from this altitude was grandiose. I could see newly discovered Gaussberg and ... gave my description via telephone to the deck of the ship. It was the only ice-free landmark in the surrounding area.' Although 600 miles (965 kilometres) of coastline would be surveyed during the expedition, there would be no sledging journeys beyond Gauss-berg from their winter quarters. Unlike many other explorers, Drygalski believed that there was no scientific value to enduring blizzards, hardship and danger simply to trudge across 'featureless wastes'.

Drygalski's time in Antarctica was shorter than he had hoped. Having managed to free the *Gauss* from its imprisonment in the ice by using an ingenious method of laying ash and garbage on the frozen surface to help melt a path to freedom, he ordered the ship home, rather than staying for another winter. 'It was a most difficult decision,' Drygalski wrote, 'cer-

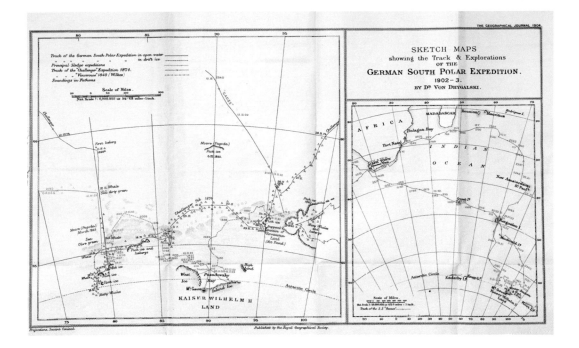

SKETCH MAPS
showing the Track & Explorations
OF THE
GERMAN SOUTH POLAR EXPEDITION.
1902-3.
BY Dᴿ VON DRYGALSKI.

tainly the most difficult one I had to make, but it was necessary. There was no safe place to spend the winter here.' To Drygalski's later disappointment, even before he returned home to Berlin he was criticized for having made his journey too late in the season, and his expedition was widely condemned as a failure and a disgrace. Some declared that a scholar should never have been appointed leader, and that the results would have been far different if a naval officer or whaling captain had been in command. As a result, Drygalski would be unable to raise the funds for a second journey south. The academic journal *Deutsche Rundschau für Geographie und Statistik* noted:

> The overflowing abundance of scientific material cannot obscure the fact that the expedition has not closed with the successes that one might have wished for in the interest of the continuation of Antarctic exploration. These require striking results, primarily, an expansion of our spatial knowledge of Antarctica .... The German expedition was able to contribute little to the solution of the interesting question whether a great connected land mass – an Antarctic continent – exists at the South Pole.

'Our time', reflected Hans Gazert, the medical officer on the expedition, 'wants the sensational, wants tales of dangers and adventures. But we did not set out to seek those and then entertain the world but to track down the secrets of the Antarctic.' Truly, times had changed and the public increasingly had a thirst for dramatic stories of heroes pitting themselves against the 'great white south' – now into the arena would step men whose adventures would shape our image of the South Pole: this was to be the 'heroic age' of exploration.

Above: The progress of the German voyage under Drygalski was followed with interest in Britain. *The Geographical Journal*, established in 1831 by the Royal Geographical Society, reported on the expedition in 1904, accompanied by these maps of routes that covered the length, from east to west, of that part of the coastline of Antarctica the expedition had named Kaiser Wilhelm II Land. The map outlines the sea journey of the *Gauss* vessel with dates, sledge journeys, plus the routes taken by the *Challenger* expedition in 1874 and the *Wilkes* expedition in 1840.

CHAPTER 3
FARTHEST SOUTH

Above: After the launch of *Discovery*, a lunch,
21 March 1901.

Never was there such a return as when we climbed on our ship
Nimrod again – we had been given up for 10 days past and killed
in a hundred different ways.

JAMESON BOYD ADAMS, FROM A LETTER TO A FRIEND, 10 MARCH 1909.

That Britain would get an official expedition to build on the discoveries of
James Clark Ross and compete with those being mounted by other European nations, owed a great deal to the determination of Sir Clements
Markham, president of the RGS. A former naval midshipman who had
joined a Franklin search expedition, Markham had long championed the
idea of a national Antarctic expedition and had become a fierce advocate
of polar exploration. From 1895 to 1899, his dogged persistence meant
that funds were raised and support agreed – until, finally, a Royal Navy
expedition was approved. What Markham lacked was a suitable leader,
although he already had a clear idea of what qualities he was looking for:

> [The Commander of the expedition] must be a naval officer ...
> and he must be young. These are essentials. Such a commander
> should be a good sailor with some experience of ships under sail,
> a navigator with a knowledge of surveying, and he should be of a
> scientific turn of mind. He must have imagination and be capable
> of enthusiasm. His temperament must be cool, he must be calm,
> yet quick and decisive in action, a man of resource, tactful and
> sympathetic.

ROBERT FALCON SCOTT

The ideal candidate presented himself to Markham in June 1899 by
chance, while walking down Buckingham Palace Road in London. Robert
Falcon Scott, a torpedo lieutenant of the battleship HMS *Majestic*, had met
Markham several years earlier in the West Indies while still a midshipman

on the training ship HMS *Rover*, and he had caught his attention by winning a cutter race. Markham later dined with the 18-year-old and had been immediately impressed by Scott's 'intelligence, information and charm of his manner'. However, to many, Scott seemed an odd choice of commander for such a prestigious expedition as this. Scott had no polar experience – indeed, he later confessed that he had had no previous interest in polar exploration before meeting Markham – and although he had risen through the ranks commendably enough, there were others who were far better qualified. Among them was eminent geologist Professor John Walter Gregory, who was in line for the role of scientific director of the expedition and unimpressed by Scott's credentials. He wrote in confidence to a colleague:

> I do not think Scott at all a good man for the post. ... It is his first command & for a man who talks so much about discipline I think it is a pity for his first command to be so unusual. I think he is a poor organizer, his departments are in arrears & he is so casual in all his plans. He appears to trust to luck things which ought to be a matter of precise calculation.

In the years to come, Scott would be roundly criticized for not taking the advice of explorers with experience in the polar regions. With Markham at

Above: The officers and scientific staff of the Royal Research Ship (RSS) *Discovery* pose for a photograph as she lies alongside in London's East India Dock on 17 July 1901. *Discovery* was designed for use in the Antarctic and was the last traditional wooden three-masted ship to be built in Britain. Commander Scott is seated in the front row (second from the left), while behind him stands a youthful-looking Ernest Shackleton (fifth from the left).

his side, Scott had paid a visit to the eminent Norwegian explorer Fridtjof Nansen, who in 1888 had become the first man to cross the Greenland icecap on skis, but he then largely ignored Nansen's recommendations about the use of dogs and skis. Scott also admitted in his journal that he was 'woefully ignorant' of polar expeditions past. The expedition ship *Discovery* would have a library of books, including some narratives by Greely, Payer, Nares, McClintock and Scoresby, but she was missing accounts by Peary and Nansen, which Scott confessed would have been extremely valuable in helping to calculate adequate provisions, sledge weights and the essentials of polar travel.

Despite this, with Markham as his champion, Scott went unchallenged as leader of the expedition. Scott's instructions were undeniably scientific in tone:

> The main objects of the Expedition are to determine, as far as possible, the nature, condition, and extent of that portion of the south polar lands which it is able to reach; to make a magnetic survey in the southern regions to the south of the 40th parallel; and to carry on meteorological, oceanographic, geological, biological, and physical investigations and researches. … With the magnetic survey, the other primary object of the expedition is geographical discovery and scientific exploration by sea and land, in two quadrants of the four into which the Antarctic regions are divided for convenience of reference, namely, the Victorian and Ross Quadrants. It is desired that the extent and configuration of the land should be ascertained by explorations inland or coastwise; that the depth, condition, and nature of the ice-cap should be investigated, as well as the nature of the volcanic regions of the mountain ranges, and especially of any fossiliferous rocks.

There was no direct mention of an attempt to reach the South Pole, although that was clearly Markham's private ambition for the expedition. Secretly, Scott saw the expedition not just as a means for advancement within the Royal Navy, but also as a chance to conquer his fears of inadequacy, and to enjoy some adventure to boot. Others, too, saw ulterior motives behind the expedition. So concerned was Gregory that there was 'no guarantee to prevent the scientific work from being subordinated to naval adventure', he promptly resigned his post.

A VOYAGE OF DISCOVERY

Among those chosen for the expedition was merchant seaman Ernest Shackleton. A competent, enthusiastic and hard-working individual, Shackleton had a decade of experience at sea, with both sail and steam. In the years to come, he would also prove to be a natural leader under the most hazardous and stressful circumstances. Louis Bernacchi was of the opinion that Shackleton was 'always alert for any new interest, energetic, full of flashing new ideas (many of them impractical)…'. Although Markham was keen for the expedition to be made up purely of Royal Navy

Above: A carte de visite of Fridtjof Nansen (1861–1930), from the studio of Carl Johansgade, 1890. Nansen was born and raised in the countryside outside Christiana (Oslo), where he developed a love of the outdoors and expertise in what would today be described as survival crafts. He was an outstanding boyhood skater and skier, and as a young man aged 18 he broke the world record for one-mile skating, and aged 19 he won Norway's cross-country skiing championship then defended it for 11 years in succession. Such activities gave him a tremendous physique with great stamina and endurance, as well as a clear understanding of the practical value of skis in snowy regions.

men, he also recognized Shackleton's strengths. 'Scott was fortunate in finding such an excellent and zealous officer,' wrote Markham. 'He is a steady, high principled young man ... hard working and exceedingly good tempered ... a marvel of intelligent energy.'

The other crucial member of Scott's party was Edward Wilson, the second-in-command and head of the scientific staff. As a doctor, zoologist, artist and ornithologist, he was possibly the most useful man on the team; as confidant, gentleman and peace-maker, he was probably the most valuable. The geologist Raymond Priestley commented that Wilson was the nearest thing to a saint that he had ever come across.

Discovery sailed from East India Dock in London at noon on 31 July 1901 to the cheers of several hundred people. Six months later, after briefly visiting Borchgrevink's hut and discovering the eastern coast of the Ross Sea, Scott rose high above the Antarctic coast at Barrier Inlet to survey the surrounding area from the balloon *Eva*. Wilson believed that the balloon ascent was a foolhardy mission:

> The Captain, knowing nothing whatever about the business, insisted on going up first and through no fault of his own came down safely. Then Shackleton went up, a good deal higher, some [800] feet and came down safely, with good photos from above. Then we went to lunch and at lunch Koettlitz and Hodgson were allowed to go up after noon. I refused. As only one can go up at a time,

Above Left: Captain Scott makes his first outing on skis over the pack-ice during the *Discovery* voyage, 5 January 1902. Scott later wrote: 'With very few exceptions we had none of us used ski before, and consequently our first trial caused vast amusement; but even in such a short time it was possible to see signs of improvement, and before the afternoon ended races were organized and figures were darting about in all directions, with constant collisions and falls and much laughter.'

Above Right: After having landed at Cape Adare on 9 January 1902, Dr Edward Wilson struck this jaunty pose for Ernest Shackleton before they went on a foray to collect specimens among the huge Adélie penguin rookery there. The pair also explored the remains of Borchgrevink's hut.

I must say I think it is perfect madness to allow novices to risk their lives in this silly way, merely for the sake of a novel sensation, when so much depends on the life of each of us for the success of the expedition. Happily, after lunch, the balloon was found to have leaked to such an extent that an ascent was impossible, so no one went up and the balloon was emptied. And then it was found that had anyone used the valve in the morning, when the balloon was up, it would not have closed properly and nothing could have prevented the whole show from dropping to earth like a stone! The whole ballooning business seems to me to be an exceedingly dangerous amusement in the hands of such inexperienced novices as we have on board.

Below: This picture was taken on 3 February 1902 as *Discovery* was moored to the edge of the Great Ice Barrier. Captain Scott took advantage of the clear weather to make the first ascent in the tethered hydrogen balloon *Eva*. Shackleton subsequently went aloft with a camera. In taking a number of shots of the scenes below him he recorded the first aerial photographs in Antarctica.

By the end of March, *Discovery* was frozen into McMurdo Sound, a sheltered inlet near the south end of Ross Island. Provisioned for three years, the men felt adequately prepared for the winter ahead. Some of them even exhibited a sense of superiority when it came to their stalwart approach to the impending darkness. After reading Cook's account of the *Belgica* expedition, the first lieutenant, Charles Royds, expressed his disgust in his journal:

To begin with, what sort of men can they be, who sit and cry over the thought of 'sweethearts' far away, who brood over their soli-

tude, who imagine every sickness possible to these regions, who grow their hair long because they are too tired to cut it, and one hundred and one things they did, which an ordinary man in the same circumstances wouldn't have thought of doing ... could anything be more hopeless; and simply because – to my mind – a little strength of mind was wanting; just a little will to fight against despondence, and a lack of moral courage to appear happy and contented when they were not.

Shackleton agreed. 'The idea that we could get ... sick of one another is foolish', he wrote. To keep themselves occupied, the men not only worked on their scientific observations but also put on amateur theatricals in what became known as the Royal Terror Theatre, and contributed to the monthly newspaper, the *South Polar Times*, which was illustrated by Wilson and edited by Shackleton. To begin with, the mood aboard ship was on the whole positive. Their accommodation, according to Wilson, was comfortable enough:

One doesn't feel the cold a bit on such a day, or night as this. In fact speaking generally of the life down in these regions, one is very seldom even uncomfortable from cold and then nearly always in doors. Of course one is acclimatized. We all feel any extra warmth at once, most uncomfortably, and if the ward-room temperature gets over 60° by any chance, every one complains and many cannot sleep at all,

Above Left: During the voyage south Edward Wilson made hundreds of sketches of the birdlife they observed and encountered. He later worked up many of these field sketches into fine watercolours, such as these studies of the royal and yellow-eyed penguins, which are still found in great numbers on Macquarie and the Auckland Islands.

Above Right: The title page of the first edition, in April 1902, of *Discovery*'s onboard journal, the *South Polar Times*. Shackleton was the editor (Nemo, as he styled himself) of this in-house magazine during its first year of existence (it lasted two, with the second under Louis Bernacchi). Set on a typewriter, the monthly was created to maintain morale and keep people occupied during the long, dark season. About 400 pages were produced, with articles about life on the ice, natural history observations, cartoons, caricatures, watercolours, the proceeds of the debating society, poetry and more.

Six weeks later, the winter quarters did not feel quite so cosy, and the men were not quite so content. Even Royds would eventually concede: 'Say what you like, the absence of the sun has, and must have, a depressing effect on the best of men.' It was not so much the unceasing darkness, but the accompanying damp. Scott was eventually forced to insulate his feet in a box of hay while sitting at his desk. 'Perhaps it is as well that there should be some difficulties to overcome', he mused. There would be far greater difficulties to face in the coming months.

TOWARDS THE POLE

With the new season approaching, Scott chose Shackleton and Wilson for the forthcoming journey towards the South Pole. In his diary Wilson expressed his delight at being chosen:

> The Capt called me in for a talk … then the Skipper told me he had taken the long journey towards the South Pole for himself, and had decided that to get a long way south the party must be a small one … Would I go with him? My surprise can be guessed. It was rather too good a thing to be true it seemed to me … I then argued for three men rather than two. 'Who then was to be the third?' he said. So I told him it wasn't for me to suggest anyone. He then said he need hardly have asked me because he knew who I would say, and added that as a matter of fact he was the man he would have chosen himself. So then I knew it was Shackleton; and I told him it was Shackleton's one ambition to go on the southern journey. So it was settled and we three are to go …

On 22 August, after four long months of darkness, Scott and Shackleton climbed 1,000 feet (300 metres) to the summit of Crater Hill and observed the first glimpse of the return of the sun. 'For [a long time],' Scott recorded in his journal, 'our blinking eyes remained fixed on that golden ball and on the fiery rack of its reflection; we seemed to bathe in that brilliant flood of light, and from its flashing rays to drink in new life, new strength, and new hope.'

After several delays, the southern party set out on the morning of 2 November. 'Dogs in splendid form, could hardly be held at first,' Scott noted with pleasure, 'but later of course had to be driven & not yet accustomed to voice, the whip was in some request. However we did very well – great enthusiasm at ship all officers & some men accompanying us a considerable distance.' At a farthest south of 78° 45′, they bade farewell to their support party and turned their attention towards the South Pole. They left behind them the dreaded winter; a number of expeditionary blunders, such as having been under-provisioned and poorly prepared; and a handful of men who were exhibiting signs of scurvy. For Scott, this was the turning point and, ignoring the weaknesses of his team so far, he wrote in his journal that their prospects of success were good:

The sun shone brightly on our last farewells, and whilst behind us we left all in good health and spirits, it is scarcely to be wondered at that our hopes ran high for the future. We are already beyond the utmost limit to which man has attained: each footstep will be a fresh conquest of the great unknown. Confident in ourselves, confident in our dog team, we can but feel elated with the prospect that is before us.

But it was not long before Scott's journal entries changed in tone. The Great Ice Barrier was 'so utterly unlike anything experienced before,' he confessed, and 'already it is evident that if we are to achieve much it will be only by extreme toil, for the dogs have not pulled well today; possibly it may be something to do with the surface, which seems to get softer, possibly the absence of the men in front to cheer them on, and possibly something to do with the temperature, which rose at one time to +20 and made the heavy pulling very warm work.'

Seven weeks into the trek, the condition of the three men had become alarmingly poor. Wilson observed that Shackleton had 'decidedly angry-looking gums' – it was a sure sign that he was suffering from scurvy. By Christmas Scott and Wilson were also suffering; Wilson's left eye was so painful that he was dosing it with drops of cocaine solution and taking mor-

Left: *The Illustrated London News* carried stories detailing the perilous adventures of the sledging journeys made from *Discovery* to locations in the south and west. This is an illustration from a feature published in July 1903 that recounts Lieutenant Armitage's 'hairbreadth escape' from a crevasse.

Above: During the period that *Discovery* was locked in the grip of the ice, the men undertook all sorts of scientific and leisure activities. This rare photograph shows one of the men standing beside a small survey sledge, which has been rigged up to carry the sounding equipment some distance over the pack-ice.

We are Awful Fools to be Here

Edward Wilson, from his diary, 1902.

Friday, 5 December Just turned in, 4 a.m. Nearly every night now we dream of eating and food. Very hungry always, our allowance being a very bare one. Dreams as a rule of splendid food, ball suppers, sirloins of beef, cauldrons full of steaming vegetables. But one spends all one's time shouting at waiters who won't bring one a plate of anything, or else one finds the beef is only ashes when one gets it, or a pot full of honey has been poured out on a sawdusty floor. One very rarely gets a feed in one's sleep, though occasionally one does. …

Thursday, 11 December … We started seal meat with our breakfast, as well as having it for lunch today. Very heavy day's work. … The dogs seem a trifle better in health for the pieces of their companion, whom I cut up and distributed among them. Not one refused to eat it, indeed most of them neglected their fish for it. There was no hesitation. 'Dog don't eat dog' certainly doesn't hold down here, any more than does Ruskin's aphorism in *Modern Painters* that 'A fool always wants to shorten space and time; a wise man wants to lengthen both'. We must be awful fools at that rate, for our one desire is to shorten the space between us and the land. Perhaps Ruskin would agree that we are awful fools to be here at all, though I think if he saw these new mountain ranges he might think perhaps it was worth it. …

Friday, 26 December Woke up at 5 a.m. and as the left eye is still uncomfortable, made a sketch, using the right eye only. About 10 a.m. we started off and made nearly 5 miles, when my left eye got so intensely painful and watered so profusely that I could see nothing and could hardly stand the pain. I cocainized it repeatedly on the march, but the effect didn't last for more than a few minutes. For two days too I have had this eye blindfold for a trifling grittiness and now it came to this, while the right eye, which I had been using freely, was perfectly well. The Captain decided we should camp for lunch and the pain got worse and worse. I never had such pain in the eye before, and all the afternoon it was all I could do to lie still in my sleeping bag, dropping in cocaine from time to time. We tried ice, and zinc solution as well. After supper I tried hard to sleep, but after two hours of misery I gave myself a dose of morphia and then slept soundly the whole night and woke up practically well.

Saturday, 27 December … From start to finish today I went blindfold both eyes, pulling on ski. Luckily the surface was smooth and I only fell twice. I had the strangest thoughts or day dreams as I went along, all suggested by the intense heat of the sun I think. Sometimes I was in beech woods, sometimes in fir woods, sometimes in the Birdlip woods, all sorts of places connected in my mind with a hot sun. And the swish-swish of the ski was as though one's feet were brushing through dead leaves, or cranberry undergrowth or heather or juicy blue-bells. One could almost see them and smell them. It was delightful. I had no pain in the eyes all day, a trifling headache. Towards evening we came in sight of a splendid new range of mountains still farther to the south.

Wednesday, 31 December … As we got deeper and deeper in among this chaos of ice, the travelling became more and more difficult, and the ice all more recently broken up, so that no snow bridges had formed and we were faced by crevasses, ten, twenty, and thirty feet across, with sheer cliff ice sides to a depth of 50 or 80 ft. Unknown depths sometimes, because the bottom seemed a jumble of ice and snow and frozen pools of water and great screens of immense icicles. A very beautiful sight indeed, but an element of uncertainty about it, as one was always expecting to see someone drop in a hole, and while keeping your rope taut in case that happened, you would suddenly drop in a hole yourself. We tried hard to cross all this and reach the rock, but after covering a mile or more of it we came to impassable crevasses … which decided us to retrace our steps, as even if we reached it, this ice foot would prevent our reaching rock.

phine in order to sleep. Increasingly weakened from physical exhaustion, exposure, scurvy and woefully inadequate provisions, the three men continued south. Despite Wilson's concerns that if they pressed on they would not have provisions enough to see them safely back to the ship, Scott persisted. He was determined to push on towards the South Pole.

On 30 December 1902, Scott and Wilson left Shackleton to guard the camp, located at 82° 15′, while they reconnoitred a nearby inlet. Wilson recorded in his journal that the weather was so thick that they were compelled to return after just one or two miles. Scott recorded their new farthest south as 82° 17′ and he wrote:

> Whilst one cannot help a deep sense of disappointment in reflecting on the 'might have been' had our [dog] team remained in good health, one cannot but remember that even as it is we have made a greater advance towards a pole of the earth than has ever yet been achieved by a sledge party.

Above: On 3 February 1903, the southern party of (from left to right) Shackleton, Scott and Wilson finally made it back to the safety of the ship after their three-month sledge journey. Wilson described the scene in his journal: '… as we turned Cape Armitage we saw the ship decorated from top to toe with flags and all the ship's company up the rigging round the gangway to cheer us, which they did most lustily as we came onboard … then came the time for a bath, and clothes came off that had been on since November the second of the year before, and then a huge dinner.'

Their return to the ship was agonizing. By mid-January, all of the dogs they had brought with them had died or been killed. As starvation set in, the condition of the men worsened. Shackleton, increasingly breathless, started to cough up blood. 'We are all terrible-looking ruffians now,' observed Scott. 'The sun has burnt us quite black, and for many days our only bit of soap has remained untouched. It is some time, too, since we clipped our beards, and our hair has grown uncomfortably long; our faces have developed new lines and wrinkles, and look haggard and worn – in fact, our general appearance and tattered clothing have been a source of some amusement to us of late.'

Amusement at their appearance aside, the men were feeling uneasy about their chances of reaching the ship. On 15 January, Wilson confided to his journal that Shackleton was worryingly sick, and although Shackleton was still walking in harness, he had been ordered, despite his protests, not to help pull the sledges. As Shackleton reluctantly took his place behind the sledges, on skis, Wilson confronted Scott. The more their companion's health had deteriorated, the more Scott's patience had worn thin. He referred to Shackleton cuttingly as the 'lame duck' and 'our invalid', which only added to Shackleton's crushing sense of shame at his lack of strength.

Ten days later Shackleton resumed sharing the load, although they were all by now suffering from 'a desperate hunger'. Then Shackleton began to suffer from violent asthma attacks, which occasionally caused him to be 'livid and speechless'. On 29 January Shackleton was fighting unconsciousness as he heard Wilson saying to Scott that he did not expect him to last the night. Four days later, Scott wrote:

We are as near spent as three persons can well be. If Shackleton has shown a temporary improvement, we know by experience how little confidence we can place in it, and how near he has been and still is to a total collapse. As for Wilson and myself, we have scarcely liked to own how 'done' we are, and how greatly the last week or two has tried us .... One and all, we want rest and peace, and, all being well, to-morrow, thank Heaven, we shall get them.

Scott's prayers were answered. The following day, on 3 February, they were intercepted by Skelton and Bernacchi, who described the three broken men: 'Long beards, hair, dirt, swollen lips & peeled complexions, & blood shot eyes [which] made them almost unrecognizable. They appeared to be very worn & tired & Shackleton seemed very ill indeed.' With almost inexpressible relief, the three rejoined the ship. They had been away for 93 days and had travelled about 850 miles (1,370 kilometres) – the longest journey so far in Antarctica, and the closest yet made to the South Pole. However, Shackleton's health raised serious questions about his suitability for any further long sledging journeys, and the tensions, still increasing, between Scott and Shackleton only made matters worse. Despite his protests, Scott decided to send Shackleton and eight others back to England aboard the relief ship *Morning*, while he remained in Antarctica.

The following sledging season, Scott and two companions ascended the Ferrar Glacier and journeyed west across the immense polar plateau. Scott, gazing over the 'wildly and awfully desolate' expanse before him, wrote:

We see only a few miles of ruffled snow bounded by a vague, wavy horizon, but we know that beyond that horizon are hundreds and even thousands of miles which can offer no change to the weary eye, while on the expanse that one's mind conceives one knows there is neither tree nor shrub, nor any living thing, nor even inanimate rock – nothing but this terrible limitless expanse of snow … and we, little human insects, have started to crawl over this awful desert, and are now bent on crawling back again. Could anything be more terrible than this silent windswept immensity when one thinks such thoughts.

The sense of human frailty in such a place would be echoed several years later in the journals of Scott's last journey.

By the time Scott returned home to Britain the expedition had attained a new farthest south, surveyed a considerable amount of fresh territory and had collected a wealth of meteorological, magnetic, geological and biological results from its scientific programme. It was, the *Times* declared on 10 September 1904, 'one of the most successful [expeditions] that ever ventured into the Polar regions, north or south'.

Left: Discovery (left), still locked in the pack-ice of McMurdo Sound when this picture was taken on 14 February 1904, is approached by the two relief ships *Morning* (right) and *Terra Nova* (centre), both ex-whalers. Within a few days they had managed to free the ship and turned their bows northwards to make for New Zealand. When Scott returned to Antarctica it would be in command of *Terra Nova*.

PRICE SIXPENCE

CANTERBURY TIMES ANNUAL 1904

SNOW QUEEN

Above: The *Discovery* voyage enjoyed good coverage in the press in New Zealand, just as it did back in Britain, 1904.

SHACKLETON THE LEADER

Having been devastated by his premature return home in 1903, Shackleton made a remarkable recovery. In response to public demand, he began a lecture tour, with funds going towards sending the relief ship *Terra Nova* south to bring Scott and his men home. The enthusiastic response of the public to his energetic tale of the southern journey gave him both the confidence and the exposure to begin planning his own expedition.

On Monday 11 February 1907, it was announced that Shackleton was preparing an Antarctic expedition, which would leave later that year with the aim of reaching both the Magnetic South Pole and the Geographic South Pole. The announcement was timed perfectly. That same night the Norwegian explorer Roald Amundsen had given a lecture at the RGS about his completion (in 1903–1906) of the Northwest Passage in the converted herring boat *Gjøa* – a pioneering feat of navigation that had been unsuccessfully attempted, with much loss of life, for three centuries. Inspired by Amundsen's achievement, Shackleton now envisioned himself winning the South Pole for England: 'I am representing 400 million British subjects,' he wrote enthusiastically to his wife Emily. Royal patronage only intensified this patriotic feeling. On 5 August 1907 a farewell dinner was held on the wooden sealer *Nimrod*. In the place of honour was Emily Shackleton, with Ernest on her right; behind them hung a Union Flag, which had been presented to Shackleton a few days earlier by Queen Alexandra, along with a note that read: 'May this Union Jack, which I entrust to your keeping, lead you safely to the South Pole.'

Although it had taken him years to realize his dream of leading his own expedition – and in the interim he had bounced from the roles of secretary of the Royal Scottish Geographical Society to journalist to parliamentary candidate – Shackleton's energy, ambition and charm had won him many supporters.

By the time *Nimrod* departed from New Zealand, on her final leg south, 50,000 people had flooded the streets of the small harbour town of Lyttleton to catch a glimpse of the charismatic explorer as he headed towards the South Pole. As Margery and James Fisher later wrote in their biography of Shackleton, in 1907 the South Pole had something of the emotional value that Everest has had in our own time: 'If it was not constantly in the minds of the general public, at least they were willing to be excited by the thought of a man setting out to reach this mysterious spot, which no doubt some of them visualised as a post stuck in a waste of snows.' Shackleton had certainly generated excitement – the surging crowds in Lyttleton threatened to push the brass bands into the water and several of the vessels choking the harbour listed dangerously as passengers rushed across the decks to cheer the explorer on his journey.

However, back in England there were a few men who watched Shackleton's progress warily – and among them was Scott. Thanks in part to the success of Shackleton's lecture tour and press coverage, Scott had returned home to find himself lionized. He received medals from numerous geographical societies around the world, was given an honorary doctorate of science from the University of Cambridge and awarded membership of France's Légion d'honneur. Scott embraced his new-found fame, frequenting society parties and taking extended leave from the Royal Navy to write a book. So at home was he with his celebrity that he was caricatured as a dandy and a roué by 'Spy' in *Vanity Fair*.

Nevertheless, Shackleton was by far the more charismatic of the two. In addition, he had intended to employ the old *Discovery* headquarters of McMurdo Sound. Scott, incensed by the news, wrote to Shackleton immediately and declared his objections to the proposed use of 'his' base:

> I feel I have a sort of right to my own field of work in the same way as Peary claimed Smith's Sound and many African travellers their particular locality ... I don't want to be selfish at anyone's expense and least of all at that of one of my own people but still I think anyone who has had to do with exploration will regard this region primarily as mine ... it must be clear to you now that you have placed yourself directly in the way of my life's work – a thing for which I have sacrificed much and worked with steady purpose ... If you go to McMurdo Sound you go to winter quarters which are clearly mine ... I do not like to remind you that it was I who took you to the South or of the loyalty with which we all stuck to one another or of incidents of our voyage or of my readiness to do you justice on our return.

Above: Scott returned to England as a hero and his image was reproduced many times in the form of souvenir prints.

Scott had some powerful backers, including the RGS's former president Sir Clements Markham, its current president Sir George Goldie and its secretary J. Scott Keltie. Markham described Shackleton as the 'black sheep' of Scott's previous expedition, and he was indignant at what he believed was Shackleton's shameful behaviour. Even Wilson, whom Shackleton counted among his friends, made clear his allegiance to Scott. 'Now Shackles,' he wrote, 'I think that if you go to McMurdo Sound & even reach the Pole – the gilt will be off the gingerbread because of the insinuation which will almost certainly appear in the minds of a good many, that you forestalled Scott who had a prior claim to the use of that base.' Wilson's advice to Shackleton was to avoid McMurdo at all costs, even if it meant that it significantly diminished his chances of successfully reaching the South Pole. Remarkably, after much deliberation, Shackleton acquiesced to Scott's demands and signed an agreement that, in the eyes of all parties privy to it, would give him only a marginal chance of a favourable outcome.

In Antarctica, trying to observe that agreement, Shackleton's plan to establish his alternative base at King Edward VII Land was soon thwarted. Barred by ice and battered by heavy seas and storms, Shackleton was forced to make his way to the 'prohibited' base. It was a decision that would torment him. Had he not agreed to Scott's demands, he would have thought nothing of going on to McMurdo Sound – 'but I had promised and I felt each mile that I went to the West was a horror to me'. But he had no

On Shackleton's Hut

SIR WALLY HERBERT, 2007.

Shackleton's hut at Cape Royds was one of the friendliest huts I have ever seen in the Antarctic. I visited it for the first time shortly after the return of the sun in 1961 with Peter Otway. Peter and I had spent the previous summer in the field, and the winter at New Zealand's Scott Base working on our maps, and taking care of our dogs, and were now preparing for a season in the field mapping in the historic territory of the Beardmore and the Axel Heiberg Glaciers – the routes taken by Shackleton, Scott and Amundsen. During the previous summer a party from the University of Wellington had come down to work on the historic huts in McMurdo Sound – to rid them of the ice which had engulfed them and generally put them back into good shape. So Peter and I had the privilege of being the first party to visit those huts since their work had been completed.

We had approached the hut from the South in pitch darkness, and on reaching a snow bank had stopped and set up camp, not knowing where we were. I was up at the first light of dawn the next day, and discovered, looming not twenty yards from the lead dog of my team, Derrick Point where Shackleton's party had hauled their stores up the ice cliffs from the sea ice on 10 February 1908.

I scrambled up a small ice-foot – a miniature glacier split with crevasses and tumbled in blocks – and on to a hard snow col between two rocky hills, across a small frozen lake and there it was to my right: a neat, warm ochre, sun-soaked hut nestling in a dip – as snug a little hut as ever I have seen. It brought from me a gasp of joy. Behind it, rising above a rock ridge, the white cone of Mount Erebus cut a fine profile against a blue sky.

It was a small pocket of kindly feeling – a shell of timber with a few relics left to taint it with the odour of age, and yet I entered that hut as Herbert Ponting had done: 'with a feeling akin to awe'. It was from that little hut that Shackleton and his three companions of the Southern Party had set off for the South Pole on 29 October 1908. Four men and four ponies, nine days later, watched their support party 'dwindling to a speck in the north'. To their south lay almost four months of dire hunger and, as Amundsen said, 'the most brilliant incident in the history of Antarctic exploration'. They sledged to within ninety-seven geographical miles of the South Pole – an advance of 353 geographical miles beyond Scott's Farthest South record of 1902. They discovered and pioneered a route on the Beardmore Glacier and discovered nearly five hundred miles of a new mountain range. The hut seemed too small to have housed such men.

Even Sir Raymond Priestley, who had been a member of Shackleton's expedition, was affected by the occult atmosphere of that place. He wrote in his diary when he visited the hut as a member of Scott's expedition in 1911: 'The whole place is very eerie, there is such a feeling of life about it. Not only do I feel it but the others do also. Last night after I turned in I could have sworn that I heard people shouting to each other. I thought that I had only got an attack of nerves but Campbell asked me if I heard any shouting, for he had certainly done so.'

That little hut was set in a delightful environment and all day we strolled around soaking in sunshine, aware of the impulsion that had driven the Pole-seekers to exercise hard where we lazily ambled. Was it any wonder that thoughts of them re-kindled my idea of dog-sledging to the Pole at the end of the field season. There, in Shackleton's hut, it was easy to dream. Time was turned back half a century by the adventurous spirits that dwelt in that place, and I was unashamedly in sympathy with them. I was more aware of atmosphere there than in any other place I have visited. It was for me a stimulating experience, although on another occasion it might not have been so, for it had caught me that day with a rising 'Pole fever'.

choice. As Captain England of *Nimrod* frankly informed him, the idea of wintering on any other part or inlet of the ice barrier was a suicidal one. Having agonized over the decision, Shackleton simply had to put his feelings to one side and press on, because, as he confided to his wife, 'my duty to the country and King since I was given the flag for the Pole and lastly but not least my duty to all who entrusted themselves to my keeping' required it of him.

Above: The kitchen area in Shackleton's hut, now restored, at Cape Royds, photographed by Ann Hawthorne. Many of the original supplies remain in place a century later.

FARTHEST SOUTH

Dividing his men into several teams, Shackleton intended to secure tangible geographical achievements. Before winter had set in, six of the party – second-in-command Jameson Boyd Adams, the two doctors Eric Marshall and Alistair Forbes Mackay, Sir Philip Brocklehurst and the two Australian members Douglas Mawson and Edgeworth David – had made the first ascent of Mount Erebus.

By October 1908, the real focus of the expedition was under way. One party, including David, Mawson and Mackay began to ascend the Victoria Land plateau towards the Magnetic South Pole. Within a month, the main party of Shackleton, Marshall, Adams and Frank Wild had commenced their trek towards the Geographic South Pole.

The going for the southern party was tough from the start. Shackleton had decided to leave the sledge-dogs behind, relying instead on four ponies and manual hauling. The ponies proved to be almost useless, sinking belly-deep into the soft snow. With regret, the ponies were shot when they floundered and weakened, and their meat was depoted for later consumption. By 1 December only one pony was left, and a vast ridge of mountains lay ahead of the party. Shackleton's one consolation was that, on 26 November, they had passed Scott's farthest south position. Two days later the four scaled a red granite rock and gazed across a magnificent scene. Dr Marshall recorded the sight:

> ... to the South a great glacier extended as far as the eye could reach, flanked on either side by rugged ice-covered mountains, until lost sight of 60 miles distant where the mountains on the East flank and the Cloudmaker on the West formed a 'narrows' or waist, which forecast great ice disturbances as the glacier flowed from the distant plateau, which we now realised guarded the secrets of the Pole itself.

They had discovered the great sweep of the Beardmore Glacier – the 'gateway' to the South Pole. 'It is all so interesting and everything is on such a vast scale that one cannot describe it well,' wrote Shackleton. 'We 4 are seeing these great designs and the play of Nature for the first time and possibly this may never be seen by man again.'

Below: From left to right, Jameson Adams, Frank Wild and Ernest Shackleton at their 'farthest south' on 9 January 1909. Of that moment, Shackleton would later write: 'The last day out and we have shot our bolt. The tale is 88° 23′S … homeward bound.'

Three days later, 'Socks', the group's last remaining pony, was lost down a crevasse. Some have speculated that had this disaster been averted, Shackleton's expedition may have been the first to reach the South Pole. By this point the men were exhausted and their rations depleted. They had travelled 550 miles (885 kilometres) from their base, and they were still 250 miles (400 kilometres) from the South Pole. On Christmas day, Wild wrote: 'May none but my worst enemies ever spend their Christmas in such a dreary God-forsaken spot as this.' Yet still he tried to keep his spirits up: 'Here we are 9,500 ft. above sea level, farther away from civilisation than any human being has ever been since civilisation was, with half a gale blowing, and drift snow flying, and a temperature of 52° of frost, and yet we are not miserable.' Shackleton, noting among his companions their 'cheerfulness and regardlessness of self', also tried to remain positive. Despite Marshall having recorded their body temperatures as 2 degrees subnormal, Shackleton declared his men were 'fit as can be' – 'It is a fine open air life!' They had reached a critical juncture, and their rations were reduced – 'it is the only thing to do for we must get to the Pole, come what may'. But Shackleton, writing in his diary, knew that the odds now were stacked against them:

> I cannot think of failure yet I must look at the matter sensibly and the lives of those who are with me. I feel that if we go on too far it will be impossible to get back over this surface and then all the results will be lost to the world. We can now definitely locate the South Pole on the highest plateau in the world and our geological work and the meteorology will be of great use to science: But all this is not the Pole and man can only do his best and we have arrayed against us the strongest forces of Nature.

At 4 a.m. on 9 January 1909, the men left a makeshift depot, which contained all the supplies they would need to take them back 150 miles (240 kilometres) to the previous depot, and made an extraordinary last-ditch attempt to get within at least 100 miles (160 kilometres) of their goal. Taking only a supply of chocolate, biscuits and sugar with them, they made a dash for it, as Wild put it, running 'as hard as we could pelt over the snow'. Then, as one, they stopped – they stood at the highest latitude ever reached, to their knowledge, by any human on the planet. Peary had claimed the farthest north of 87° 06′ in 1906, now they were closer to the ends of the Earth than anyone in history. However, it was not elation they felt, but crushing exhaustion, disappointment and hunger. Shackleton recorded: 'we have shot our bolt and the tale is 88.23 S. 162 E.'

Unfurling the Union Jack that had been presented to them by Queen Alexandra, they quietly congratulated one another. They were within 97 miles (156 kilometres) of the South Pole, but they could go no further with any certainty that they would make it home alive. Later, Adams would comment: 'If we'd gone on one more hour, we shouldn't have got back.' 'Whatever regrets may be we have done our best,' Shackleton wrote philosophically. 'Beaten the South Record by 366 miles the North by 77 miles. Amen.'

Above: After he returned to England, Shackleton gave a huge number of public lectures to audiences hungry to hear more about his exploits to the 'farthest south'.

THE NIMROD SHACKLETON'S ANTARCTIC EXPEDITION. 1907-1909.

ICEMOUND OF CONDENSED VAPOUR, Mt EREBUS.

THE START FROM CAPE ROYDS, SHACKLETON'S EXPEDITION.

THE AURORA AUSTRALIS SHACKLETON'S EXPEDITION.

NORTHERN PARTY AT S.MAGNETIC POLE, SHACKLETON'S EXPEDITION.

Shackleton's decision to turn away from the South Pole – which was so tantalizingly close – to ensure the safe return of his men may be reckoned as one of the greatest moments of courage and good sense in polar history. As J. Gordon Hayes pointed out in 1932 in his book *The Conquest of the South Pole*:

> Shackleton had a remarkable gift for making correct and swift decisions that averted disaster, and his greatness as an explorer is largely attributable to this intuition. Success on his expeditions was very near to his heart, but the safety and health of those who served under him came first; and the fact that he never lost a life may be regarded as the finest of all his feats and the greatest of all his triumphs.

Nevertheless, now Shackleton and his men had to face 700 gruelling and uncertain miles to safety. Despite their exhaustion, hunger, bouts of dysentery and exposure, the men managed to stagger safely back to base. Remarkably, Shackleton immediately continued on with Wild to search for the missing party assigned to reach the magnetic pole. Finally, with all the men accounted for, *Nimrod* headed home. Shackleton's British Antarctic Expedition, more popularly known as the *Nimrod* Expedition, had been successful in many respects – the approximate location of the Magnetic South Pole had been discovered, Mount Erebus had been summited for the first time, the south polar plateau had been ascended, the 'gateway' to the South Pole had been discovered and charted, a wealth of scientific data had been collected and a new farthest south had been reached. No matter that the South Pole itself had not been claimed   Shackleton's decision to turn back from his goal for, as he described it, the sake of his men and their families was heroic in itself, and it struck a chord with the British public. In years to come, his statement to his wife Emily that 'a live donkey is better than a dead lion, isn't it?' came to be the burning question many explorers had to face: whether fame was worth the cost of the lives of oneself and others.

A HERO'S RETURN

On the afternoon of 14 June 1909, the gates of Charing Cross Station were closed to prevent the crowds of well-wishers from surging through. 'No one who was present,' wrote Shackleton's close friend Hugh Robert Mills, 'is ever likely to forget the roar of cheering from the crowd which filled the Strand and Trafalgar Square as the open carriage, with Shackleton, his wife and children, made its way slowly along the streets where no attempt had been made to keep a passage open, for the police had failed to foresee this burst of enthusiasm. The newspapers put the crowd at 10,000, and telegraph boys had delivered 400 telegrams at the door by the time the party had arrived.' According to popular reports of the day, the horses were taken out of their shafts and the carriage hauled by teams of men through the streets into the city. The *Illustrated London News* called Shackleton 'The Hero of the Moment' and the *Daily Telegraph* proclaimed:

Left: The *Nimrod* voyage was celebrated at home in all manner of popular souvenirs. This set of collectible cigarette cards shows the greatest hits of the expedition, in particular the 'conquest' of the South Magnetic Pole. On 16 January 1909, Alistair Mackay, Edgeworth David, and Douglas Mawson finally raised the Union Jack there at 72° 15′S, 155° 16′E. Having taken a few photographs and 'claimed the area for the Empire', they had little time to rest in their desperate struggle to return to the safety of a rendezvous with the ship *Nimrod* before their supplies ran out.

Below: Ernest Shackleton made a triumphant return to London, where he was overwhelmed by a wave of admirers at Charing Cross Station on 14 June 1909.

We cannot make too much of him … Let us remember at this moment that in our age, filled with vain babbling about the decadence of the race, he has upheld the old fame of our breed; he has renewed its reputation for physical and mental and moral energy; he has shown that where it exerts itself under fit leadership it is still second to none … and at a critical time in the fortunes of all the Britains he has helped to breathe new inspiration and resolve into the British stock throughout the world.

Meanwhile, history was also being made in the Arctic. On 2 September it was announced in the *New York Herald* that Dr Frederick Cook, a friend of Roald Amundsen and the physician on Gerlache's *Belgica* expedition, was claiming that he had reached the North Pole. With spectacular timing, five days later a cable from Labrador asserted that Robert Peary was the first to the North Pole. The civilized world seemed consumed with polar fever, and still the prize of the South Pole lay unclaimed.

Three months after Shackleton's return, at an elegant reception at the Savage Club, London, in honour of the *Nimrod* Expedition, Scott took the opportunity to announce his own plans to conquer the South Pole. 'All I have to do now,' he added, 'is to thank Mr Shackleton for so nobly showing me the way.'

This page: Shackleton's heroics appeared on the front cover of many periodicals. He toured the country that summer to give numerous lectures and put on shows.

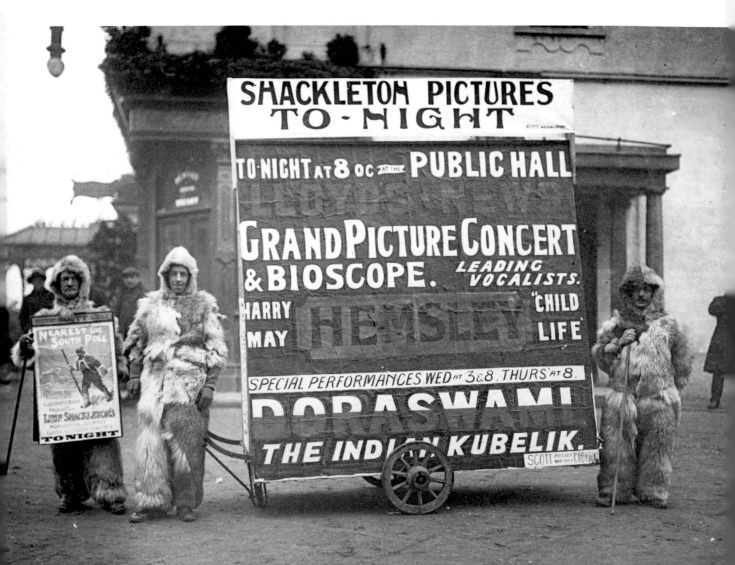

The Lure of Little Voices

Robert W. Service, 1907.

There's a cry from out the loneliness--oh, listen, Honey, listen!
  Do you hear it, do you fear it, you're a-holding of me so?
You're a-sobbing in your sleep, dear, and your lashes, how they glisten--
  Do you hear the Little Voices all a-begging me to go?

All a-begging me to leave you. Day and night they're pleading, praying,
  On the North-wind, on the West-wind, from the peak and from the plain;
Night and day they never leave me--do you know what they are saying?
  'He was ours before you got him, and we want him once again.'

Yes, they're wanting me, they're haunting me, the awful lonely places;
  They're whining and they're whimpering as if each had a soul;
They're calling from the wilderness, the vast and God-like spaces,
  The stark and sullen solitudes that sentinel the Pole.

They miss my little camp-fires, ever brightly, bravely gleaming
  In the womb of desolation, where was never man before;
As comradeless I sought them, lion-hearted, loving, dreaming,
  And they hailed me as a comrade, and they loved me evermore.

And now they're all a-crying, and it's no use me denying;
  The spell of them is on me and I'm helpless as a child;
My heart is aching, aching, but I hear them, sleeping, waking;
  It's the Lure of Little Voices, it's the mandate of the Wild.

I'm afraid to tell you, Honey, I can take no bitter leaving;
  But softly in the sleep-time from your love I'll steal away.
Oh, it's cruel, dearie, cruel, and it's God knows how I'm grieving;
  But His loneliness is calling, and He knows I must obey.

CHAPTER 4
A RACE TO THE POLE

*You shall go to the S. Pole. Oh dear, what's the use of having energy
& enterprise if a little thing like that can't be done. It's got to be done,
so hurry up.*

KATHLEEN BRUCE IN A LETTER TO HER FUTURE HUSBAND, ROBERT FALCON
SCOTT, 11 JULY 1908.

Below: Scott and his wife Kathleen, accompanied by Scott's long-time supporter Sir Clements Markham, on board *Terra Nova* in May 1910 prior to its departure from London's West India Dock.

The tumultuous applause that greeted Shackleton's achievements, which included a knighthood bestowed on him by King Edward VII, may not have sat well with Scott, but he could take comfort from the fact that the South Pole had remained unclaimed. Scott had wanted to mount another expedition to Antarctica for some time, but sponsors were in short supply and many of his supporters at the RGS now believed that Shackleton was the more worthy explorer. Some even thought that Scott should not embark on the mission at all, including the RGS's vice-president Admiral Sir Lewis Beaumont, who expressed his concerns in private:

> Scott would make a very great mistake … by trying to compete with Shackleton on a Pole-hunting expedition … the [RGS] Council's attitude ... ought ... to be ... opposed to it.

> The more I think of the difference between what Shackleton has done, and the mere act … of standing at the position of the Pole itself – the less I think of it!

> Let [Scott] lead another Antarctic expedition if he will … but let it be a scientific expedition …. He is looking at the thing now from too close, individually …. All this is to incline you to put Scott off from making … a mistake – that is, competing with Shackleton in organizing an expedition to go over the old route merely to do that 97 miles….

With funding unforthcoming from either the RGS or Britain's Admiralty,

other sources had to be found. To secure sponsorship Scott knew he would have to appeal to the public's thirst for adventure. 'People whose knowledge is derived from the sensational press count success in degrees of latitude,' Scott conceded. It had become clear from Shackleton's reception that there were now certain expectations of a polar explorer – as *Macmillan's Magazine* declared:

> It is well that popular triumph should be accorded to other than military heroes. Lieutenant Shackleton and his companions have been the lions of the month, and never did a lion roar more modestly and more becomingly than the gallant hero, who in his speeches has shown a fund of dry humour not usually found among such men.

If such praise for his former subordinate was hard to swallow, it nevertheless confirmed to Scott what kinds of expedition and man would attract the public's attention. Adventure had to be a crucial part of any popular undertaking. 'I admit that the main object of the expedition is to reach the South Pole,' he said, before adding, 'but this is largely a matter of sentiment.' To reassure potential financial backers in the scientific community, Scott made it clear that furthering knowledge of the world remained a fundamental part of his plans, declaring that it was the duty of the explorer: '... to bring back something more than a bare account of his movements ... He must take every advantage of his unique position and opportunities to study natural phenomena.' To that end Scott intended to have a comprehensive research programme, and for his team to contain a proper

Above: Scott sought many ways to raise funds for the *Terra Nova* voyage – from individuals, such as schoolboys sponsoring one sleeping bag at a time, to corporations, in the form of support from food suppliers. F.J. Hooper was persuaded by Ponting to pose for publicity shots on a number of occasions; in this instance, Hooper is photographed sampling beans supplied by the American company Heinz, which offered its wares in return for good exposure.

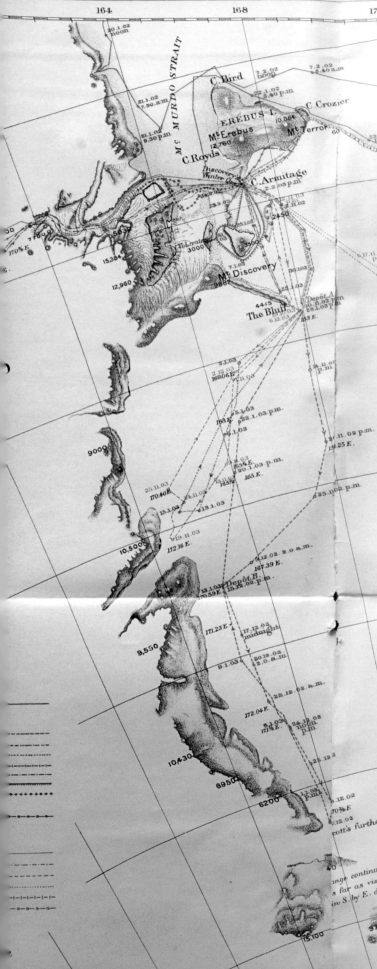

complement of experts in cartography, geology, glaciology, meteorology, marine biology and other scientific disciplines.

A RETURN TO THE SOUTH

In September 1909 when the sensational news broke of the competing claims (controversial, to this day) of Cook and Peary to have reached the North Pole six months previously, Scott was able to benefit from a swelling tide of patriotism. Despite their illustrious history in polar exploration, the British had lost a major geographical prize to the Americans, and there were rumours that Peary was now planning to head south. For national dignity's sake, the South Pole had to be claimed for Britain. To Admiral Sir Arthur Moore, Scott wrote, 'I don't hold that anyone but an Englishman should get to the S. Pole.' Fearful that someone would beat him to his dreamed-of destination, rather than the two years or more of careful planning that a venture of this magnitude normally required, Scott gave himself just nine months to achieve the following targets: to raise the finances needed; to secure the use of a ship; to find and vet a team of scientists and crew; to calculate what supplies the expedition would require; and to order then test a vast store of clothing, equipment and supplies. Last but not least, he would plan the route.

Scott's second Antarctic expedition was formally announced on 13 September 1909, within a week of the announcement that Peary was claiming to have reached the North Pole. The following day, Scott's wife Kathleen gave birth to their son Peter. By now Scott was unabashed about declaring that the goal was to attain the South Pole and 'to secure for the British Empire the honour of that achievement'. He needed £40,000 and he targeted commercial sponsors, as well as the public – even schools were invited to contribute to the purchase of everything from ponies and dogs, to socks and sleeping bags.

THE NATIONAL A

Two members of Scott's crew reduced the fund target by 'donating' £1,000 to join: the independently wealthy Lawrence Oates ('Titus' or 'the soldier') and Apsley Cherry-Garrard ('Cherry', a friend of Wilson's, appointed as assistant zoologist). Eventually the expedition was to have a total of more than 60 men serve in the ship and shore parties. There were five officers, all (except Oates) with Royal Navy experience: Scott, second-in-command Edward ('Teddy') Evans, Henry ('Birdie') Bowers, surgeon and parasitologist Edward ('Atch') Atkinson and Oates. The scientific team was seven strong, under the leadership of Edward ('Billy') Wilson: meteorologist George ('Sunny Jim') Simpson, geologists Thomas ('Griff') Taylor and Frank ('Deb') Debenham, biologist Edward ('Bronte') Nelson, physicist and glaciologist Charles ('Silas') Wright, and Cherry-Garrard. The men contributed a variety of skills, including Herbert ('Ponco') Ponting the photographer or 'camera artist' (as he preferred it), Cecil Mears and Siberian Demetri Gerof the dog experts, Tryggve Gran the prize skier (recommended by Nansen) and Bernard Day, a *Nimrod* veteran, the mechanic. From the ranks of the officers and the men – who included another geologist, later to join them in Sydney, Raymond Priestley; the naval gunner Edgar ('Taff') Evans; and the Londoner Able Seaman Harry Dickason – Scott would pick his 'twelve good men and true' to form the crucial parties. A Dundee-built whaler, the *Terra Nova*, was selected as the expedition vessel.

Although Scott's appeal attracted a lot of coverage – and 8,000 men had applied to join the crew – the expedition was still £8,000 short of its target by the time that it departed from England in July 1910, which meant that Scott had only sufficient money to pay the wages of his team up to their arrival in New Zealand. Another problem was that the planning had been rushed and poor decisions had been made; in particular, Scott's choice of Manchurian ponies instead of dogs would prove to be a significant handicap on the southern journey – yet it was a choice he felt unnecessary to justify. After all, Shackleton had established a new farthest south record without relying wholly on teams of dogs. Furthermore, although five of the crew he assembled had been on the *Discovery* expedition, few others had any polar experience; for example, only two of the four later selected to march to the pole had visited Antarctica previously, and only one, the Norwegian Gran, had skiing expertise.

The news of the apparent conquest of the North Pole had another consequence for Scott. Waiting for him upon his arrival in Melbourne on 10 October was a telegram: 'Beg leave to inform you *Fram* proceeding Antarctic. Amundsen.' The telegram was dated 3 October and had been sent from Christiania (the then name of Oslo), even though the *Fram* had left Norway on 7 June with Roald Amundsen on board. It was mystifying.

AMUNDSEN THE COMPETITOR

From an early age, Amundsen had been fascinated by tales of adventure, in particular the tragic tale of the disappearance of the Franklin expedition in the ice-choked labyrinth of islands that make up part of the sea route between the Atlantic and Pacific oceans through the Arctic waters of Canada, Alaska and Greenland, which is known as the Northwest Passage. Although his parents always wanted him to become a doctor, Amundsen privately visualized a future for himself as a polar explorer.

Amundsen's boyhood hero, his fellow countryman Nansen, offered a role model, and in 1893 when Nansen had set out in his specially designed ship *Fram*, in an attempt to drift with the pack-ice across the Arctic Ocean, Amundsen felt that he had found his calling. Amundsen had failed his exams in medicine and both parents had passed away, which left him free to decide his own future. Embarking on a series of sealing voyages only gave him more of a taste for the polar wilds, so when the opportunity presented itself he volunteered to join Gerlache's expedition and was accepted as first mate. Having acquired confidence in the polar environment, Amundsen returned home and earned his master mariner's certificate, before spending several years in the Arctic and becoming the first man to successfully navigate the Northwest Passage, doing so between 1903 and 1906 in his sloop *Gjøa*. The knowledge that he gained from living alongside the Inuit peoples during this expedition, such as driving dogs, the use of fur clothing and how to build snow igloos, would be put to good use in Antarctica.

Amundsen's next goal had been to reach the North Pole, until the declarations of both Peary and his old friend Cook shattered those plans. 'This was a blow indeed!' he confessed. 'If I was to maintain my prestige as an explorer I must quickly achieve a sensational success of some sort.' Having been thwarted in his intended mission, Amundsen decided quickly that instead of using his vessel, *Fram*, to explore the northern polar basin he would change fronts and, as he put it, 'solve the last great problem – the South Pole'.

Because Amundsen's northern enterprise was heavily in debt and he was unwilling to risk upsetting his backers, he decided against informing anyone of his plans: neither Nansen, who had lent him the *Fram*, nor the majority of his crew. From Christiana, Amundsen set a course for Buenos Aires – the crew were not the least bit surprised at the route because the Panama Canal was not yet open and going around South America was necessary in order to reach the Bering Strait. Only when *Fram* docked in Madeira did he unburden his audacious secret and reveal his plans to the group, many of whom were in the Norwegian navy: second-in-command Thorvald Nilsen; Fredrick Gjertsen, the first mate; Kristian Prestrud, the first officer of the *Fram* and the expedition's navigator; Fredrick Hjalmar Johansen, Nansen's partner in 1895; Adolf Lindstrøm and Karinius Olsen, cooks and carpenters; Olav Bjaaland, a ski champion of Norway; Helmer Hanssen, an experienced ice pilot and dog driver, who had accompanied Amundsen as second mate aboard the *Gjøa*; Sverre Hassel, an expert dog driver and navigator; Oscar Wisting, a former naval gunner; Ludvig Hansen, an ice pilot and skilled maker of paraffin tanks; Martin Rønne, a sailmaker; Jørgen Stubberud, a carpenter, who built a prefabricated hut for the pack-ice; Andreas Beck, an ice pilot; Knut Sundbeck, Jacob Nödtvedt and H. Kristensen, all engineers; and Alexander Kutchin, an oceanographer.

Amundsen handed to his brother Leon letters of announcement and personal messages to both the King of Norway and Nansen, along with strict instructions that the announcement of Amundsen's change of plan would be timed so that there was no possibility of the sponsors being able to recall the expedition. Once Leon had arrived back in Christiania he was also to send a telegram to Scott. As soon as Leon had gone ashore with his instructions, Amundsen turned *Fram* south and, in his typical understated style, he recorded:

September 9 – Friday

... At 6 pm I called all the men together and told them my intention to go for the South Pole. When I asked if they were willing to go with me, I got a unanimous yes .... We left at 9.30 using the engine. It was clear and starry, a wonderful night. Half an hour later we were in the NE trade wind, good and fresh. Set sails and made fine speed for the South Pole. The dogs were given two big meals with fresh food during our stay at Madeira. We bought two horses and slaughtered them in a dingy alongside the vessel. Very appetising.

The news 'astonished us all', wrote Alexander Kutchin. 'Nobody had suspected it ... weariness soon overcame us – a kind of drunkenness – new thoughts, new plans, as far from the old ones as the South Pole from the

Above: This portrait of Roald Amundsen was taken in 1906, upon his safe arrival in Nome, Alaska, having successfully navigated a Northwest Passage. Now a proven explorer and leader of men, Amundsen was determined to embark upon another challenge and to do so he turned his attention southwards.

North.' 'Before going North,' wrote one of the men to his wife, 'we will make a small excursion to the South Pole.' Astonishment gave way to excitement, 'Hurrah', cheered another member of the crew, Olav Bjaaland: 'That means we'll get there first!'

Because Scott's plan to claim the South Pole was well known, Amundsen felt that secrecy and speed on his part were important – if Scott became aware of a rival expedition it would impel him to organize his own even more quickly. In addition, Amundsen had concerns that if he announced his intentions too soon 'it would only have given occasion for a lot of newspaper discussion, and possibly have ended in the project being stifled at its birth' – and he believed that an attempt to reach the South Pole would serve his sponsors well. Amundsen was already well placed to start the expedition: he had the funding, the equipment and a carefully chosen crew in place, and it would take little effort to set his sights for the South instead of the North. He was in a favourable position to make the South Pole first, and he knew it. Whether Scott would be annoyed at there being a competitor in the field was of no concern to Amundsen. 'I do not belong to that class of explorer who believes that the Polar sea has been created for myself alone', he wrote. 'First come, first served is an old saying.' Although he had no scruples about challenging Scott, Amundsen was aware that he would be reproached for not having announced his revised plan earlier, and in his own account of the expedition he wrote:

> I knew I should be able to inform Captain Scott of the extension of my plans before he left civilization, and therefore a few months sooner or later could be of no great importance. Scott's plan and equipment were so widely different from my own that I regarded the telegram that I sent him later, with the information that we were bound for the Antarctic regions, rather as a mark of courtesy than as a communication which might cause him to alter his programme in the slightest degree. The British expedition was designed entirely for scientific research. The Pole was only a side-issue, whereas in my extended plan it was the main object. On this little detour science would have to look after itself …

As Amundsen suspected, his latest goal became headline news in Norway: 'Sensational announcement by Roald Amundsen' … 'With a single blow … Roald Amundsen … reawakens the attention of the world when the exciting fight for the South Pole is on.' The reaction of Nansen, one of the world's best polar explorers, to the change of focus was immediate: 'The idiot!' he exclaimed at the news. 'Why couldn't he have told me. He could have had all my plans and calculations.' Nansen had tremendous respect for his younger countryman, recognizing the mettle he possessed and the ambition that drove him (the same qualities that had enabled Nansen to achieve some of the greatest journeys in history) – and although Nansen wished he was young and fit enough to attempt the journey to the South Pole himself, he acknowledged that Amundsen was perfectly placed to achieve his goal. A devoted patriot, Nansen also quietly enjoyed the idea of a fellow Norwegian challenging the British expedition.

Above: Amundsen (left) watches as Martin Rønne operates the sewing machine on the deck of *Fram* in 1910 as the vessel makes her journey through the tropics, heading south to the Antarctic. The dogs loll in the shade, providing a sharp contrast to the collective effort they would soon have to make.

Notwithstanding Scott's suspicion that there might be competitors, the actual news of a rival – a 'bolt from the blue', as Tryggve Gran put it – was a devastating blow to Scott, who appeared to block out the possibility that Amundsen was heading for the South Pole; after all, Amundsen's telegram stated that he was heading to Antarctica. It was only when a local reporter in Wellington pressed Scott on his reaction to the challenge – letting slip that there was a rumour that the Norwegian was intending to use McMurdo Sound as his base – that the penny seemed to drop. According to Gran:

> Scott fell silent. But the interviewer did not give up. Then Scott became angry and brushed the man off by saying, 'If, as [your] rumour says, Amundsen wants to try for the South Pole from some part of the coast of the West Antarctic, I can only wish him good luck.'

Scott reiterated that the primary reason for his expedition was scientific research, but there was still the question of where Amundsen was at that

moment, and where he intended to make his base. A month after he had received the telegram from Amundsen, Scott sent a message to Nansen asking where Amundsen planned to land. 'I do not believe the report that he is going to McMurdo Sound – the idea seems to me preposterous in view of his record,' Scott wrote, anxiously trying to determine whether Amundsen might appropriate the base Scott claimed as his own: '... but the fact that he departs with so much mystery leaves one with an uncomfortable feeling that he contemplates something which he imagines we should not approve.' Nansen replied succinctly: 'Unknown.' There was nothing to do other than for Scott to continue on as best he could. 'None can foretell our luck,' Scott said. 'We may get through, we may not. We may have accidents to some of the transports, to the sledges, or to the animals. We may lose our lives. We may be wiped out. It is all a question that lies with providence and luck.'

Amundsen was not the only competitor making his way to Antarctica. The aspirant Japanese explorer Nobu Shirase also had dreams of being the first to reach the South Pole. His first expedition to Antarctica had sailed from Tokyo in December 1910, only to return to Sydney five months later having made no landings and with only bad weather to report. The unfortunate Shirase and his men were regarded with a mixture of hostility and amusement. Shirase wrote in his memoirs:

> The New Zealand press viewed our attempt with ridicule. The
> *New Zealand Times* was particularly poignant in its comments upon
> us. It remarked that we were a crew of gorillas sailing about in a
> miserable whaler, and that the polar regions were no place for
> such beasts of the forest as we. The zoological classification of us
> was perhaps to be taken figuratively, but many islanders interpret-
> ed it literally, because crowds of people came to our tents daily to
> observe the 'sporty gorillas' misguided with the crazy notion of
> conquering the South Pole.

Shirase's second expedition would be more successful, with his vessel *Kainan Maru* even dropping anchor alongside Amundsen's *Fram* in the Bay of Whales, yet, perhaps unsurprisingly, Scott did not appear to take the Japanese threat seriously. Amundsen, however, was in a different league. In Lyttleton, Scott oversaw the remaining preparations for the journey south. The *Terra Nova* was painstakingly loaded with a vast array of equipment: three motor-sledges, 460 tons of coal, collapsible huts, an ice-house with 162 carcasses of mutton, 35,000 cigars, 32 tons of pony fodder, 5 tons of dog food and a menagerie of animals: 15 ponies, 35 huskies, three rabbits, a fantail pigeon and a guinea pig, not to mention the ship's cat, with its own hammock. Although Scott took pains to make it appear that it was business as usual, members of the expedition party could see that the introduction of a competitor had unsettled their leader. Oates wrote to his mother:

> What do you think about Amundsen's expedition? If he gets to the
> Pole first we shall come home with our tails between our legs and
> no mistake. I must say we have made far too much noise about

ourselves all that photographing, cheering, steaming through the fleet etc. etc. is rot and if we fail it will only make us look more foolish. They say Amundsen has been underhand in the way he has gone about it but I personally don't see it is underhand to keep your mouth shut – I myself think these Norskies are a very tough lot they have 200 dogs ... also they are very good ski-runners while we can only walk, if Scott does anything silly such as underfeeding his ponies he will be beaten as sure as death.

ATTENTION TO DETAIL

All of Amundsen's expeditions were executed with meticulous precision. He was well read and well tested in polar travel, had trained hard and was fully prepared to face even the most extreme obstacles. Amundsen was a 'professional' explorer – objective and ambitious about his goals and how to achieve them. Even during his first experience as part of the *Belgica* expedition, Amundsen had shown a flair for tackling challenges head on, such as setting out to investigate a strange apparition in the dead of the polar night (see page 46).

On 1 December 1910, Amundsen chose the seven members of the team who would trek with him towards the South Pole. Olav Bjaaland, Helmer Hanssen, Sverre Hassel, Oscar Wisting, Jørgen Stubberud, Hjalmar Johansen and Kristian Prestrud. In addition, he decided to increase the wages of his small crew by 50 percent, as an incentive. Now, with his goal clear he urged the *Fram* quickly south, for even with a head start, poor weather conditions or any number of other obstacles could prevent them from beating Scott. They needed to make the most of every possible advantage – 'At all costs we had to be first at the finish', Amundsen recalled. 'Everything had to be concentrated on that.'

Meanwhile, Scott's expedition seemed jinxed. On 2 December, Wilson wrote: 'Dawn came ... and with it everything began to go wrong'. The *Terra Nova* had crossed into the Furious Fifties, and had been greeted with hurricane winds that had whipped the sea into swells 35 feet (11 metres) high. The overladen ship pitched helplessly on soaring mountains of froth, then plunged into green black chasms; the tiny amount of air trapped inside the flailing vessel was the only thing keeping her afloat. With the pump broken and the engine stalled, the men – crew, scientists and gentlemen staff alongside one another – desperately baled water in two-hour shifts as they vomited, some managing to sing as they did so ('I went to bale with a strenuous prayer in my heart, and a 'Yip-I-Addy' on my lips...'). Stacks of coal sacks and fuel cans were torn from their lashings and smashed together; men clung desperately to anything they could to prevent being swept away; and dogs and ponies slid back and forth, gulping for air. Oates attempted to keep the ponies calm and on their feet, but struggled alone without the companionship of singing comrades. 'About 4 in the morning the fo'castle got half-full of water and on looking out I found the whole forrard part of the ship deserted and one solitary dog washing about. I began then to think

Top: Helmer Hanssen and Oscar Wisting make some repairs to a sledge in a workshop that they have dug out of the snow around their base at Framheim, the Bay of Whales, in 1911.

Above: Adolf H. Lindstrom in the small kitchen in the hut at Framheim, 1911

An Oriental Encounter

NOBU SHIRASE, *NANKYOKUKI*, 1913.

At 2 a.m. we made out a faint pale grey line on the horizon to port, which we thought must be either a mountain or a cloud. Not until 4:20 a.m. did we see that it was actually the undulating wall of the Great Ice Barrier itself. As we drew nearer we could see it more and more clearly. At first sight the Barrier appeared as a sweeping crescent of ice about 150 *shaku* [150 feet/45 metres] high; it was like a series of pure white folding screens, or perhaps a gigantic white snake at rest. The sea was fortunately clear of ice, and as we looked about us we were surrounded by the rippling greasy blue-green waters so characteristic of the Ross Sea. The ship was by now surging forward, with all sails set and engine full ahead.

… After a general discussion about where to land, it was agreed that only the Main Landing Party would go ashore at the Bay of Whales, and that *Kainan-maru* would then take a Coastal Party back to explore King Edward VII Land. We altered course at 10 a.m., and started to steam westwards.

During the afternoon the sky gradually clouded over. The wind blew mournfully, the temperature dropped, and snow squalls drove sporadically across the deck. Then suddenly we realised that the dark shape we could just make out about twenty miles ahead was a ship. 'Look! Pirates!' said one of the sailors to Yoshino, who happened to be on deck.

Total panic ensued! Yoshino was so astonished he went round telling the whole ship, and everyone crowded on deck in disbelief. As we drew nearer, we could see that it was a lone sailing ship, but we were still uncertain where she was from. Just as the Japanese flag flew from the mast of *Kainan-maru*, this vessel was also flying a flag, but because of the distance and poor visibility we were unable to see it properly.

Eventually when only about five miles remained between the two ships, we managed to identify their flag. It was a blue cross on a red ground, and we were now in no doubt that she was *Fram*, the ship of the Norwegian Polar Expedition.

Soon after this we sailed into the Bay of Whales as planned …. On examining our surroundings we saw that the sea ice extended all the way to where the Barrier rose at the end of the bay, which was about fifteen miles from the ice edge. The bay was indeed enormous, and we had a truly panoramic view. The sea ice was thick and smooth and stretched rigid across from east to west, linking the ice cliffs of the Barrier which rose on either hand ….

It was 11 p.m. when we left the ship and set off …. Our group advanced in a straight line towards the Barrier ahead, our feet making strange and ghostly squeaks as we trod on the half-frozen snow …. We were all dressed alike with three shirts and two pairs of long underpants, over which we wore our uniforms complete with hoods, snow goggles, ear-muffs and gloves. On our feet we wore soft felt boots with metal crampons, and we each carried a long bamboo pole to steady us as we walked. As we advanced further and further onto the ice, the heat of the sun beat down on us from above and reflected up at us from the snow, and we began to feel uncomfortably hot. Soon the sweat was streaming off us and we were completely soaked. Those with overcoats took them off and walked on panting, with the coats slung over their shoulders. To make matters worse, the steam rising from our bodies condensed so as to form an extremely disagreeable mist on the dark lenses of the goggles we wore as protection against snowblindness. However, as we couldn't take them off, we just had to carry on walking in increasing discomfort, occasionally mopping the lenses as we went.

Eventually … we reached the foot of the Barrier. A great wall of ice towered steeply more than two hundred shaku [200 feet/60 metres] above us with blue and purple lights rising like flames overhead, and as we gazed up in horror our skin turned to goose flesh at the sight that met our eyes. We could see that anything much stronger than a breeze would bring some of the steepest parts crashing straight down. Protruding blocks of ice, avalanches past and yet to come, precariously jutting chunks and lumps, all these contrasted with strangely carved shapes of a polished chalky whiteness. The blocks of ice continually falling from this cliff had smashed the sea ice below to such an extent that in places you could even see the water beneath it. Some of the floes were ratted on top of one another and as the great swells of the ocean surged to and fro beneath them they moved slowly up and down, sending strange rending noises like ripping silk echoing across the silent land and the sky. From holes in the ice seals occasionally showed their heads, baring their cruel fangs as they came up for air. Such awesome sights and stirrings are unique to the polar regions.

… Muramatsu, Yoshino and Hanamori took the lead and started to advance. They struck out with caution, their poles in their hands, picking their way across the rotten sea ice, scrambling on their bellies to climb atop a huge block of fallen ice, then leaping a yawning chasm …. Ahead of them a recent mighty avalanche had left a terrifying scar, and this was where their labours really started. The ice ahead was steep, smooth and slippery, but before they could even start their assault on the cliff they had to cross a deep crevasse which barred their way. Glancing up they saw above them an overhanging section of the Barrier which showed every sign of imminent collapse, and they knew they were in mortal danger. To put it bluntly, the slightest lapse of attention and their fates would be sealed, either crushed beneath a block of ice or sent plummeting into the depths of a crevasse. However, only by surmounting the obstacle of the ice cliff would there be any further advance, and as they had already pledged their very lives to this venture they gathered their courage and determination in both hands and fought with all

their might, brandishing their snow-shovels as weapons …. They did not dare to raise their voices. They took their turns to lead the way with apprehensive awe, as if looking into the depths of a bottomless pool, or walking on tip-toe across very thin ice.

However, their patient labours brought them step by step towards the top. On reaching a smooth plateau of ice they looked down, and saw a narrow path which they had cut snaking endlessly through the snow like a sheep's intestines. Then, turning around, they suddenly realised that they had at last arrive on the Barrier itself! Without a moment's pause to catch their breath or mop away the sweat which now drenched their bodies, they shouted loud Banzais!, raising both hands high in triumphal salute. The second and third units echoed their Banzais! from below, and soon to a succession of Banzai! Banzai! their fellow explorers emerged to join them at the top. Glancing at their watches they saw it was precisely midnight ….

As we all looked back at the way we had come, we saw the blue sea lying in an almost flat calm, the white ice floes scattered on its surface, and the two ships *Kainan-maru* and *Fram*, floating in lonely isolation alongside the expanse of sea ice which covered the entire bay. This was a sumie world painted in Indian ink on white paper. On the ice around *Kainan-maru* we could just make out the black shapes of people dotted about and moving hither and thither to the sound of occasional gun shots, and surmised that the ship's crew were out and about on the ice, hunting penguins, seals and suchlike to dissipate the weariness of the long voyage, like little birds let out of their cage.

Turning to look in the other direction, we saw a boundless plain of white ice stretching undisturbed into infinity, meeting the blue sky and continuing beyond. Though we could sense the many secrets hidden in its depths, there was not a shadow to be seen. The sun was reflected off the white snow with dazzling brightness, and we were all struck to the very heart by a feeling of awe.

that things were getting a bit serious.' The young Australian geologist
Frank Debenham staggered back below decks after glimpsing the vast
terror of water outside, which was like 'an abomination of watery desolation, giant waves … racing towards me whipped by a shrieking wind'. Birdy
Bowers, who later wrote that 'none of our landsmen who were working so
hard knew how serious things were', did his best to encourage them – 'Isn't
that a wonderful sight', he laughed, slapping Debenham on the back.
'Didn't I tell you that a sailor's life is the only one worth living?'

The storm finally broke. Then came the ice. The *Terra Nova* became locked
into a barrage of ice-floes, which at times were so obstinate that 'one would
almost believe [them] possessed of an evil spirit'. Scott wrote that the ship
seemed 'like a living thing fighting a great fight'. It seemed to take an eternity for them to reach Antarctica, but the first sight of the desolate
continent seemed ample reward for the challenges the crew had met so far.

As they steamed towards Cape Royds, Scott wrote: 'The sky was quite clear and the sun brilliant, the blue shadows were sharply marked on the distant mountains, and the great fields of snow on land and sea seemed to flash in the bright light.' The crew were mesmerized; instead of sleeping, the men wrapped themselves in blankets and sat drinking in the extraordinary sight in front of them: 'Many watched all night', wrote Cherry-Garrard, 'as this new world unfolded itself, cape by cape and mountain by mountain.'

A MEETING IN THE ICE

In January 1911 the *Terra Nova* anchored off Ross Island in McMurdo Sound. After establishing winter quarters at Cape Evans, the ship then sailed along the Great Ice Barrier to deposit a party on King Edward VII Land, under the command of Victor Campbell, to conduct scientific work. To the astonishment of Scott's crew, they discovered *Fram* lying at anchor in the Bay of Whales. Amundsen had made his camp, called Framheim, on the barrier itself, a full 60 miles (96 kilometres) closer to the South Pole than Scott's base. Putting aside his earlier fears that the Norwegians would use his old base as their starting point, Scott had begun to convince himself that Amundsen would base himself on the shores of the Weddell Sea – a more obvious place to land if he was sailing south from the Americas. Therefore it was astonishing to find *Fram* in their 'backyard'. Suddenly the threat posed by the Norwegians was all too apparent. The British were quickly, and courteously, welcomed aboard the famous ship, where they saw for themselves the efficiency of Amundsen's operation. After their polite but brief exchange of greetings, *Terra Nova* sailed back to Cape Evans to report their encounter. Harry Dickason concluded: 'It appears Capt. Amundsen ... is going to have a run for the Pole so it will prove a very exciting affair .... He has dogs for sledge work and all his men are good on ski.' Scott, as he confided in a letter to his wife some months later, knew early on that he simply had to continue at the pace he had originally set himself:

> I don't know what to think of Amundsen's chances. If he gets to
> the Pole, it must be before we do, as he is bound to travel fast with
> dogs and pretty certain to start early. On this account I decided at
> a very early date to act exactly as I should have done had he not
> existed. Any attempt to race must have wrecked my plan, besides
> which it doesn't appear the sort of thing one is out for.

Right: Terra Nova (background) and *Fram* in the Bay of Whales on Saturday, 4 February 1911. Scott's vessel entered the bay around midnight, with Scott surprised to find that Shackleton had been proved right about the bay's existence. Priestley recorded: 'Man proposes but God disposes and I was waked at one o'clock by Lillie with the astounding news that we had sighted a ship at anchor to the sea ice in the Bay. All was confusion on board for a few minutes, everybody rushing up on deck with cameras and clothes. It was no false alarm, there she was within a few hundred yards of us and what is more, those of us who had read Nansen's books recognized the *Fram*.'

… you can rely on my not saying or doing anything foolish – only I'm afraid you must be prepared for finding our venture much belittled.

After all, it is the work that counts, not the applause that follows.

Scott had realized that the use of dogs may give Amundsen the advantage. The veteran Norwegian explorer Otto Sverdrup had once stated: 'Polar exploration has two natural requirements: Skis and dogs.' Amundsen was also a firm believer in the benefits of running the two together. Unlike Scott, Amundsen was emotionally detached from his dogs, simply seeing them unsentimentally as tools that were essential for his progress – and to be discarded, quite ruthlessly, whenever necessary. Aboard *Fram* were more than 100 prime sledge-dogs, which had been carefully chosen and shipped from northern Greenland to Norway before the ship's departure, and three men in his team were experienced dog drivers, in particular Sverre Hassel. If one of the animals became exhausted, troublesome or a burden for the rest of the team, Amundsen intended to feed dog to dog, thereby giving strength to the others. It was an anticipated order of events, with a dispassionate solution.

In contrast, Scott refused to rely on dogs for his southern journey. Ignoring the advice of veteran explorers such as Nansen and Peary, Scott asserted that the only 'manly' way to travel in the polar environment was to man-haul: 'No journey ever made with dogs can approach the height of that fine conception ... when men go forth ... with their own unaided efforts and … succeed in solving some problems of the unknown.' However, this time Scott intended to use a combination of power from men, Manchurian ponies, motorized sledges and, as a last resort, a few token huskies.

FINAL PREPARATIONS

Over the following weeks, both expeditions laid depots for their journeys. Scott was following Shackleton's route over the Beardmore Glacier, while Amundsen was pioneering his own, direct course for the pole across the Great Ice Barrier via the previously unexplored Axel Heiberg Glacier. On paper the Norwegian's choice of base might have looked foolhardy, given the potentially unstable surface of the Great Ice Barrier, but in practice it proved to be an excellent decision. As Amundsen recorded in his diary, skis were the key:

The skiing on the Barrier is splendid. Every day we had reason to praise our skis. We often asked each other where we would have been without these excellent devices. The answer was mostly: probably at the bottom of some crevasse or hole. Already on reading the various reports of the Barrier's appearance and nature, it was clear to all of us, who were bred and born with skis on our feet, that these must be considered indispensable .... Many a time

we moved over parts so crevassed and broken that it would have
been impossible to negotiate on foot. I need not elaborate on the
advantage of skis in deep, loose snow.

Superbly proficient in the polar environment, the Norwegians had moved
half a ton of supplies to an advanced camp some 80 nautical miles (92
miles/148 kilometres) closer to the pole, and they had returned within just
five days, exhilarated and in confident mood, to Framheim. More journeys
and depot-laying would follow, with part of the trail festooned with pen
nants marking the way home. Scott's group, on the other hand, had
struggled for 24 days over nearly 140 miles (222 kilometres) with his ponies

Cinematographing the Antarctic

HERBERT G. PONTING, *PEARSON'S MAGAZINE*, 1914

Captain Scott decided to establish winter quarters on Ross Island, and when we arrived at the appointed spot, there was a wonderful wealth of subjects for my camera, for the ship was moored to the ice about a mile from the shore, and there were magnificent bergs and ice cliffs close at hand. … I soon began to reap a rich harvest of negatives.

I was, however, most vividly impressed with the dangers of photographing in these regions during the 48 hours following our arrival at our base ….

The morning after our arrival I was just about to start across the ice, with a sledge well packed with photographic apparatus, when eight 'killer' whales appeared, heading towards the ship, blowing loudly …. The whales dived under the ice, so, estimating that they would rise again from under it at a certain place near at hand, I ran for the spot, and got to within 6 feet of the ice edge, when what was my consternation to find the ice suddenly heave up under my feet, and split into fragments all around me; whilst the eight whales, lined up with sides touching each other, slid their heads up from under

the ice and blew, one of them within only a few feet of my face. … By good luck I was thrown backwards instead of being precipitated into the water, or I should never have lived to tell this story.

When the whales rose from under the ice there was a loud 'booming' sound – to use the expression of Captain Scott, who was a witness to the incident – as they struck the ice with their backs; and immediately they had cleared it, a rapid movement of their flukes made a great wave, which set the floe, on which I was isolated, rocking so furiously that once more I had all I could do to keep my feet. Then the whales turned about with the deliberate intention of attacking me. My friends were watching within 50 yards of me. I heard frantic shouts of 'run,' but I could not run, it was all I could do to keep my feet as I leapt from fragment to fragment of the rocking ice, with the whales a few feet behind me, snorting and blowing among the ice blocks, in close pursuit. I heard later that not a man on the ship thought I could escape.

I remember my own sensations at this time very well – they were of disappointment of having failed to secure a photograph, and of conjecture as to whether or not I could reach safety before the whales got me. The ice had already started to drift away with the current, and as I reached the last fragment I saw that I could not jump to the firm ice, for the 'lead' was too wide. I stood for a moment or two hesitating what to do. Frantic shouts of 'Jump, man, jump,' reached me from my friends.

Just then, by great good luck, the floe on which I stood turned slightly and lessened the distance. I was able to leap across, not, however, a moment too soon, for as I reached security and looked back,

a huge 'killer' pushed his head out of the water and rested it on the ice, looking around with his little pig-like eyes to see what had become of me. As he did so, he opened his jaws wide, and I then saw what Captain Scott has described in his journal in writing of this incident – 'the most terrible array of teeth in the world.' There can be no doubt that this was an organised attack on me. It is the only instance known of these whales having deliberately attacked a human being.

I shall never forget Captain Scott's expression as I reached him in safety. During the next year, I several times saw that same look on his face, when he thought someone was in danger. It always showed

how deeply he felt the responsibility for life, which he thought rested so largely on himself. He was deadly pale as he said to me: 'My God, old chap, that was the nearest squeak I ever saw.'

Above & Left: Ponting (seen here posing proudly with his camera and its 'novel telephoto apparatus' in 1912), lectured daily in London with a combination of film and slides when he returned from the South. His photographs were first exhibited by the Fine Art Society at their fashionable gallery in New Bond Street – the 'final perfection of the photographer's art' according to *Country Life.* His celebrated shows in 1914 at London's Philharmonic Hall were, by all accounts, a huge success and within two months he had performed over 100 times to an estimated audience of 120,000 people.

Above: One of Ponting's most famous photographs, 'Ice reflections with the *Terra Nova* in the distance', 7 January 1911.

Right: Getting the camp at Cape Evans in order on 23 January 1911, when 'the weather was calm and beautiful'. Ever keen to the needs of the expedition's sponsors, Ponting was sure to feature their brands whenever possible – in this instance the Norwich-based food company Colman's, providers of mustard and cornflour.

floundering up to their bellies in the snowdrifts to establish the One Ton camp at 79° 29´S. Although he travelled the same distance in just five days when using dogs to return from laying the depot, it seems remarkable that Scott persisted with the clearly less effective ponies for his southern journey. Perhaps blinded by particular notions of manliness, Scott's transport decision was to prove a crucial, and fatal, one.

As winter approached, Scott's party focussed primarily on the scientific side of the expedition, with Wilson, Bowers and Cherry-Garrard making an extraordinary five-week winter journey to the emperor penguin rookery at Cape Crozier – an experience later immortalized in Cherry-Garrard's classic book *The Worst Journey in the World*. Christmas was spent surrounded by the ice: 'We had the most splendid dinner, with soup, stewed penguin, plum pudding and mince pies, asparagus, champagne, and liqueurs, and afterwards everyone sang. I may say at once that there is very little talent … but the absence of talent doesn't deter our merry party at all. Everyone has to sing his turn, and the choruses are deafening.' The scientific team gave lectures on their fields of experience, and the expedition photographer Herbert Ponting became 'an immense source of entertainment', holding the crew spellbound with his exotic tales, such as 'the pretty amusement of flying pigeons with Aeolian whistling pipes attached to their tail feathers'.

All in all, spirits were high but, crucially, by the time the sun had set in Antarctica on 22 April, flaws were beginning to show in Scott's plans. Ten of the 19 ponies were dead and the few dogs they had were poorly trained and not as strong as those Amundsen had brought with him. One of the motor-sledges had been lost through the ice, and there were doubts as to whether the machines were suited for the expedition. However, Scott remained positive: a number of depots had been laid for the journey south, the equipment had been tested and the scientific programme had started. They would press on.

Amundsen spent the long, dark months perfecting his equipment – making his sledges lighter and more flexible, redesigning the tents, and refining their skis and bindings. In their downtime the Norwegians read from their extensive polar library and attended compulsory lectures in navigation. As the returning sun cast its first rays over the ice barrier, Amundsen was ready. On Friday 8 September 1911 he set out at the front of the party. 'The skiing has been brilliant today', he wrote jubilantly. 'I have rarely had such good skiing.'

As Amundsen began his sprint south, Scott was still preparing for his journey, but the Englishman, writing on 11 September, was feeling positive about the season ahead:

Above: Using block and tackle suspended from the yardarm, the men haul the motorized sledge off the *Terra Nova* and onto the ice, 8 January 1911. 'A day of disaster', Scott wrote in his journal that night. Within 20 minutes the sledge had disappeared through the ice – '. . . half a minute later nothing remained but a big hole. Perhaps it was lucky that there was no accident to the men, but it's a sad incident for us in any case. It's a big blow to know that one of the two best motors, on which so much time and trouble have been spent, now lies at the bottom of the sea.'

A whole week since the last entry in my diary. I feel very negligent of duty, but my whole time has been occupied in making detailed plans for the Southern journey. These are finished at last, I am glad to say; every figure has been checked by Bowers, who has been an enormous help to me. If the motors are successful, we shall have no difficulty in getting to the Glacier, and if they fail, we shall still get there with any ordinary degree of good fortune. … I have tried to take every reasonable possibility of misfortune into consideration, and to so organise the parties as to be prepared to meet them. I fear to be too sanguine, yet taking everything into consideration I feel that our chances ought to be good.

… Of hopeful signs for the future none are more remarkable than the health and spirit of our people. It would be impossible to imagine a more vigorous community, and there does not seem to be a single weak spot in the twelve good men and true who are chosen for the Southern advance. All are now experienced sledge travellers, knit together with a bond of friendship that has never been equalled under such circumstances.

_430._

… If the Southern journey comes off, nothing, not even priority at the Pole, can prevent the Expedition ranking as one of the most important that ever entered the polar regions.

The following day, on 12 September, Amundsen found his pace checked by terrible conditions. It was possible that his party's advance was too early in the season, and they may have to quit and start again. From now on prudence was the watchword:

Poor visibility. Horrible breeze from S. -52° Dogs obviously weakened by the cold. People stiff in their frozen clothes – more or less content after a night of frost – prospects of milder weather doubtful – all this persuaded me to settle for reaching the depot at 80°

Above: One of Amundsen's camps with dogs, sleds and other equipment as well as a stash of supplies, marked with a flag (visible in the background, next to the tent). This picture is probably of the first depot at 80°S, which was as far as he was able to reach on his abortive first journey in September 1911.

The Winter Journey

APSLEY CHERRY-GARRARD, *THE WORST JOURNEY IN THE WORLD*, 1922.

The horror of the nineteen days it took us to travel from Cape Evans to Cape Crozier would have to be re-experienced to be appreciated; and anyone would be a fool who went again: it is not possible to describe it. The weeks which followed them were comparative bliss, not because later our conditions were better – they were far worse – but because we were callous. I for one had come to that point of suffering at which I did not really care if only I could die without much pain. They talk of the heroism of the dying – they little know – it would be so easy to die, a dose of morphia, a friendly crevasse, and blissful sleep. The trouble is to go on.

It was the darkness that did it. I don't believe minus seventy temperatures would be bad in daylight, not comparatively bad, when you could see where you were going, where you were stepping, where the sledge straps were, the cooker, the primus, the food; could see your footsteps lately trodden deep into the soft snow that you might find your way back to the rest of your load; could see the lashings of the food bags; could read a compass without striking three or four different boxes to find one dry match; could read your watch to see if the blissful moment of getting out of your bag was come without groping in the snow all about; when it would not take you five minutes to lash up the door of the tent, and five hours to get started in the morning. …

I have met with amusement people who say, 'Oh, we had -50 temperatures in Canada; they didn't worry me,' or 'I've been down to minus sixty something in Siberia.' And then you find that they had nice dry clothing, a nice night's sleep in a nice aired bed, and had just walked out after lunch for a few minutes from a nice warm hut or an overheated train. And they look back upon it as an experience to be remembered. Well! Of course as an experience of cold this can only be compared to eating a vanilla ice with hot chocolate cream after an excellent dinner at Claridge's. But in our present state we began to look upon minus fifties as a luxury which we did not often get ….

Birdie always lit the candle in the morning – so called, and this was an heroic business. Moisture collected on matches if you looked at them … sometimes it was necessary to try to four or five boxes before a match struck. The temperature of the boxes and matches was about a hundred degrees of frost, and the smallest touch of the metal on naked flesh caused frostbite. If you wore mitts you could scarcely feel anything – especially since the tips of our fingers were already very callous. To get the first light going in the morning was a beastly cold business, made worse by having to make sure that it was at last time to get up ….

There are those who write of Polar Expeditions as though the whole thing was as easy as possible. They are trusting, I suspect, in a public who will say, 'What a fine fellow this is! We know what horrors he has endured, yet see, how little he makes of all his difficulties and hardships.' Others have gone to the opposite extreme. I do not know that there is any use in trying to make a -18° temperature appear formidable to an uninitiated reader by calling it fifty degrees of frost. I want to do neither of these things. I am not going to pretend that this was anything but a ghastly journey, made bearable and even pleasant to look back upon by the qualities of my two companions who have gone. At the same time I have no wish to make it appear more horrible than it actually was: the reader need not fear that I am trying to exaggerate ….

More than once in my short life I have been struck by the value of the man who is blind to what appears to be a common sense certainty: he achieves the impossible. We never spoke our thoughts: we discussed the Age of Stone which was to come, when we built our cosy warm rock hut on the slopes of Mount Terror, and ran our stove with penguin blubber, and pickled little Emperors in warmth and dryness. We were quite intelligent people, and we must all have known that we were not going to see the penguins and that it was a folly to go forward. And yet with quiet perseverance, in perfect friendship, almost with gentleness those two men led on. I just did what I was told. …

As we approached Terror Point in the fog we sensed that we had risen and fallen over several rises. Every now and then we felt hard slippery snow under our feet. Every now and then our feet went through crusts in the surface. And then quite suddenly, vague, indefinable, monstrous, there loomed something ahead. I remember having a feeling as of ghosts about as we untoggled our harnesses from the sledge, tied them together, and thus roped walked upwards on that ice. The moon was showing a ghastly ragged mountainous edge above us in the fog, and as we rose we found that we were on a pressure ridge. We stopped, looked at one another, and then bang – right under our feet. More bangs, and creaks and groans; for that ice was moving and splitting like glass. The cracks went off all round us, and some of them ran along for hundreds of yards. Afterwards we got used to it, but at first the effect was very jumpy. From first to last during this journey we had plenty of variety and none of that monotony which is inevitable in sledging over long distances of Barrier in summer. Only the long shivering fits following close one after the other all the time we lay in our dreadful sleeping bags, hour after hour and night after night in those temperatures – they were as monotonous as could be. Later we got frostbitten even as we lay in our sleeping bags. Things are getting pretty bad when you get frostbitten in your bag.

There was only a glow where the moon was; we stood in a moonlit fog, and this was sufficient to show the edge of another ridge ahead, and yet another on our left. We were utterly bewildered. The deep booming of the ice continued, and it may be that the tide has something to do with this, though we were many miles from the ordinary coastal ice …. We were clearly lost ….

When we started next morning (July 15) we could see on our left front and more or less on top of us the Knoll, which is a big hill whose precipitous cliffs to

seaward form Cape Crozier. The sides of it sloped down towards us, and pressing against its ice-cliffs on ahead were miles and miles of great pressure ridges, along which we had travelled, and which hemmed us in. Mount Terror rose ten thousand feet high on our left, and was connected with the Knoll by a great cup-like drift of wind-polished snow …. For three miles we slogged up, until we were only 150 yards from the moraine shelf where we were going to build our hut of rocks and snow. This moraine was above us on our left, the twin peaks of the Knoll were across the cup on our right; and here, 800 feet up the mountain side, we pitched our last camp.

We had arrived.

Below: Cherry-Garrard, photographed by Ponting, having returned to base from his journey across the Barrier in support of Scott's polar party, 29 January 1912.

Below: From left to right, Scott, George Simpson, Teddy Evans and Birdie Bowers, photographed by Ponting before they left for a sledging trek to the Western Mountains on 15 September 1911. It was probably during this journey that Scott settled on which men he would choose as his companions for the push to the South Pole later that year.

Right: Christmas 1911 and (from left to right) Robert Forde, Frank Debenham, Griffith Taylor and Tryggve Gran – forming the Western Geological Party – pose for a group shot during their fieldwork. This photograph is actually taken by Debenham, who can be seen pulling the string to release his camera's shutter.

this time – deposit our things and then return as quickly as possible to await the arrival of spring. To risk men and animals out of sheer obstinacy and continue, just because we have started on our way – that would never occur to me. If we are to win this game, the pieces must be moved carefully – one false move, and everything can be lost ....

Amundsen's comrade Olav Bjaaland recorded his relief that the decision had been made to turn for home: '... just as well, otherwise we would have frozen to death .... Sleeping bags and clothes are wet through; in fact as stiff as iron, but when one has finally got into them, one just has to stay there. God help me it was just shit and best forgotten.'

At 9.30 a.m. on 20 October, after several false starts due to bad weather, a smaller team of five – Amundsen, Bjaaland, Wisting, Hanssen and Hassel – set out once again through fog and mist on their southern journey. Within two days the team of five were running the gauntlet of a crevasse field that almost claimed Bjaaland and several dogs. All were saved from a yawning crevasse – a hole that 'looked foul and bottomless, room for 100

sledges'. It was a 'filthy terrain' Amundsen wrote, one not to be navigated in thick fog. 'This place had been crumpled with such violence, that huge slabs were piled up against each other like rafting in the pack ice .... It is quite extraordinary.'

Once through the crevasse field, Amundsen and his men made good progress, finding their depots precisely, even through the thickest spindrift, by using sledge meter and compass. With characteristic sang froid, Amundsen recorded them having a 'splendid time' – they were comfortable in their tent, the men were well fed, the dogs were pulling well and were 'bursting with health'. By 31 October the men were firmly in their stride, having made considerable ground, they rested, rebuilt their depot, and then indulged in caramel pudding. Prospects were good.

Back at Cape Evans, Scott was finally ready to embark on the long trek to the South Pole. On 29 October, Scott, Wilson, Crean and Evans donned their sledging kit and made a trial camp by some icebergs nearby for the benefit of Ponting, his cinematograph and posterity. With ponies well-fed and the motor sledges ready, there was nothing left to do but pen letters home. Bowers wrote reassuringly to Kathleen Scott that although the expedition had already had its trials, perhaps Amundsen's 'little game to the eastward' had all been the 'best thing for our object'. Ever loyal to Scott, he shared the belief that manhauling was the best and most noble way forward. 'Certainly to trust the final dash to such an uncertain element as dogs would be a risky thing, whereas man-haulage, though slow, is sure …'.

Scott, too, felt encouraged as he made his final preparations on the journey that would prove to be his last. 'The future is in the lap of the gods', he wrote in his diary. 'I can think of nothing left undone to deserve success.'

Overleaf: Inside the hut at Cape Evans (clockwise from bottom left): Tom Crean and Petty Officer Evans mend the reindeer-skin sleeping bags, 16 May 1911. The jumble of bunks that was known as 'The Tenements' and which was home to (from left to right) Cherry-Garrard, Bowers, Oates, Meares (with pipe) and Atkinson, photographed on 9 October 1911. 'These five are all special friends', Scott wrote in his journal, 'and they have already made their dormitory very habitable.' Thomas Clissold, described as an 'excellent cook', baking the daily fresh bread on 25 March 1911. Captain Scott in his 'den' on 7 October 1911 – he spent much of his time in the evenings making entries in his journals and writing letters.

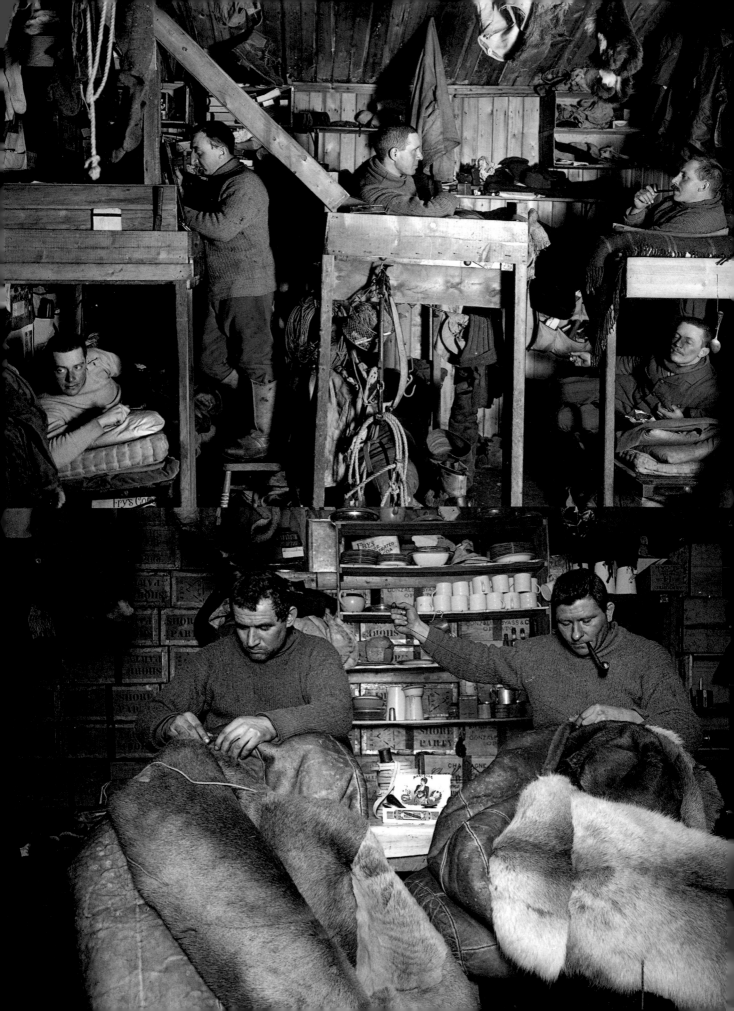

CHAPTER 5
THE FINAL MARCH

Victory awaits those who have everything in order – people call it luck. Defeat is certain for those who have forgotten to take the necessary precautions in time – people call that bad luck.

ROALD AMUNDSEN FROM *THE SOUTH POLE*, 1927.

Wednesday 1 November 1911 was a bad day for both Scott and Amundsen. For Scott it should have been a time to celebrate, because it marked the beginning of his great southern journey. In fact, the start was shambolic. Leaving the base in three detachments, Scott's South Pole team and their support parties set off – Meares leading the teams of dogs and Teddy Evans, Day, Lashly and Hooper in the motorised sledges – and made slow progress under a threatening sky with the obstinate ponies. 'The ponies hate the wind', Scott observed as he catalogued the bucking, kicking and general devilment of the beasts. The different paces of the ponies were causing unforeseen difficulties: 'It reminded me of a regatta', he confessed, 'or a somewhat disorganised fleet with ships of very unequal speed.'

Elsewhere, after a rest day at 81°, Amundsen had problems of his own and was struggling with his dogs, fog and crevasses. After covering about 14 miles (23 kilometres), Hilmer Hanssen caught his ski in a dog-sled trace as he ran over a crevasse. Within moments, he was spreadeagled across the chasm, with his sledge sliding downwards and his huskies erupting into a vicious fight on the brink of the abyss; shortly after that, Sverre Hassel fell through a snow-bridge. It was perilous terrain they were now crossing – Amundsen observed that:

> These crevasses are impressive when one lies at the edge and stares down in them. A bottomless chasm goes from light blue into the thickest darkness. The ugliest formations we have found here are huge holes that could swallow *Fram* and a lot more besides. These holes are covered by a thin wind crust, and the little hole that is visible doesn't seem so menacing. But if one gets on to such a

delightful spot, one is irrevocably lost …. We go with our lives in our hands each day. But it is pleasant to hear – nobody wants to turn back. No – these boys want to press on, cost what it will.

Amundsen's team pushed on, even though the skiing was 'sticky as fish glue' and they had lost sight of their flags in the fog. By 5 November the sun appeared briefly enough for them to see their southernmost depot, just two miles (three kilometres) away. Everything in the store was in perfect order. They were now fully fitted out for the next 100 days, and both the dogs and equipment were in the finest condition. 'I am now sitting in the tent and writing and it is so warm that thoughts stray now and then to the tropics', Amundsen recorded.

Their stride was now unchecked. 'We are running like greyhounds over the endless flat snow plain', Amundsen wrote. Travelling over such a surface was so easy that there was almost no effect on the dogs after a full day's pulling, and their speed was picking up to a gratifying four and a half miles per hour (seven kilometres per hour), with the dogs galloping across the smooth, flat ice. Snow cairns were now built every third nautical mile (every 18,225 feet/5,556 metres) as markers, with a final-leg depot placed at each whole degree so that an easy return was virtually guaranteed – and it also meant that they were running with increasingly lighter sledges.

Top Left: Captain Oates enjoying his pipe in the freezing conditions of midwinter as he inspects the Siberian ponies in their stables on 23 May 1911.

Bottom Left: Krisravista the sledge dog inspects the gramophone in another shot that was created by Ponting to please a supplier, in this case the Gramophone Company (in imitation of Nipper the dog, His Master's Voice).

Above: Scott's South Pole party ready themselves for departure, pulling a sledge laden with tent and sleeping bags towards Three Degree Depot. The photograph was most likely taken by the party's fifth member, Bowers.

ONTO THE PLATEAU AND BEYOND

On 21 November, Amundsen and his team attained the polar plateau after a pioneering ascent up the ice-falls of the Axel Heiberg Glacier. It was a wild icescape they had encountered en route, with enormous blocks of ice and mighty abysses, making their camp on a shattered ledge, listening to the 'foul rumbling of avalanches of vile blocks of ice on Olavs Høy'. Now, camped on the plateau at an altitude of 10,000 feet (3,050 metres), Amundsen ordered the killing of 24 of the dogs, leaving 18 of the strongest and best alive for the final phase – as a result, the men called the camp the Butcher's Shop. 'Heigh ho,' mused Bjaaland, 'polar life is a grind.' From their position here at 85° 36′ S they would make the dash to the pole, with three sledges and supplies for 60 days.

While Amundsen raced further ahead, Scott was remarking glumly that his team's marches were 'uniformly horrid'. The ponies were struggling over a surface of hard sastrugi and deep pits of granular snow, and one by one they were starting to weaken and fall. 'The weather was horrid', Scott continued. 'Overcast, gloomy, snowy. One's spirits became very low.' In a moment of sudden panic at their slow progress, Scott decided that they were carrying too much weight and ordered that they offload any bags of supplies he considered to be surplus to requirements. It was a risky move, particularly when – unlike Amundsen – they were not establishing enough depots for their return trek.

As December dawned, Amundsen's team negotiated the Devil's Glacier and Scott's team faced the prospect of having to dispatch his floundering ponies. Unusually, Amundsen had made a vital mistake by ordering his team to leave their crampons at the Butcher's Shop – now they found themselves facing a climb of sheer ice. The way ahead looked impossible: 'A thousand thoughts ran through my brain', he wrote in his journal on 1 December. 'The pole lost, perhaps, because of such an idiotic blunder.' All, too, were suffering the effects of frostbite to differing degrees. Bjaaland recorded that the raging Antarctic gales were like naked flames that burned their skin, rendering their faces as white and hard as wax candles: 'The Chief's nose is like that of a country bumpkin, Wisting's jaw looks like the snout of a Jersey cow. Helmer has thick scabs and skin as rough as a file.'

Below: Scott's sledge flag made of heavyweight sateen. The flag bears the Cross of St George nearest the hoist, which is divided white over blue, with the Scott family crest of a stag's head and motto: 'Ready Aye Ready'. Scott flew this flag at the South Pole – it can be seen beneath his gloved left hand in the photographs made that day – and the treasured object was recovered from his tent after the tragedy had played out.

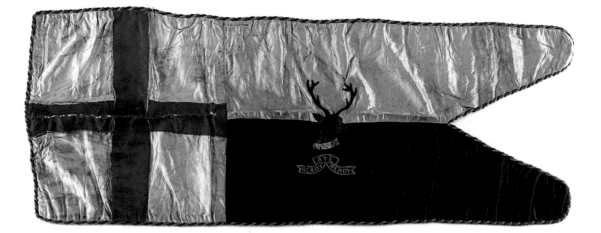

Meanwhile, Scott, comparing his own team's journey to that of Shackleton's during his *Nimrod* expedition, gloomily noted that whereas Wild had recorded mostly fine weather, they had endured quite the opposite. 'It is dreadfully dismal work marching through the blank wall of white', Scott lamented. 'Our luck in weather is preposterous.' The weather lifted only occasionally, and along with it the moods of the party so that once in a while laughter would be heard in the tent – but then the blizzards would rage again, with a fine powdery snow that covered men and animals from head to foot in an uncomfortable crust, making Scott feel thoroughly depressed:

> What on earth does such weather mean at this time of year? It is more than our share of ill-fortune, I think, but the luck may turn yet. I doubt if any party could travel in such weather even with the wind, certainly no one could travel against it. Is there some widespread atmospheric disturbance which will be felt everywhere in this region as a bad season, or are we merely the victims of exceptional local conditions? If the latter, there is food for thought in picturing our small party struggling against adversity in one place whilst others go smilingly forward in the sunshine: How great may be the element of luck! No foresight – no procedure – could have

prepared us for this state of affairs. Had we been ten times as experienced or certain of our aim we should not have expected such rebuffs.

Although Amundsen had also experienced challenging weather conditions, his head start and the speed he was moving at ensured that he outran the worst of it. Scott and his men, who were to become severely weakened from exhaustion, exposure and chronic hunger, were being battered by conditions that were extreme, even for Antarctica.

The following day, 6 December, was no better: 'Noon. Miserable, utterly miserable. We have camped in the "Slough of Despond". The tempest rages with unabated violence … the ponies look utterly desolate. Oh! but this is too crushing and we are only 12 miles from the Glacier. [Beardmore Glacier] A hopeless feeling descends on one and is hard to fight off. What immense patience is needed for such occasions …. Resignation to misfortune is the only attitude, but not an easy one to adopt.'

Amundsen, his men and his dogs were all exhausted – they had pushed themselves hard, but their persistence was paying off. For days there had been no visibility and they had navigated by dead reckoning, but by 8 December the cloud began to clear and the sun appeared – 'not in all her glory, but modest and pretty'. Enough, in fact, for a good shot. They discovered, to their amazement, that even though they had travelled through thick fog and snowdrift, they were exactly where they thought they were, to the very minute: at 88° 16´S, just seven nautical miles (13 kilometres) from Shackleton's farthest south record. It was masterful navigation, and perhaps some degree of intuition, that had brought them to this point. 'So we are ready to take the Pole in any kind of weather on offer', challenged Amundsen. Leading on skis, Amundsen pushed on quickly:

Right: Amundsen and Helmer Hanssen had to undertake a number of measurements to confirm their position, during their time in the vicinity of the South Pole from 14 to 17 December 1911. Here, the pair pose as if they are taking observations with a sextant and an artificial horizon.

Opposite: With more than 800 miles (1,300 kilometres) to travel to reach safety, Scott and his four companions stand exhausted and dejected at the South Pole on 17 January 1912. 'Great God!', Scott wrote that night. 'This is an awful place and terrible enough for us to have laboured to it without the reward of priority …'

Then suddenly I heard a stout, hearty cheer behind me. I turned round. In the light breeze from the S., the brave, well-known colours were flying from the first sledge, we have passed and put behind us the Englishman's record. It was a splendid sight. The sun had just burst through in all its glory and illuminated in a lovely manner the beautiful little flag …. My goggles clouded over again, but this time it was not the south wind's fault.

As the Norwegians celebrated with an extra ration of chocolate, Scott was in despair. 'Our case is growing desperate', he recorded. The snow was almost impassably deep and Wilson had advised that the ponies were finished. Two miles (three kilometres) from the foot of the Beardmore Glacier, at a place they called Shambles Camp, all the ponies were shot. The group still had dogs, but Scott was still not using them to their best advantage. Now Scott believed that using skis was the only way forward, but this was a lesson he had learned rather late. Having ignored the advice of men such as Nansen, and not having trained his men fully, Scott found that some of his Southern Party were far from confident with the equipment. 'It is most awfully trying', he confided in frustration to his journal. 'I had expected failure from the animals but not from the men …. Ski are the thing, and here are my tiresome fellow-countrymen too prejudiced to have prepared themselves for the event.'

TRIUMPH AND HEARTACHE

On Thursday 14 December, Bjaaland wrote: 'We now lie and look towards the Pole, and I hear the axle creaking, but tomorrow it will be oiled. The excitement is great. Shall we see the English flag – God have mercy on us, I don't believe it.'

The following day the Norwegians discovered that the South Pole was theirs: 'Thanks be to God!' Amundsen wrote in his journal, recording the date as 15 December. It was actually 14 December because they had crossed the International Date Line and hadn't adjusted their logs and journals – a mistake later remedied by Amundsen. Celebrating under an overcast sky, the small party knew that they would have to make more observations to confirm their position. It took them a couple of days to be sure, taking observations all night and painstakingly recording the results. Finally, there was no doubt and the Norwegian flag was planted, its delicate silk fluttering in the wind, with the frostbitten hand of each man on the pole:

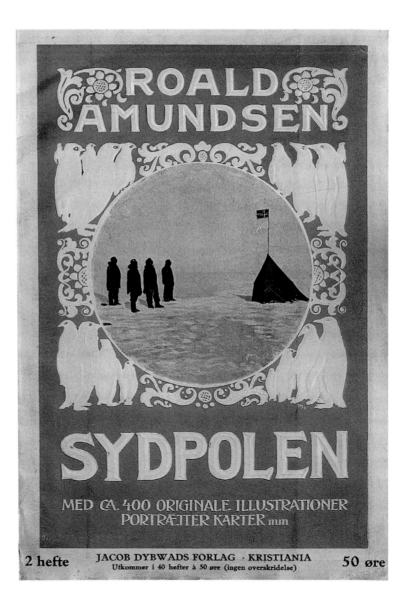

Right: Amundsen's account of his adventure to the South Pole – *Sydpolen* – was a best-seller in Norway and was immediately published in London in an English language version. In this Norwegian advertisement, Amundsen and his men are seen offering their farewell to the Pole, leaving behind a reserve tent along with letters for Scott and the King of Norway, proof of their success in the event that they failed to return.

CAPTAIN ROALD AMUNDSEN
discoverer of the Sth Pole.
on board The "FRAM"
at Hobart. — March —
1912

Here we lie on the South Pole, an exceptionally flat snow plain. Not a single uneven bit to see .... It is still this evening and so peaceful. The dogs lie happily stretched out in the baking sun .... We have all been busy with the binoculars to see if there is any sign of life anywhere, but in vain. We are definitely the first here .... We have set up the little tent with the Norwegian flag and '*Fram*'s' flag below it, waving from the top of the tent pole. Several things were deposited in the tent: my sextant with glass horizon, a hypsometer, three reindeer foot bags, some reindeer fur boots, and a pair of mittens. I left a letter to the King, and a few words to Scott, who I presume will be the first to come here after us. On the tent pole we fastened a plate on which we all wrote our names. And so farewell, dear Pole, we won't meet again.

A full month later, on Tuesday 16 January, after travelling for a body-shattering 77 days over almost 800 miles (1,300 kilometres) of sastrugi, crevasses and wild white desert, Scott, Wilson, Bowers, ('Taff') Evans and Oates were confronted with a heart-stopping discovery. Ahead of them, Bowers spied what he initially thought was a cairn. When they drew closer, the men discovered a black flag. All around were the sights of a busy camp — dog tracks and impressions in the snow where sledges had lain. Scott wrote in his diary:

First to the Pole

ROALD AMUNDSEN, *THE SOUTH POLE*, 1912.

December 7 … The warmth of the past few days seemed to have matured our frost-sores, and we presented an awful appearance. It was Wisting, Hanssen and I who had suffered the worst damage in the last south-east blizzard; the left side of our faces was one mass of sore, bathed in matter and serum. We looked like the worst type of tramps and ruffians, and would probably not have been recognized by our nearest relations. These sores were a great trouble to us during the latter part of the journey. The slightest gust of wind produced a sensation as if one's face were being cut backwards and forwards with a blunt knife. They lasted a long time, too; I can remember Hanssen removing the last scab when we were coming into Hobart – three months later. We were very lucky in the weather during this depot work; the sun came out all at once, and we had an excellent opportunity of taking some good azimuth observations, the last of any use that we got on the journey.

December 9 … arrived with the same fine weather and sunshine. … Every step we now took in advance brought us rapidly nearer the goal; we could feel fairly certain of reaching it on the afternoon of the 14th. It was very natural that our conversation should be chiefly concerned with the time of arrival. None of us would admit that he was nervous, but I am inclined to think that we all had a little touch of that malady. What should we see when we got there? A vast, endless plain, that no eye had yet seen and no foot yet trodden; or – No, it was an impossibility; with the speed at which we had travelled, we must reach the goal first, there could be no doubt about that. And yet – and yet – Wherever there is the smallest loophole, doubt creeps in and gnaws and gnaws and never leaves a poor wretch in peace. 'What on earth is Uroa scenting?' It was Bjaaland who made this remark, on one of

these last days, when I was going by the side of his sledge and talking to him. 'And the strange thing is that he's scenting to the south. It can never be –' Mylius, Ring, and Suggen showed the same interest in the southerly direction; it was quite extraordinary to see how they raised their heads, with every sign of curiosity, put their noses in the air, and sniffed due south. One would really have thought there was something remarkable to be found there.

… The weather during the forenoon had been just as fine as before; in the afternoon we had some snow-showers from the south-east. It was like the eve of some great festival that night in the tent. One could feel that a great event was at hand. Our flag was taken out again and lashed to the same two ski-sticks as

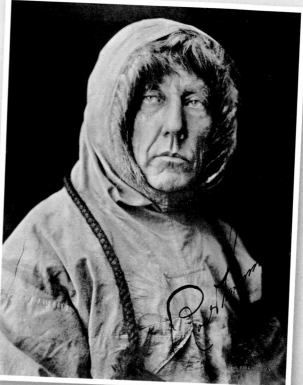

before. Then it was rolled up and laid aside, to be ready when the time came. I was awake several times during the night, and had the same feeling that I can remember as a little boy on the night before Christmas Eve – an intense expectation of what was going to happen. Otherwise I think we slept just as well that night as any other.

On the morning of December 14 the weather was of the finest, just as if it had been made for arriving at the Pole. I am not quite sure, but I believe we dispatched our breakfast rather more quickly than usual and were out of the tent sooner, though I must admit that we always accomplished this with all reasonable haste. We went in the usual order – the foreunner, Hanssen, Wisting, Bjaaland, and the reserve forerunner. By noon we had reached 89° 53´ by dead reckoning, and made ready to take the rest in one stage. At 10 a.m. a light breeze had sprung up from the south-east, and it had clouded over, so that we got no noon altitude; but the clouds were not thick, and from time to time we had a glimpse of the sun through them. The going on that day was rather different from what it had been; sometimes the ski went over it well, but at others it was pretty bad. We advanced that day in the same mechanical way as before; not much was said, but eyes were used all the more. Hanssen's neck grew twice as long as before in his endeavor to see a few inches farther. I had asked him before we started to spy out ahead for all he was worth, and he did so with a vengeance. But, however keenly he stared, he could not descry anything but the endless flat plain ahead of us. The dogs had dropped their scenting, and appeared to have lost their interest in the regions about the earth's axis.

At three in the afternoon a simultaneous 'Halt!' rang out from the drivers. They had carefully examined their sledge meters, and they all showed the full distance – our Pole by reckoning. The goal was reached, the journey ended. I cannot say – though I know it would sound much more effective – that the object of my life was obtained. That would be romancing rather too barefacedly. I had better be

honest and admit straight out that I have never known any man to be placed in such a diametrically opposite position to the goal of his desires as I was at that moment. The regions around the North Pole – well, yes, the North Pole itself – had attracted me from childhood, and here I was at the South Pole. Can anything more topsy-turvy be imagined?

Above: Amundsen's English narrative of his success, *The South Pole*, naturally remains a classic in polar literature. This treasured copy belonged to the explorer Sir Wally Herbert, who carried it with him on his sledge when he became the first man to retrace Amundsen's route on the Axel Heiberg Glacier in 1962.
Left: Roald Amundsen, the first man to reach the South Pole, a signed publicity photograph, 1920.

This told us the whole story. The Norwegians have forestalled us and are first at the Pole. It is a terrible disappointment, and I am very sorry for my loyal companions. Many thoughts come and much discussion have we had. To-morrow we must march on to the Pole and then hasten home with all the speed we can compass. All the day dreams must go; it will be a wearisome return.

The following day, he continued in his journal:

The Pole. Yes, but under very different circumstances from those expected. We have had a horrible day – add to our disappointment a head wind 4 to 5, with a temperature -22°, and companions labouring on with cold feet and hands. We started at 7.30, none of us having slept much after the shock of our discovery …. Great God! This is an awful place and terrible enough for us to have laboured to it without the reward of priority ….'

While Amundsen's team celebrated their return to their well-stocked depot at 82° with a fine meal of seal steak and chocolate pudding, Scott divvied out his team's scant rations and contemplated the long journey back. Scott had woefully miscalculated the rations they would need, and had misjudged the effect that man-hauling would have on their speed and condition – they were chronically malnourished and psychologically beaten. Meares had returned to Cape Evans with the dogs in mid-December. Had Scott instead used dogs for the dash to the Pole, and retained the bags of food so casually offloaded earlier in the journey, the tale may have been different. Thus, in spite of a full sail on the sledge and a following wind, their pace was slow. It was essential for the men to keep their spirits up, but without the prize of the South Pole they felt the strain of the tiring and monotonous daily slog.

The journey was beginning to mark them all. Wilson, despite suffering from snowblindness, kept medical notes that gave an indication of their state: 'Evans has got 4 or 5 of his finger-tips badly blistered by the cold. Titus also his nose and cheeks … Evans' finger-nails all coming off, very raw and sore … Titus' toes are blackening, and his nose and cheeks are dead yellow … Evans' fingers suppurating …'

Of all of them, Evans was affected the worst – badly frostbitten and fatally weakened from malnutrition and exposure. By mid-February, Scott was deeply concerned by the man who he noted was clearly broken in body and 'nearly broken down in brain'. 'God knows how we are going to get him home,' confided Oates to his journal, 'we could not possibly carry him on the sledge.' After continually falling behind the team, Evans collapsed and died. 'It is a terrible thing to lose a companion in this way,' Scott continued in his journal, yet: 'calm reflection shows that there could not have been a better ending to the terrible anxieties of the past week. Discussion of the situation at lunch yesterday shows us what a desperate pass we were in with a sick man on our hands at such a distance from home.'

Right: A map showing the extent of operations for the *Terra Nova* voyage, and the tracks of the main southern journey out across the Ross Barrier, up the Beardmore Glacier route pioneered by Shackleton, and along the King Edward VII Plateau to the Pole. Scott's march south, with his caravan of dogs, ponies and motorized sledges, began on 1 November 1911. Over the coming weeks, the party would reduce in size as successive support teams turned back. Meares returned to base on 12 December with the dogs, leaving the man-hauling Southern Party – Scott, Wilson, Oates, Bowers and Evans – to continue to the Pole.

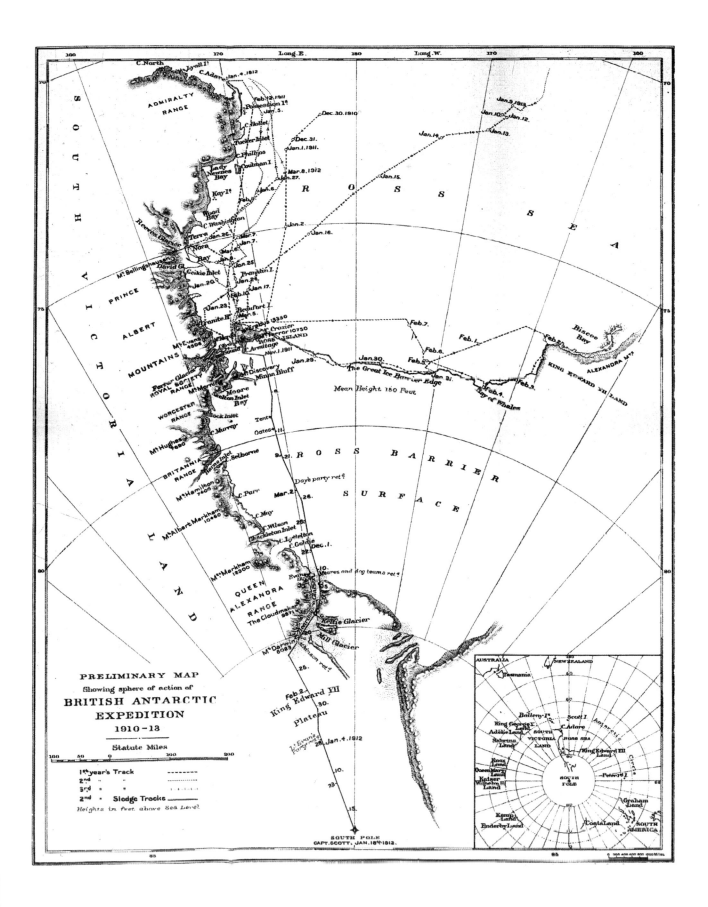

Breaking camp within just half an hour of Evans's burial, the group made rapid strides down the Great Ice Barrier to Shambles Camp, where the last of their ponies had been shot. At the camp, they feasted on horsemeat and welcomed a 'more plentiful era', but even these extra provisions were not enough. 'Cold, very cold ... desperately cold', Scott wrote. 'We want more food yet and especially more fat .... We talk of little but food.' Fuel, too, was now dangerously low and Oates's strength was ebbing fast, with his feet desperately frostbitten. Things, Scott noted in his journal on 5 March, were 'looking very black indeed'. 'We mean to see the game through with proper spirit,' he continued, 'but it's tough work to be pulling harder than we ever pulled in our lives for long hours, and to feel that the progress is so slow. One can only say God help us & plod on our weary way, cold and very miserable, though outwardly cheerful.'

Two days later, at 11 a.m. on Thursday 7 March 1912, *Fram* was quietly dropping anchor outside Hobart, Tasmania. Amundsen, dressed in a modest sailor cap and sweater, stepped into the harbourmaster's boat and went ashore clutching his telegram briefcase. Almost immediately, the *Fram* was surrounded by reporters, but they left empty-handed. Amundsen had sworn the crew to secrecy. After visiting the Norwegian consul and checking into a 'miserable little room' at the Orient Hotel, Amundsen dispatched three coded telegrams: the first to the King of Norway, the second to Nansen and the third to his brother Leon.

The following morning, on the advice of Leon, Amundsen sent exclusive news of his victory to the *Daily Chronicle* in London. By 10 p.m. telegrams of congratulation began to pour in after the story of the conquest of the South Pole had been published. 'Journalists tried to break open the door of my bedroom,' Amundsen noted in his diary, 'but did not get in.'

THE LEGEND BEGINS

Three days after the news of Amundsen's conquest of the South Pole was speeding across the globe, Oates reached crisis point. For some days he had been unable to pull the sledge and had been reduced to sitting on it. Despite being 'wonderfully plucky', it was clear that he was near the end. An open discussion by the men about their future ended in Scott ordering Wilson to 'hand over the means of ending our troubles'. Such was their suffering that even Scott contemplated suicide, albeit only briefly. They were all now feeling the cold dreadfully. 'We *must* go on,' Scott recorded, 'but now the making of every camp must be more difficult and dangerous. It must be near the end, but a pretty merciful end ... must fight it out to the last biscuit.' Days merged into each other as they staggered on until around 16 or 17 March. Still far from safety, Scott wrote:

> Should this be found I want these facts recorded. Oates' last thoughts were of his Mother, but immediately before he took pride in thinking that his regiment would be pleased with the bold way in which he met his death. We can testify to his bravery.

He has borne suffering for weeks without complaint, and to the very last was able and willing to discuss outside subjects. He did not – would not – give up hope to the very end. He was a brave soul. This was the end. He slept through the night before last, hoping not to wake; but he woke in the morning – yesterday. It was blowing a blizzard. He said, 'I am just going outside and may be some time'. He went out into the blizzard and we have not seen him since.

Scott, Wilson and Bowers made no effort to stop Oates leaving the tent, even though they knew he was walking to his death, considering it to be 'the act of a brave man, and an English gentleman'. Scott added that he hoped they would all meet the end with a similar spirit, for assuredly the end was not far.

Within a week, Scott was suffering from a gangrenous right foot. He had begun writing his last letters. Wilson and Bowers, appearing to be faring better, contemplated marching the 11 miles (18 kilometres) to their vital stash of supplies at One Ton depot to retrieve more fuel and food, but a ferocious, whirling drift prevented them. Later meteorological studies have shown that there were unusually violent katabatic winds. The distance to the depot, which seemed so short on their outward journey, now seemed tragically beyond reach. On around 24 March Scott wrote a message to the public in which he detailed the last stages of their trek:

> We are weak, writing is difficult, but for my own sake I do not regret this journey, which has shown that Englishmen can endure hardships, help one another, and meet death with as great a fortitude as ever in the past. We took risks, we knew we took them; things have come out against us, and therefore we have no cause for complaint, but bow to the will of Providence, determined still to do our best to the last. But if we have been willing to give our lives to this enterprise, which is for the honour of our country, I appeal to our countrymen to see that those who depend on us are properly cared for.
>
> Had we lived, I should have had a tale to tell of the hardihood, endurance, and courage of my companions which would have stirred the heart of every Englishman. These rough notes and our dead bodies must tell the tale, but surely, surely, a great rich country like ours will see that those who are dependent on us are properly provided for.

On 29 March he wrote his last entry: 'We shall stick it out to the end, but we are getting weaker, of course, and the end cannot be far. It seems a pity, but I do not think I can write more.'

A TERRIBLE DISCOVERY

Confined to the hut by the darkness and debilitating cold of the long winter, the men endured an uneasy eight months of waiting for Scott's polar team to return. When spring arrived, Edward Atkinson, who had been left in command of the base at Cape Evans, mounted a search for the missing party. Although Atkinson had been 'morally certain' since March 1912 that Scott's team had perished, for weeks the appearance of a distant seal or penguin had raised hopes that the men were alive and on their way home. The expedition's northernmost party, the scientific team under the command of Campbell, was also missing. Those at Cape Evans knew that Scott's team had to be the priority, even if they were convinced the men were already dead. As Charles Wright observed: 'The first object of the expedition had been the Pole. If some record was not found, their success or failure would for ever remain uncertain. Was it due not only to the men and their relatives, but also to the expedition, to ascertain their fate if possible?'

It was Wright who first saw the tent, although at first he thought it was an object of little significance, as so much of it had been buried by snow. He tried to signal to the rest of the party to join him but 'my alphabetical signals could not be read by the navy and I considered it would be a sort of sacrilege to make a noise. I felt much as if I were in a cathedral and found myself with my hat on'. Atkinson, Gran and Cherry-Garrard joined Wright, but were confused by what they had found. 'Cherry' recalled later:

> I do not know how he knew .... Just a waste of snow: to our right the remains of one of last year's cairns, a mere mound and then three feet of bamboo sticking quite alone out of the snow; and then another mound of snow, perhaps a trifle more pointed. We walked up to it. I do not think we quite realized – not for very long – but someone reached up to a projection of snow, and brushed it away. The green flap of the ventilator of the tent appeared, and we knew that the door was below.

Above: A cherished print of Captain Oates as he walks out into the blizzard, after the 1913 painting 'A Very Gallant Gentleman' by John Charles Dollman. Oates had been struggling for some time, but by the evening of Friday 16 March, as Scott wrote in his diary, Oates simply could not go on. He sacrificed himself for the benefit of the others, leaving the tent while uttering the now immortal words: 'I am just going outside and may be some time.'

Finding the Dead

EDWARD L. ATKINSON, *SCOTT'S LAST EXPEDITION*, 1923.

Eight months afterwards we found the tent. It was an object partially snowed up and looking like a cairn. Before it were the ski sticks and in front of them a bamboo which probably was the mast of the sledge. The tent was practically on the line of cairns which we had built in the previous season. It was within a quarter of a mile of the remains of the cairn, which showed as a small hummock beneath the snow.

Inside the tent were the bodies of Captain Scott, Doctor Wilson and Lieutenant Bowers. Wilson and Bowers were found in the attitude of sleep, their sleeping bags closed over their heads as they would naturally close them.

Scott died later. He had thrown back the flaps of his sleeping bag and opened his coat. The little wallet containing the three notebooks was under his shoulders, and his arm flung across Wilson. They had pitched their tent, and it had withstood all the blizzards of an exceptionally hard winter. Each man of the expedition recognized the bodies. From Captain Scott's diary I found his reasons for this disaster. When the men had been assembled I read to them these reasons, the place of death of Petty Officer Evans, and the story of Captain Oates' heroic end.

We recovered all their gear and dug out the sledge with their belongings on it. Amongst these were 35 lbs. of very important geological specimens which had been collected on the moraines of the Beardmore Glacier; at Doctor Wilson's request that he had stuck to these up to the very end, even when disaster stared them in the face and they knew that the specimens were so much weight added to what they had to pull.

When everything had been gathered up, we covered them with the outer tent and read the Burial Service. From this time until well into the next day we started to build a mighty cairn above them. This cairn was finished the next morning, and upon it a rough cross was placed, made from the greater portion of two skis, and on either side were up-ended two sledges, and they were fixed firmly in the snow, to be an added mark. Between the eastern sledge and the cairn a bamboo was placed, containing a metal cylinder, and in this the following record was left:

'November 12, 1912, lat. 79 degrees, 50 mins. South. This cross and cairn are erected over the bodies of Captain Scott, C.V.O., R.N., Doctor E.A. Wilson, M.B., B.C. Cantab., and Lieutenant H.R. Bowers, Royal Indian Marine – a slight token to perpetuate their successful and gallant attempt to reach the Pole. This they did on January 17, 1912, after the Norwegian expedition had already done so. Inclement weather with lack of fuel was the cause of their death. Also to commemorate their two gallant comrades, Captain L.E.G. Oates of the Inniskilling Dragoons, who walked to his death in a blizzard to save his comrades about eighteen miles south of this position; also of Seaman Edgar Evans, who died at the foot of the Beardmore Glacier. "The Lord gave and the Lord taketh away; blessed be the name of the Lord."'

This was signed by all the members of the party. I decided then to march twenty miles south with the whole of the expedition and try to find the body of Captain Oates.

For half that day we proceeded south, as far as possible along the line of the previous seasons march. On one of the old pony walls, which was simply marked by a ridge of the surface of snow, we found Oates' sleeping bag, which they had brought along with them after he had left.

The next day we proceeded thirteen more miles south, hoping and searching to find his body. When we arrived at the place where he had left them, we saw there was no chance of doing so. The kindly snow had covered his body, giving him a fitting burial. Here, again, as near to the site of the death as we could judge, we built another cairn to this memory, and placed thereon a small cross and the following record:–

'Hereabouts died a very gallant gentleman, Captain L.E.G. Oates of the Inniskilling Dragoons. In March 1912, returning from the Pole, he walked willingly to his death in a blizzard, to try and save his comrades, beset by hardships. This note is left by the Relief Expedition of 1912.'

It was signed by Cherry and myself.

Above: The wintering party outside the hut at Cape Evans – a rare panoramic shot by Frank Debenham, taken in 1912.

The men dug the tent out and found the three frozen bodies. Under Scott's sleeping bag they discovered his diaries and last letters, with instructions to take them home. The relief party sat silent, spellbound, as Atkinson read from Scott's journal, revealing the full scale of the tragedy.

At midnight on 12 November 1912, beneath a 'blazing sky', Atkinson read the lesson from *The Book of Common Prayer's* burial service from *Corinthians*, followed by some prayers, before collapsing the tent over the bodies of Scott and his companions. Lastly, a snow cairn was erected, marked by a pair of skis lashed together as a cross. Carrying the precious literary relics, the men returned back to base to await the return of *Terra Nova*, which would take them and their news to New Zealand, and then home.

A NATION MOURNS

It was not until 12 February 1913 that news reached London of the deaths of Scott and his team. It prompted an almost unprecedented national outpouring of grief.

On Valentine's Day a memorial service was held for Scott and his party at St. Paul's Cathedral. The crowd of 10,000 was greater than the gathering for those who had perished on the *Titanic* the previous year. In an unprecedented act, King George V, dressed in the uniform of an admiral of the fleet, joined the grieving masses. A correspondent from the *Times* reported:

> Within the Cathedral all is hushed and dim. The wintry light of the February morning is insufficient to illuminate the edifice, and circles of electric light glow with a golden radiance in the choir and nave and transepts. Almost every one attending the service is in mourning or dressed in sombre garments. Gradually the building fills, and as it does so one catches glimpses of the scarlet tunics

of distinguished soldiers, of scarlet gowns, the garb of City alder-
men, and of the golden epaulettes of naval officers shining out
conspicuously against the dark background of their uniforms. The
band of the Coldstream Guards is stationed beneath the dome …
and this, too, affords a vivid note of colour.

The public grieved on behalf of Scott's absent widow who, unaware of the
dreadful reality, was on a ship between California and Tahiti, en route to
New Zealand where she planned to meet her husband and lend him her
support. Knowing that Scott would stay in Antarctica until he felt his work
was done well enough, she had no reason to believe that his party had failed
to return to Cape Evans. About the memorial service, the *Evening Standard*
reported: '[I doubt if St. Paul's] ever contained a congregation so profoundly moved as that which gathered here today.' And the newspaper
reminded its readers of the one who is: '… still ignorant of the frightful
tragedy, that hapless woman, still on the high seas, flushed with hope and
expectation, eager to join her husband and to share in the triumphs of his
return. It made one feel that the service was rather unreal.' It was not until
19 February that Kathleen Scott heard the news.

Before Scott had left, Kathleen had urged him to reach the South Pole no
matter what, and not to hold himself back for the sake of her and Peter –
perhaps it was an oblique reference to Shackleton's decision to return home
without the prize. To Kathleen, the journey to the South Pole had the
romance of a mythical quest; the pole was the grail, and her husband the
hero who would have to face all manner of adversity to reach it. She had
made these feelings clear to her husband, scribbled in pencil in a note that
Scott would carry with him to his death:

I left off just where I was going to tell you a very difficult thing.
Look you when you are away South I want you to be sure that if
there be a risk to take or leave, you will take it, or if there is a dan-

ger for you or another man to face, it will be you who face it, just as much as before you met Doodles [Peter] and me. Because man dear we can do without you please know for sure we can. God knows I love you more than I thought could be possible, but I want you to realise that it won't [crossed out] wouldn't be your physical life that would profit me and Doodles most. If there's anything you think worth doing at the cost of your life – Do it. We shall only be glad. Do you understand me? How awful if you don't.

Although she must have been devastated, Kathleen took the news with grace, and was inspired by her husband's last words to the nation: 'That was a glorious courageous note and a great inspiration to me,' she wrote in a journal she had kept since he left for Antarctica. 'If he in his weak agony-wracked condition could face [death] with such sublime fortitude how dare I possibly whine. I will not. I regret nothing but his suffering.'

In the coming days, the full scale of the tragedy was revealed to a rapt public. It was clear from the reports of Atkinson that Scott had been the last to die. It must have been unimaginable agony for him in those final hours. Oates was already dead somewhere in the snows, and Bowers and Wilson were rigid and lifeless beside him. In the weak light from a makeshift lamp burning methylated spirit, and with the strength he had left in him ebbing away, he wrote a letter to the mother of Bowers, and then one to the wife of Wilson: 'If this letter reaches you, Bill and I will have gone out together. We are very near it now and I should like you to know how splendid he was at the end – everlastingly cheerful …. His eyes have a comfortable blue look of hope … I can do no more to comfort you than to tell you that he died as he lived, a brave, true man – the best of comrades and the staunchest of friends. My whole heart goes out to you in pity.'

Scott had managed to tie the sleeping bags of his dead companions, then had waited for his own death. With his feet frozen and his body weakened with hunger and exposure, there was no possible escape for Scott – the tent was a canvas tomb. Finally, he could bear it no longer. Cherry-Garrard wrote: 'Scott had thrown back the flaps of his bag at the end. His left hand was stretched over Wilson, his lifelong friend … I feel sure that he had died last – and one I had thought that he would not go so far as some of the others. We never realized how strong that man was, mentally and physi-cally, until now.' The poignancy of this act was profound. There were six men that had discovered the tent, and all were greatly disturbed by what they found: 'It was clear [Scott] had had a very hard last minutes', Gran wrote of the sight of the body in the tent. 'It was a horrid sight.'

The British public felt the loss of their gentleman-hero keenly, and, extraordinarily, this grief seemed to be echoed across the globe. When the last of Scott's rescue party returned to England, Cherry-Garrard wrote: 'We landed to find the Empire – almost the civilized world, in mourning. It was as though they had lost great friends.'

SCOTT'S APOTHEOSIS

If ever there was a story epitomizing patriotism, then the deaths of Scott and his companions was it. The newspaper headlines ran bold: 'A Nation's Tribute to its Heroic Sons Dead in the White Wastes of the Far South' and 'His Dying Appeal to England'. This quintessential tale of companionship, self-sacrifice – in the case of Oates – and strength of mind and purpose in the face of seemingly inevitable death was an immensely powerful narrative. Some sources exulted in the upright example the tragedy offered to the public: 'The calamity has its consolations in that it has proved once more the inherent heroism of British men of action. Like other great deeds it will brace the moral nerve of the nation.'

Scott's eloquent appeal to the nation, written in his death-throes from the vast impenetrable South, had elevated him to heights he would never have achieved had he returned home safely. In life he may have been a Royal Navy officer beleaguered by depression, self-doubt and almost unforgivably bad planning, but in death he became a nation's shining hero.

Within a couple of years, countless thousands of British men would suffer in the trenches during the carnage of the First World War. Examples of bravery and steadfastness in action, such as the failed expedition to the South Pole, did a great deal to help men to face up to their worst fears and to find their own inner courage to draw upon. During that conflict, Kathleen Scott and Apsley Cherry-Garrard would receive steams of letters from soldiers, who said that the stories of Oates and Scott had inspired them to face danger, fear and death with strength and resolve: 'It just shows how one can face death', read one typical example. 'This is indeed a case of death where is thy sting.'

Scott's metamorphosis was secured by dint of the extensive written and visual record, and it was sustained by the press. Stories of the courage of his men, their valiant struggle against the ghostly whiteness of the South and the nobleness of their deaths were serialized alongside the achingly poignant images of the team broken by defeat at the South Pole and the memorial cairn built over the bodies of the three explorers. The result was a massive surge in circulation. A record 1,340,000 copies of a special memorial edition of the *Daily Mirror* had been sold on the day of the service at St. Paul's Cathedral, and for weeks on end Fleet Street ensured that the story remained at the forefront of the minds of the reading public. The Scott story attained myth-like status. 'It is a splendid tragedy', declared the *Daily Mail*. 'A splendid epic, written like many another British epic dotted over the globe in a language which every creed and race and tongue of man can understand.' According to the *Times*, the real value of the deaths of Scott and his men was:

> … moral and spiritual, and therefore in the truest sense national. It is proof that in an age of depressing materialism men can still be found to face known hardship, heavy risk, and even death, in pursuit of an idea, and that the unconquerable will can carry them through, loyal to the last to the charge they have undertaken.

Left & Above: On 10 February 1912 news of the 'disaster following Scott's success' (as the *Daily Graphic* put it) was cabled around the world. Every newspaper in London devoted many pages to the tragedy in the Antarctic. On 14 February a national memorial service was held in St Paul's Cathedral; the mourners in attendance included King George V (as shown by the *Illustrated London News*) and a crowd of some 10,000 people stood outside on the street.

Above: When the search party returned to what is now known as McMurdo, they climbed Observation Hill where they erected a large wooden cross, inscribed with the names of Scott and his companions. It also bore the words of Tennyson: 'To strive, to seek, to find, and not to yield'.

That is the temper of men who build empires, and while it lives among us we shall be capable of maintaining the Empire that our fathers builded .... So we owe honour and gratitude to Captain Scott and his companions for showing that the solid stuff of national character is still among us, and that men are still willing to be 'killed in action' for an idea.

The polar exploration community was particularly affected by the news of the deaths during Scott's expedition. It was a reminder of both the danger of their profession and the underlying reason behind their exploits – the quest for fame. Almost every polar explorer dreamed of being elevated to such heights as Scott. The French explorer Dr Jean Charcot wrote: '... a halo of glory, shedding a reflecting glow upon his country, will surround his name.' Privately, some confided that they were unsurprised at the tragic outcome of the expedition. Leon Amundsen was among them, and he wrote to his brother:

This awful tragedy is of course here too the topic of the day. Many had expected this as the entire expedition was organised in such a way as to invite disaster. I consider now that for all parties it is an advantage that you were at the South Pole otherwise one can be certain that a new British expedition would be organised without delay and probably without changing anything of the old style. And the result could be catastrophe upon catastrophe like in its time the North West Passage was.

Others who had foreseen that Scott's party would encounter difficulties were diplomatic enough to ignore the errors and focus instead on Scott's heroic endeavour. One such was Robert Peary, who had once tried to convince Scott to use dogs and had pointed out to him the foolhardiness of relying on ponies: 'They died like Englishmen, fighting against the most abnormal conditions, and meeting their death after a dogged struggle worthy of the highest traditions of their profession.' Refreshingly honest, Tryggve Gran, the young Norwegian skier who had tried to teach Scott's party to ski, said: 'No polar explorer of historical stature has escaped blunders. Nansen, Peary, Amundsen, Shackleton, Ross, Borchgrevink – all of them messed up one way or the other, and others followed them, but they were able to overcome their mistakes. Scott was the unlucky one. His false step brought him a catastrophe, but also glory.'

All those who had been to the Arctic and the Antarctic felt a connection in some way with Scott's death, but perhaps none more than Amundsen. The Norwegian explorer, who had been celebrating his success, was floored by the tragic news: 'I am unwilling to believe the report its true. I was announced to have perished, so was Shackleton … I am grieved beyond measure at the report.'

Message to the Public

Robert Falcon Scott, entry from his journal, 24 or 25 March 1912.

The causes of the disaster are not due to faulty organization, but misfortune in all risks which had to be undertaken.

The loss of pony transport in March 1911 obliged me to start later than I had intended, and obliged the limits of stuff transported to be narrowed.

The weather throughout the outward journey, and especially the long gale in 83° S., stopped us.

The soft snow in lower reaches of glacier again reduced pace.

We fought these untoward events with a will and conquered, but it cut into our provision reserve.

Every detail of our food supplies, clothing and depots made on the interior ice-sheet and over that long stretch of 700 miles to the Pole and back, worked out to perfection. The advance party would have returned to the glacier in fine form and with surplus food, but for the astonishing failure of the man whom we had least expected to fail. Edgar Evans was thought the strongest man of the party. The Beardmore Glacier is not difficult in fine weather, but on our return we did not get a single completely fine day; this with a sick companion enormously increased our anxieties.

As I have said elsewhere, we got into frightfully rough ice and Edgar Evans received a concussion of the brain — he died a natural death, but left us a shaken party with the season unduly advanced.

But all the facts above enumerated were as nothing to the surprise which awaited us on the Barrier. I maintain that our arrangements for returning were quite adequate, and that no one in the world would have expected the temperatures and surfaces which we encountered at this time of year. On the summit in lat. 85°/86° we had -20°, -30°. On the Barrier in lat. 82°, and 10,000 feet lower, we had -30°in the day, -47° at night pretty regularly, with continuous head wind during our day marches. It is clear that the circumstances come on very suddenly, and our wreck is certainly due to this sudden advent of severe weather, which does not seem to have any satisfactory cause. I do not think human beings ever came through such a month as we have come through, and we should have got through in spite of the weather but for the sickening of a second companion, Captain Oates, and a shortage of fuel in our depots which I cannot account, and finally, but for the storm which has fallen on us within 11 miles of the depot at which we hope to secure our final supplies. Surely misfortune could scarcely have exceeded this last blow. We arrived within 11 miles of our old One Ton Camp with fuel for one last meal and food for two days. For four days we have been unable to leave the tent — the gale howling about us. We are weak, writing is difficult, and but for my own sake I do not regret this journey, which is shown that Englishmen can endure hardships, help one another, and meet death with as great a fortitude as ever in the past. We took risks, we knew we took them; things have come out against us, and therefore we have no cause for complaint, but bow to the will of Providence, determined still to do our best to the last. But if we have been willing to give our lives to this enterprise, which is for the honour of our country, I appeal to our countrymen to see that those who depend upon us are properly cared for.

Had we lived, I should have had a tale to tell of the hardihood, endurance, and courage of my companions which would have stirred the heart of every Englishman. These rough notes and our dead bodies must tell the tale, but surely, surely, a great rich country like ours will see that those who are dependent on us are properly provided for.

CHAPTER 6
OF ICE AND MEN

We had pierced the veneer of outside things. We had 'suffered, starved and triumphed, grovelled down yet grasped at glory, grown bigger in the bigness of the whole.' We had seen God in his splendours, heard the text that Nature renders. We had reached the naked soul of man.

ERNEST SHACKLETON, FROM *SOUTH*, 1919.

On 8 March 1912 the news reached London that Amundsen had won the South Pole for Norway. Of Scott, as yet there was no word. In time, the tragedy of Scott's defeat and death would take centre stage but in the meantime a remarkable example of survival had unfolded elsewhere in Antarctica.

Two months before Amundsen's victory had been announced, a veteran of Shackleton's *Nimrod* expedition had stepped onto the rugged coast of eastern Antarctica. Australian geologist Douglas Mawson had been invited by Scott to join the *Terra Nova* expedition but he had chosen instead to lead his own scientific expedition to the Magnetic South Pole and the virtually uncharted area of Adélie Land and King George V Land, which had remained unexplored since the expeditions of d'Urville and Wilkes in 1840. Mawson's *Aurora* sailed into Commonwealth Bay on 8 January 1912 and dropped anchor at Cape Denison, before she ferried a secondary party to a camp 1,500 miles (2,400 kilometres) to the west, at the Shackleton Ice Shelf. The aim was not to achieve any great 'firsts' or to return as heroes, but simply to conduct a thorough scientific programme.

Unwittingly, Mawson had chosen one of the most inhospitable places on the continent at which to establish his main base. Cape Denison was a place where winds regularly oscillated between gale and hurricane force; it was, as the explorer later put it, 'the home of the blizzard'. As winter descended, ice granules bombarded the hut with the velocity of shotgun pellets. The men had to move with their bodies bent double, forced to use ice-axes at

every step as they fought to stay on their feet. Virtually imprisoned in the hut as the winter swirled furiously about them, there was little Mawson could do but focus on the spring journeys that lay some ten months ahead.

In November 1912, taking advantage of a relative lull in the strength of the winds, five separate exploring parties set out in different directions: three would travel to the east, one south to the magnetic pole and one to the west. Mawson and two companions – the Swiss skier and mountaineer Xavier Mertz and the Australian Belgrave E.S. Ninnis – headed farthest east to survey King George V Land. Their journey was to consist of a catalogue of terrifying ordeals and near-misses as they crossed giant glaciers and hazardous crevasse fields. After a month of arduous travel, the men decided to abandon one of the sledges and they loaded most of the supplies, with their tent, onto Ninnis's sledge. The following day, Ninnis disappeared without a sound into a crevasse along with his sledge, his dogs and their things.

Mawson and Mertz were more than 300 miles (500 kilometres) from safety, and without a single depot between them and their destination. Weakening

Left: The *Aurora*, photographed in 1912 by Frank Hurley, within a cavern of the Mertz Glacier. This photograph was taken during the Australasian Antarctic Expedition and is from the personal album of expedition leader Douglas Mawson.

Above: Rare photographs from Hurley's presentation album, detailing the adventures of Mawson's Australasian Antarctic Expedition, 1909–1913. Passing through the pack-ice, *Aurora* reached Commonwealth Bay and the men landed stores ashore with which to build their main base hut at Cape Denison.

So This is the End

DOUGLAS MAWSON, *THE HOME OF THE BLIZZARD*, 1915.

Outside, the bowl of chaos was brimming with drift-snow and as I lay in the sleeping bag beside my dead companion I wondered how, in such conditions, I would manage to break and pitch camp single-handed. There appeared to be little hope of reaching the Hut, still one hundred miles away. It was easy to sleep in this bag, and the weather was cruel outside. But inaction is hard to bear and I braced myself together determined to put up a good fight.

… From the start my feet felt curiously lumpy and sore. They had become so painful after a mile of walking that I decided to examine them on the spot, sitting in the lee of the sledge in brilliant sunshine. I had not had my socks off for some days for, while lying in camp, it had not seemed necessary. On taking off the third and inner pair of socks the sight of my feet gave me quite a shock, for the thickened skin of the soles had separated in each case as a complete layer, and abundant watery fluid had escaped saturating the sock. The new skin beneath was very much abraded and raw. Several of my toes had commenced to blacken and fester near the tips and the nails were puffed and loose.

I began to wonder if there was ever to be a day without some special disappointment. However, there was nothing to be done but make the best of it. I smeared the new skin and raw surfaces with lanoline, of which there was fortunately a good store, and then with the aid of bandages bound to the old skin casts back in place, for these were comfortable and soft in contact with the abraded surface. Over the bandages was slipped six pairs of thick woollen socks, then fur boots and finally crampon over-shoes. The latter, having large stiff soles, spread the weight nicely and saved my feet from the jagged ice encountered shortly afterwards.

So glorious was it to feel the sun on one's skin after being without it so long that I next removed most of my clothing and bathed my body in the rays until my flesh fairly tingled – a wonderful sensation which spread throughout my whole person, and made me feel stronger and happier.

… The day following passed in a howling blizzard and I could do nothing but attend to my feet and other raw patches, festering fingernails and inflamed frostbitten nose. Fortunately there was a good supply of bandages and antiseptic. The tent, spread about with dressing and the meagre surgical appliances at hand, was suggestive of a casualty hospital.

… January 17 was another day of overcast sky and steady falling snow. Everything from below one's feet to the sky above was one uniform ghostly glare. The irregularities in the surfaces not obliterated by the deep soft snow blended harmoniously in colour and in the absence of shadows faded into invisibility. … A start was made at 8am and the pulling proved more easy than on the previous day. Some two miles had been negotiated in safety when an event occurred which, but for a miracle, would have terminated the story then and there. Never have I come so near to an end; never has anyone more miraculously escaped.

I was hauling the sledge through deep snow up a fairly steep slope when my feet broke through into a crevasse. Fortunately as I fell I caught my weight with my arms on the edge and did not plunge in further than the thighs. The outline of the crevasse did not show through the blanket of snow on the surface, but an idea of the trend was obtained with a stick. I decided to try a crossing about fifty yards further along, hoping that there it would be better bridged. This time I shot through the centre of the bridge in a flash, but the latter part of the fall was decelerated by the friction of the harness ropes which, as the sledge ran up, sawed back into the thick compact snow forming the margin of the lid. Having seen my comrades perish in diverse ways and having lost hope of ever reaching the Hut, I had already many times speculated on what the end would be like. So it happened that as I fell through into the crevasse the thought 'so this is the end' blazed up in my mind, for it was to be expected that the next moment the sledge would follow through, crash on my head and all go to the unseen bottom. But the unexpected happened and the sledge held, the deep snow acting as a brake.

… In my weak condition, the prospect of climbing out seemed very poor indeed, but in a few moments the struggle was begun. A great effort brought a knot in the rope within my grasp, and, after a moment's rest, I was able to draw myself up and reach another, and, at length, hauled my body on to the overhanging snow-lid. Then, when all appeared to be well and before I could get to quite solid ground, a further section of the lid gave way, precipitating me once more to the full length of the rope.

There, exhausted, weak and chilled, hanging freely in space and slowly turning round as the rope twisted one way and the other, I felt that I had done my utmost and failed, that I had no more strength to try again and that all was over except the passing. It was to be a miserable and slow end and I reflected with disappointment that there was in my pocket no antidote to speed matters; but there always remained the alternative of slipping from the harness. There on the brink of the great Beyond I well remember how I looked forward to the peace of the great release – how almost excited I was at the prospect of the unknown to be unveiled. From those flights of mind I came back to earth, and remembering how Providence had miraculously brought me so far, felt that nothing was impossible and determined to act up to [Robert] Service's lines: Just have one more try – it's dead easy to die, It's the keeping-on-living that's hard.

My strength was fast ebbing; in a few minutes it would be too late. It was the occasion for a supreme attempt. Fired by the passion that burns the blood in the act of strife, new power seemed to come as I applied myself to one last tremendous effort. The struggle occupied some time, but I slowly worked upward to the surface. This time emerging feet first, still clinging to the rope, I pushed myself out extended at full length on the lid and then shuffled safely on to the solid ground at the side. Then came the reaction from the great nerve strain and lying there alongside the sledge my mind faded into a blank.

When consciousness returned it was a full hour or two later, for I was partly covered with newly fallen snow and numb with the cold. I took at least three hours to erect the tent, get things snuggly inside and clear the snow from my clothes. …

I was confronted with this problem: whether it was better to enjoy life for a few days, sleeping and eating my fill until the provisions gave out, or to 'plug on' again in hunger with the prospect of plunging at any moment into eternity without the supreme satisfaction and pleasure of the food. …

On the 19th it was overcast and light snow falling; very dispiriting conditions after the experience of the day before, but I resolved to go ahead and leave the rest to Providence.

Above: Sir Douglas Mawson, legendary Australian geologist and explorer, pictured in 1930. His scientific career in Antarctica spanned three decades.

rapidly as they trudged wearily back to Cape Denison the men were forced to feed dog to dog, and even to eat dog meat themselves. By early January 1913 Metz was unable to sit up and was mumbling incoherently. Eating dog liver had poisoned both men, and with toxic amounts of Vitamin A in his bloodstream Mertz was soon dead. With more than 100 miles (160 kilometres) still between him and Cape Denison, Mawson sawed the remaining sledge in half with his small pocketknife and made a sail from his companion's Burberry jacket. Ignoring the pain from his severely frostbitten feet, and enduring numerous bone-rattling falls down crevasses, Mawson staggered on. Against extraordinary odds, he made it back to Cape Denison, only to find that his relief ship *Aurora* had departed the previous day. Antarctica had dealt him the cruellest of hands. He would have to face yet another winter there before making it out in December 1913.

SHACKLETON RETURNS

Back in England, with the resurgence of public interest in the Antarctic following the news of the conquest of the South Pole, Shackleton quickly jumped back on the lecture circuit, having retired from it in the years since the voyage of the *Nimrod*. Shackleton had lost his way. Haunted by mounting debts, and restless for a new adventure, Shackleton's days had become joyless and lonely. He was becoming, as the British ski pioneer Sir Harry Brittain put it, 'a bit of a floating gent'.

With any dreams of being the first to the South Pole now dashed, Shackleton had to decide whether he was willing to allow his former glories to fade into the shadows cast by Amundsen's conquest and Scott's (soon to be heroic) defeat, or aim for yet greater heights. He had to find a new quest, bigger and better than before, if he was to maintain a profile as one of the world's leading explorers. 'The discovery of the South Pole', he had been quoted as saying in the *Daily Mail* in March 1911, 'will not be the end of Antarctic exploration.' But only one great journey was now left to complete in Antarctica: a 1,800-mile (2,900-kilometre) crossing of the continent, from coast to coast, over the vast plateau, through the South Pole and beyond. The Scot William Speirs Bruce and the German Wilhelm Filchner had both conceived and unsuccessfully attempted similar plans, but Shackleton was convinced that he had the experience to pull it off. His plan would become known officially as the Imperial Trans-Antarctic Expedition, or more popularly as the *Endurance* voyage, going down in the annals of polar history as an epic of survival against all odds and becoming an example of fine leadership.

After many months of planning and cajoling of sponsors, Shackleton's new enterprise was announced in early 1914. It was timed fortuitously to benefit from the country's eagerness to emulate Scott's heroism, yet salve some of the wounds left open by his failure. Shackleton had government support, a handful of wealthy patrons and a loyal team of men. The expedition would utilize two ships: the *Endurance*, which would carry the main party into the Weddell Sea, a treacherous region of the Southern Ocean due east of the

Antarctic Peninsula, and the *Aurora* (bought from Shackleton's friend, Australian explorer Douglas Mawson), which would take a party to the southwest region of the continent, penetrating McMurdo Sound via the Ross Sea. Shackleton proposed to land a shore party near Vahsel Bay, then trek to the Ross Sea by way of the South Pole. His support team, known as the Ross Sea party, would establish a base at McMurdo Sound and from there a series of depots would be laid across the Great Ice Barrier to the foot of the Beardmore Glacier. These depots, which were to be used in the latter part of the trek, were essential for the survival of the crossing party, because it would be impossible for the team to carry enough provisions and fuel for the entire journey.

But the future of Shackleton's new enterprise was suddenly uncertain. On 3 August 1914 Shackleton heard the news that the First World War had begun. Immediately, he offered to put the resources of the expedition at the disposal of Britain's Admiralty, only to be advised by Winston Churchill to proceed. The following day the King gave the expedition his blessing. Shackleton felt duty-bound to continue with his plans.

Left: In November 1909 a series of films about Shackleton's expedition to the Antarctic played for two nights at Barnfield Hall in Exeter, as advertized on this poster. Reaching provincial cities like this was a reflection of the immense effort Shackleton put in to capitalize on his celebrity and raise money to pay off his debts. When the news broke that Amundsen had finally claimed the South Pole, Shackleton had to think of a bold new expedition to reclaim his place in the spotlight.

Above: A 1914 chart of Antarctica with Shackleton's proposed route penned energetically across the empty spaces of unexplored land. Saved for posterity, a menu card bears a simple sketch by Shackleton that represents his ambitious plan to cross the continent.

By November 1914 *Endurance* had reached the South Atlantic, and on 5 December she sailed out of the whaling station of Grytviken on South Georgia, heading for Vahsel Bay. Within just three days the ship ran into a belt of heavy pack-ice considerably further north than Shackleton had anticipated. For the next few weeks progress was frustratingly slow, as ice constantly crowded in on the ship. Their battle with the southern pack ended when on 21 February the *Endurance* was beset at 76° 58´S – the same area where Nordenskjöld's *Antarctic* had been crushed by ice and lost in 1903. Attempts to force a channel for the ship with chisels and ice-axes failed, therefore Shackleton calmly instructed his men to prepare for a winter in the ice. Come spring, he hoped the pack would break up sufficiently to release them. Although he knew that the expedition and the safety of the men was now in jeopardy, Frank Worsley was able to recall a Shackleton who 'laughs & jokes as tho' he'd never a care in the world' – an attribute the ship's surgeon, Alexander Macklin described as 'one of his sparks of real greatness'.

Shackleton worked tirelessly to keep everyone's spirits up during their imprisonment on the prone ship, but by the end of July the ice was rifting alarmingly and rising up in pressure ridges that marched towards her. On 18 October the *Endurance* was picked up by the ice and thrown over to her port side, and on 27 October the order was given to abandon ship. Photographer Frank Hurley described the awful moment:

> We have just finished lunch and the ice-mill is in motion again. … Irresistibly this stupendous power marches onward, grinding through the five-foot ice-floe surrounding us. Now it is within a few yards of the vessel. We are the embodiment of helpless futility and can only look impotently on. … The line of pressure now assaults the ship, and she is heaved to the crest of the ridge like a toy. Immense fragments are forced under the counter and wrench

Right: Shackleton relaxes at the wheel of *Nimrod* during her return from the Antarctic in 1909. It was an expedition that established his credentials as a polar leader of the first rank and his skills would be tested to their utmost on his next voyage.

away the stern-post. Sir Ernest and Captain Worsley are surveying the ship's position from the floe when the carpenter announces that the water is gaining rapidly on the pumps. All hands are ordered to stand by to discharge equipment and stores on to the ice. The pumps work faster and someone is actually singing a chanty to their beat. The dogs are rapidly passed down a canvas chute and secured on the floe, followed by cases of concentrated sledging rations, sledges and equipment. The ship is doomed.

Above. A remarkable still photograph taken by Frank Hurley on his 'grand cinema camera', who captured the men relaxing by playing football on the sea-ice astern of *Endurance* on 16 February 1915.

With all the essential equipment offloaded, the men returned to the ship to enjoy their last meal aboard, accompanied by the groans of twisting timber and squealing ice. As they disembarked to set up home on the floe, *Endurance* continued to buckle. 'You could hear the ship being crushed up, the ice being ground into her,' Commander Greenstreet recalled many years later in a conversation with biographer James Fisher, 'and you almost felt your own ribs were being crushed, and suddenly a light went on for a moment and then went out. It seemed the end of everything.' On 21 November 1915, the men saw the last of their ship. Worsley described the events in his diary:

> At 4.50 p.m. Sir Ernest on the floe sees her funnel moving down-wards & hails me in No. 5 Tent. Without hearing what he said, I somehow knew she was going, rushed out & up the lookout, where we watched the death of the ship that had carried us so far & so well & then put up the bravest fight that ever a ship had fought before yielding crushed by the remorseless Pack. Nothing is now visible of her but 20 feet of her stern pointing pitifully up to Heaven. She remains like this a few minutes & then slowly slips down beneath her icy shroud & is seen no more. A slight gap shows in the pack but this soon closes up & no one could tell that a gallant ship had floated there.

Top & Right: Two marvellous and rare original colour Paget plate photographs of the *Endurance* voyage by Frank Hurley. Although the vessel was trapped and crushed by the ice, Hurley was able to salvage the glass photographic plates by diving into the freezing water inside the sinking ship. (Top) the bosun John Vincent mends a net while seated on deck. (Right) *Endurance* under full sail, although held up by the ice.

Above: 'Ocean Camp' – life on the ice of the Weddell Sea after the *Endurance* was abandoned, 1915.

THOUGHTS OF ESCAPE

The men were 180 miles (290 kilometres) from the nearest land, 360 miles (580 kilometres) from the nearest possible depot of food and 1,000 miles (1,600 kilometres) from the nearest inhabited spot. 'I pray God I can manage to get the whole party to civilization', Shackleton wrote in his diary.

After five months of camping on drifting, splitting and rafting ice-floes, the men saw their chance to escape when they drifted marginally closer to land. Their aim was to haul and then sail their boats and supplies to Paulet Island or Snow Hill, where Nordenskjöld's Swedish expedition of 1902 had built huts and possibly left behind depots. From there they could make their way to Wilhelmina Bay, known to be frequented by whalers. Instead, with heavy seas and strong currents making it impossible to reach their goal, they set foot – finally – on the barren shores of Elephant Island on 15 April 1916. It had been more than 16 months since the 28 souls had felt anything but keel or ice under their feet.

Shackleton knew that no relief expedition would be likely to find them if they remained where they were, and that their chance of survival on the island for any length of time was slim. An attempt at an ocean voyage in the small open boats with all the men was impossible. Their only chance, and a slim one at that, was for Shackleton to take a handful of the strongest men to seek help before the winter was once again upon them. Leaving Frank Wild in charge of the party on Elephant Island, Shackleton, Tom Crean, Harry 'Chippy' McNish, Timothy McCarthy, John Vincent and Frank Worsley clambered into a 22-foot (7-metre) whaleboat, the *James Caird*, and set out on 24 April to navigate a perilous 800-mile (1,300-kilometre) voyage to South Georgia, which was now the nearest inhabited place.

The harrowing 15-day journey in a tiny, open, whaleboat across the mountainous, storm-frenzied waters of the Southern Ocean is one of the most astonishing in polar history. Those aboard had already endured a brutal winter on the ice – their skin was blistered and torn, and they were suffering from exposure, hunger, thirst and exhaustion. The six men could not lie down comfortably in the boat, nor could they stand for more than a few moments. Innumerable times the boat threatened to capsize as it pitched and careered through the towering waves.

On 8 May, after brilliant navigation by Worsley, South Georgia came into view. The men were still far from safe because hurricane-force winds were smashing the waves onto the rocky shore, which made it too dangerous to attempt to land. Powerless, the six had to ride out the storm. Finally, on 10 May, the *James Caird* entered King Haakon Fjord. Although they had reached land safely, they were on the opposite side of the island from the whaling station where they could raise the alarm. Two of the men were too ill to move and the conditions remained too perilous to attempt another boat journey around the island. Shackleton would have to cross the island on foot.

Above: Another of Hurley's Paget plate photographs showing *Endurance* in the 'midwinter glow in the Weddell Sea', before her demise.

Right: Frank Wild surveys what is left of *Endurance* on 8 November 1915, when he, Shackleton and Hurley, as photographer, paid the last official visit to the wreck.

Shackleton, Crean and Worsley set out to negotiate South Georgia's ragged mountains, crevasse-fields and glaciers, but they were hopelessly ill-equipped for such an endeavour. Their clothes were thin and ripped, they had no sleeping bags, they used makeshift crampons in the form of battered boots with screws from the *James Caird* hammered through the soles, and each man had to carry his food in a canvas boot strung about his neck with lamp wick.

After walking continuously for 36 hours over extraordinarily tough terrain, three wild-looking men arrived at the whaling station of Stromness – only for the two boys they encountered to flee in terror at the sight of them. 'We were', Worsley recalled, 'perhaps more terrifying than primitive savages.' When they walked into the office, the manager said: 'Who the hell are you?' 'My name is Shackleton', came the quiet reply. A man called Mansell who happened to be in the office that day, recalled: 'Me – I turn away and weep. I think manager weep too.'

The Imperial Trans-Antarctic Expedition may have failed in its primary purpose, but it resulted in another spectacular tale of leadership, endurance and loyalty. With assistance from the Chilean Navy, Shackleton rescued all his men on South Georgia and Elephant Island – as well as, later, the men of the Ross Sea party, who had suffered their own traumatic

experience on the ice after the departure of the *Aurora*. 'Their great physical suffering went deeper than their appearance', remembered Captain John King Davis of the rescue party sent to the Ross Sea group. 'Their speech was jerky, at times semi-hysterical, almost unintelligible ... these events had rendered these hapless individuals as unlike ordinary human beings as any I have ever met. The Antarctic had given them the full treatment.'

The *Endurance* episode took its toll on Shackleton. He must have found the near-death experience profoundly moving, and in a visitor's book in the Chilean settlement of Punta Arenas, Shackleton inscribed these lines of poetry by St. John Lucas that were close to his heart:

> We were the fools who could not rest
> In the dull earth we left behind,
> And burned with passion for the south,
> And drank strange frenzy from its wind.
> The world where wise men sit at ease
> Fades from our unregretful eyes,
> And thus across uncharted seas,
> We stagger on our enterprise.

The Boat Journey

ERNEST SHACKLETON, *SOUTH*, 1919.

I had not realised until the sunlight came how small our boat really was. So low in the water were we that each succeeding swell cut off our view of the skyline. At one moment the consciousness of the forces arrayed against us would be almost overwhelming, and then hope and confidence would rise again as our boat rose to a wave and tossed aside the crest in a sparkling shower.

… We still suffered severely from the cold, for our vitality was declining owing to shortage of food, exposure, and the necessity of maintaining our cramped positions day and night. … One of the memories which comes to me of those days is Crean singing at the tiller. He always sang while he was steering, but nobody ever discovered what the song was.

On the tenth night Worsley could not straighten his body after his spell at the tiller. He was thoroughly cramped, and we had to drag him beneath the decking and massage him before he could unbend himself and get into a sleeping bag.

A hard north-westerly gale came up on the eleventh day (May 5th), and in the late afternoon it shifted to the south-west. The sky was overcast and occasional snow-squalls added to the discomfort produced by a tremendous cross-sea – the worst, I thought, which we had encountered. At midnight I was at the tiller, and suddenly noticed a line of clear sky between the south and south-west. I called to the other men that the sky was clearing, and then, not a moment later, realised that what I had seen was not a rift in the clouds but the white crest of an enormous wave.

During twenty-six years' experience of the ocean in all its moods I had not encountered a wave so gigantic. It was a mighty upheaval of the ocean, a thing quite apart from the white-capped seas that had been our tireless enemies for many days. I shouted, 'For God's sake, hold on! It's got us!' Then came a moment of suspense that seemed drawn out into hours. White surged the foam of the breaking sea around us. We felt our boat lifted and flung forward like a cork in breaking surf. We were in a seething chaos of tortured water; but somehow the boat lived through it, half-full of water, sagging to the dead weight and shuddering under the blow. We baled with the energy of men fighting for life, flinging the water over the sides with every receptacle that came to our hands, and after ten minutes of uncertainty we felt the boat renew her life beneath us. She floated again and ceased to lurch drunkenly as though dazed by the attack of the sea. Earnestly we hoped that never again would we encounter such a wave.

… Things were bad for us in those days, but the end was approaching. The morning of May 8th broke thick and stormy, with squalls from the north-west. …

We gazed ahead with increasing eagerness, and at 12.30 p.m., through a rift in the clouds, McCarthy caught a glimpse of the black cliffs of South Georgia, just fourteen days after our departure from Elephant Island. It was a glad moment. Thirst-ridden, chilled, and weak as we were, happiness irradiated us. The job was nearly done.

… At 5 a.m. the wind shifted to the north-west, and quickly increased to one of the worst hurricanes any of us had ever experienced. A great cross-sea was running and the wind simply shrieked as it converted the whole sea-scape into a haze of driving spray. Down in to the valleys, up to tossing heights, straining until her seams opened, swung our little boat, brave still but labouring heavily. We knew that the wind and set of the sea were driving us ashore, but we could do nothing.

The dawn revealed a storm-torn ocean, and the morning passed without bringing us a sight of the land; but at 1 p.m., through a rift in the flying mists, we got a glimpse of the huge crags of the island and realised that our position had become desperate. We were on a dead lee shore, and we could gauge our approach to the unseen cliffs by the roar of the breakers against the sheer walls of rock.

… The *James Caird* was bumping heavily, and the water was pouring in everywhere. Our thirst was forgotten in the realisation of our imminent danger, as we bailed unceasingly and from time to time adjusted our weights; occasional glimpses showed that the shore was nearer. … The chance of surviving the night seemed small, and I think most of us felt that the end was very near. Just after 6 p.m., as the boat was in the yeasty backwash from the seas flung from this iron-bound coast, just when things looked their worst, they changed for the best; so thin is the line which divides success from failure.

… Dusk was approaching. A small cove, with a boulder-strewn beach guarded by a reef, made a break in the cliffs on the south side of the bay, and we turned in that direction. … The entrance was so narrow that we had to take in the oars, and the swell was piling itself right over the reef into the cove. But in a minute or two we were inside, and in the gathering darkness the *James Caird* ran in on a swell and touched the beach.

I sprang ashore with the short painter, and held on when the boat went out with the backward surge. When the boat came in again three men got ashore and held the painter while I climbed some rocks with another line. A slip on the wet rocks 20 feet up nearly closed my part of the story, just when we were achieving safety. A jagged piece of rock held me and also sorely bruised me. I, however, made fast the line, and in a few minutes we were all safe on the beach, with the boat floating in the surging water just off the shore.

We heard a gurgling sound which was sweet music in our ears, and, peering round, we found a stream of fresh water almost at our feet. A moment later we were down on our knees drinking the pure, ice-cold water in long draughts which put new life into us. It was a splendid moment.

Left: This Burberry helmet was worn by Shackleton on the *Nimrod* expedition, but the equipment used during the *Endurance* mission was similar. Shackleton gave it away as a gift to a supporter, with a personal message.
Above: Stores being transferred to the ship's boat *James Caird* as Shackleton and his companions prepare to leave Elephant Island on 24 April 1916 in a heroic bid to reach safety and raise a rescue party.

Shackleton never attained his dream of reaching the South Pole, but despite the failures of both the *Nimrod* and *Endurance* expeditions he had established himself as one of the world's greatest polar travellers and his example inspired some of his men to return time and again to Antarctica. On 5 January 1922, during a swan song journey south, he had a fatal heart attack aboard *Quest* in the waters surrounding South Georgia – fittingly, his wife Emily requested that he be buried on the island that had played such a significant part in his life.

A MODERN AGE OF EXPLORATION

The 'heroic age' of exploration with its grand plans, tragic deaths and epic tales of survival was drawing to a close and a new era of exploration was beginning. Although Scott, Shackleton and Mawson had tried to introduce modern methods of travel – Scott had used motorized sledges, Shackleton attempted to use a car and Mawson had been the first to take an aeroplane to Antarctica – none had been particularly successful. A new breed of explorer would now shatter the silence of Antarctica with the whir of propellers and engines that heralded the mechanical age.

Heading the vanguard were Australian Sir Hubert Wilkins and American Richard Evelyn Byrd. Roundly skilled Sir Hubert – variously described as polar explorer, geographer, climatologist, balloonist, decorated war hero, secret agent, submariner, navigator, ornithologist and author – was the first, arriving in the Antarctic in 1928 with the aim of flying across the continent over the same route proposed by Shackleton in 1914. Wilkins failed twice to achieve his dream, but he did discover and chart long stretches of coastline.

Following Wilkins's lead was the charismatic United States Navy aviator Richard Evelyn Byrd. Formidably well connected, Byrd had easy access to financial and logistic support, and he used it to great effect to make what he claimed to be the first flight to the North Pole in 1926. His expeditions attracted global coverage in the press, film and exhibitions, which all promoted his celebrity as the newest polar media hero. At his celebrations at Kings Bay, at that time the northernmost community in the world, Byrd met veteran explorer Roald Amundsen who had also taken to the air with Umberto Nobile to fly across the Arctic via the North Pole in the airship *Norge*. 'Well, Byrd, what shall it be now?' Amundsen reportedly asked. 'Flying over the South Pole', Byrd replied. There were many that doubted the viability of that aspiration. Captain Charles S. Wright, who had been among the team to discover Scott's frozen body, feared for Byrd being able to take off again if he landed on the ice.

The Byrd Expedition of 1928–1930 was the first American one to Antarctica since the Charles Wilkes voyage of 1840. Four ships and three aircraft were involved and a base named Little America was established on the Bay of Whales, from where Byrd defied expectations and became the first to fly to the South Pole. The journey, which had taken Amundsen three months to complete, took Byrd just 16 hours.

Byrd was unafraid of being alone and he redrew the boundaries of the possible. Like others before him, he experienced the eerie quiet of Antarctica – a silence 'so deep one could almost reach out and take hold of it'. During a second expedition in 1933–1935, Byrd endured five solitary winter months operating a meteorological station, Advance Camp, from which he barely escaped with his life after suffering carbon monoxide poisoning. 'I was the inspector of snowstorms and the aurora, the night watchman, and father confessor to myself', Byrd wrote of his isolation. His radio provided comfort, connecting him to events in the outside world. Curiosity one day made him ask Little America for the stock market quotations – it was, he confided to his diary, 'a ghastly mistake'. Eventually, he concluded that a lengthy stay was not a good thing, reflecting: 'The Antarctic is the last stronghold of inertness. On this continent, whence all life has been driven, save for a very few primitive or microscopic forms, inertia governs a vast empire.'

Byrd's new approach to travel and communication in Antarctica transformed the way that expeditions could operate. He was the first explorer to initiate radio communication on the continent, and in doing so he removed much of the sense of isolation that had so overpowered many of the men on the historic voyages to the 'great silent south'. 'The loneliness of exploration is gone', declared the *Times*. Moreover, it was a triumph for journalism claimed the *New York Times*: 'Over the sub-zero fields of crackling ice, over the gray and restless desolation of berg-infested seas ... through blinding blizzards that drive across the Pole and through the terrific gales that sweep the floor of the world, radio, fleet messenger ... will carry the story.'

A natural showman and a master publicist, Byrd brought the Antarctic into the homes of the American public with weekly broadcasts on CBS radio from Russell Owen, one of Byrd's team stationed at Little America. Owen's dispatches, sent by Morse code to New York (and published in London in the following day's *Times*), enthralled readers and eventually earned him a Pulitzer Prize. Remarkably, given the economic depression gripping the country at the time, these voices from the frozen continent sustained popular support for an American presence in the Antarctic.

There was good reason for Americans to feel proud of their fellow countryman. Byrd returned from his flights with extensive charts and aerial photographs, as well as a host of new discoveries named for his well-known supporters, such as the Rockefeller Mountains. Byrd proved that the Ross and Weddell seas were unconnected and he was the first to conduct seismic tests to determine the

Below: The *Daily Chronicle* announces the news that the *Endurance* has been lost but Shackleton and all his men are safe.

depth of the ice on both the plateau and the Ross Ice Shelf, hitherto called the Great Ice Barrier.

The American aviator inaugurated what may be called the 'scientific age' of Antarctic exploration, although it could easily also be described as a period of mechanical innovation during a time of adventure. Now, with motorized sledges and small planes capable of enduring the severe Antarctic climate and geography, there would be little need for explorers to rely solely on man-hauling, dog-sledding, or indeed the use of ponies.

THE COMMONWEALTH EXPEDITION

Byrd, who eventually led five expeditions from the 1930s to the 1950s, has been crediting with doing more for the exploration of Antarctica than any other man. But with the exception of the American Geographical Society-supported expedition in 1947–1948, mounted by Byrd's one-time officer Captain Finn Ronne, during which he travelled a great deal and made many discoveries, there was no further significant activity in the region until the mid-1950s. The boldest of this new wave of Antarctic adventure on the ground was the Commonwealth Trans-Antarctic Expedition of 1955–1958, led by British geologist Dr Vivian Fuchs, which would cross the continent via the South Pole using a route similar to the one that Shackleton had proposed some 40 years before. American aviator Lincoln Ellsworth had become the first to fly across the continent in 1935, but no one had so far managed to tackle the hazards of an overland crossing.

The expedition was an ambitious, avowedly modern enterprise, timed to capitalize on the global interest that it was anticipated would be generated by the International Geophysical Year (IGY) programme of 1957–1958. Using the very latest in technology and polar-adapted vehicles, the private expedition – yet supported by the governments of Britain, New Zealand, South Africa and Australia as well as many corporate sponsors – included a strong scientific team that would carry out seismic soundings and glaciological, meteorological and geological research. With many nations and many interests, this was an expedition that changed the game.

The careful planning took two years and bases were built in advance of the actual crossing: Shackleton Base, constructed near Vahsel Bay on the Weddell Sea, and Scott Base at McMurdo Sound on the Ross Sea. Another smaller base about 300 miles (500 kilometres) inland to the south was called South Ice.

In addition to the scientific contingent, the expedition contained two teams that would make the overland journey: a crossing party, led by Fuchs, and a supporting party travelling from the Ross Sea, which was led by Sir

Above: The Burroughs Wellcome and Co. 'tabloid' medicine chest that was used by Richard E. Byrd during his explorations in Antarctica, including the first flight to the South Pole in 1929. The term 'tabloid', which the company registered as a trademark, referred to both the case and the compressed drugs and products it contained. Burroughs Wellcome and Co. kits were used by many explorers, including H.M. Stanley in Africa and Amundsen, Peary and Scott at the poles. In 1929 Byrd established a 'Wellcome Dispensary' at his Little America base on the Ross Ice Shelf.

Edmund Hillary – the New Zealander who had conquered Everest in 1953, capturing the hearts of millions in the process. Hillary's group would build the new Scott Base at McMurdo Sound and from there lay supply depots and establish a safe vehicle route from the polar plateau back to the sea.

Fuchs set out from Shackleton Base on 24 November 1957. He wore Captain Scott's watch, hanging on a leather thong around his neck. At South Ice the team paused to listen to the Queen's Christmas Day broadcast before moving on. As Fuchs recalled in his account of the epic journey, *The Crossing of Antarctica*: '... at five minutes to three we were all congregated in the tiny living room. Bulky forms filled every chair, sat on bunks and table, or leaned against the walls, then in silence we listened to that far away voice speaking across the world. To us, who were, perhaps, the most isolated listeners, there seemed to be special encouragement.'

It was a colourful and noisy departure towards the South Pole, with a caravan of orange-painted tracked vehicles pulling a weighty 32 tons of provisions and equipment. On the other side of the continent, Hillary set out from Scott Base, at the head of a fleet of converted tractors. Having laid a string of depots for Fuchs's party, Hillary then pressed on, controversially reaching the South Pole ahead of Fuchs on 3 January 1958 to be welcomed at the newly built US Amundsen–Scott station with hot showers, followed by a breakfast of hot dogs and baked beans. When questioned why he raced Fuchs to the Pole, Hillary replied in typical style: 'Because I wanted to. Some people have to have a scientific reason. Not me.'

Meanwhile, Fuchs had made frustratingly slow progress, with concerns for his safety being raised by the British press – a matter immediately played down by the expedition committee's chairman Sir John Slessor: 'I think [Fuchs' party] will make it and if there were any prospect of disaster we should tell them to get out. But these are not the days of Captain Scott when there was nothing but gallant hearts, flat-feet and dogs. There are aircraft available, and in this matter the Americans are being very good ...'. A modern era for exploration had indeed dawned, when explorers could just be airlifted out of trouble.

Just over two weeks later, after making frustratingly slow progress and being forced to abandon four vehicles, Fuchs joined Hillary at the South Pole. Waiting for him was a 40-strong party of international journalists. Among them was writer Geoffrey Lee Martin, who recalls flying in to the established, albeit not luxurious, American base:

> It was hard to imagine just what those ten early pioneers had experienced. I could not help but reflect on the fact that once something is achieved it soon becomes commonplace, whether it is breaking the four-minute mile, climbing Everest or reaching the South Pole. As I write this, reaching the South Pole has become almost routine, certainly by much stronger aircraft than we had, and even by adventurers who prefer to walk, including Ed Hillary's son Peter. The Pole, I wrote in my diary at the time, is a

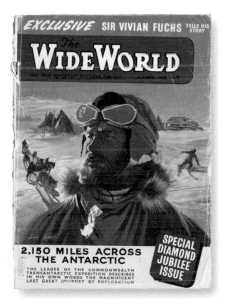

Top: Byrd made five expeditions to Antarctica. His first, which included his successful flight to the South Pole, ensured he entered the history books, and after his second expedition in 1934 his fame grew immeasurably, justified by films and public appearances. *Above:* The success of the Commonwealth Trans-Antarctic Expedition made its leader Sir Vivian Fuchs a hero at home. His adventures were serialized in best-selling instalments in the 'true adventure magazine' *The Wide World* throughout 1958.

Sextants North & South

Tom Griffiths, 2011.

In Antarctica, the return of the Sun – the beginning of its journey back south, the shaft of its first rays across the ice, the full bloom of its brief, erotic reign – shapes the polar year and its celebrations. Latitude is an earthly measure of a cosmic fact. It describes not only our place on the globe but also maps our relationship to the Sun. It is a dynamic, rhythmical relationship, this dance of the seasons, because our globe tilts on its axis as it circles the Sun, presently at an angle of 23.5 degrees. For half the year, each hemisphere basks under the most direct sunshine until planetary progress bears it off into the twilight again. The Sun seems directly overhead at the Equator, and the tropics of Capricorn and Cancer (at 23.5 degrees latitude, of course) mark the limits of its apparent seasonal wanderings. Latitude was calculated simply, by measuring with a sextant, theodolite or astrolabe the angle between the horizon and the Sun at midday.

When Roald Amundsen beat Robert Falcon Scott to the South Pole in 1911, he left him a gift should he too arrive there. The gift was his sextant. Perhaps he chose to leave this object because it

was the most potent symbol of his triumph over latitude. I think the most unexamined and astonishing fact about the race to the South Pole in 1911–12 is that the two sledging parties located the same featureless acre of ice on that vast continent. Reaching the North or South Poles is the most abstract of goals: 90°. Scott had a gift for Amundsen, too – an unwilling and tragic gift. Scott's arrival at the same spot on the endless ice, and his journal accounts of the misery of discovering the Norwegian tent with its gift of a sextant, and the miraculous discovery of those diaries under his head when he and his companions were found dead in their tent later that year – this grim, written evidence was to make Amundsen's triumph indisputable. The attainment of the North Pole a few years earlier is still subject to endless doubt and controversy, but at the South Pole, Scott's navigation and documentation corroborated Amundsen's achievement.

In 1925, Roald Amundsen and the North American Lincoln Ellsworth flew within a few degrees of the North Pole, and in May 1926, Amundsen was preparing another assault on the north, by airship. Suddenly he found he had a competitor. The North American Richard Byrd and his co-pilot Floyd Bennett were also attempting to fly to the North Pole, leaving from the same place as Amundsen. When Byrd and Amundsen had first met the year before, their companions had been struck by the contrast between the two men; Amundsen 'shaggy-haired and rugged and seasoned as an oak-

mast', and Byrd 'immaculately groomed and slender and every inch the cultured gentleman'. Amundsen was half a head taller than Byrd and, sensing the American's discomfort, invited everyone to be seated. When they met again in Spitzbergen, apparently racing one another to the Pole, Amundsen made sure his rival got his flight in first, and he also supplied Byrd and Bennett with survival gear in case their plane was forced down. Scott's death still shadowed Amundsen's life and he wanted no further resentment or controversy. On 9 May 1926, Byrd and Bennett returned from a fifteen-and-a-half-hour flight in their Fokker Trimotor plane with the news that they had indeed become the first to fly over the North Pole. Amundsen graciously welcomed them back and warmly embraced them. The news of Byrd's feat was greeted with some satisfaction in England, for many saw it as Scott's revenge. Three days later, Amundsen himself flew over the Pole. The true significance of that event remained, for the moment, hidden.

Just as Scott was eventually debunked, so was Byrd's reputation savaged within a couple of decades of his death. Doubts that had dogged his life hardened into public challenges. Had Byrd really reached the North Pole on that 1926 flight? Even at the time, attentive observers had wondered if his plane had been in the air long enough to cover the distance, especially as it returned with a leaky engine. It's possible that Byrd was initially mistaken in believing he had reached the Pole.

But he had also been under immense public and financial pressure to make that urgent flight successful – and as well, Amundsen had been there awaiting his return, like a giant shadow. Byrd's only sextant fell and was damaged on the home journey, so his surprisingly rapid return flight had not been plotted. Inexplicably, he had failed to drop over the Pole any of the 100 small and several large American flags he had carefully packed in the plane, territorial signatures which Amundsen might have sighted and confirmed on his own flight just days afterwards. Byrd's family impounded his papers and expedition records for three decades after his death, so it is only relatively recently that historians have scrutinised his flight record, which some have judged to be doctored.

Aging compatriots condemned Byrd as cold, ambitious, deceitful, even cowardly. Stories emerged that he had rolled out of the plane drunk on his return to Little America from his successful 1929 flight over the South Pole. Good friends, conscious of their debt to him, sometimes chose a judicious silence. In fact, for a while Byrd was almost forgotten because his defenders preferred to stifle research and writing on him than be party to a complex portrait. Even his contemporaries said of Byrd: 'He is very well known, but nobody knows him very well'. The man was contradictory: he could inspire love and loyalty as well as envy and resentment; he was egalitarian yet egotistical; he made a business of personal fame yet craved solitude.

This revisionist historiography belatedly awards Amundsen a rare honour. If Byrd did not fly over the North Pole in 1926, then Amundsen flew over it first. If – as also now seems possible neither Frederick Cook nor Robert Peary made it to the North Pole across the ice in 1908 and 1909 respectively (it has been argued that they too may have fabricated their claims), then Amundsen was the first there by any means, and therefore the first to both Poles of the Earth. It would also mean, astonishingly, that the South Pole was attained before the North.

Left: The sextant used by Sir Wally Herbert during his explorations in Antarctica, northern Greenland, and the pioneering crossing of the Arctic Ocean in 1968–1969.

Above: 'At the South Pole, in summer the sun never sets but moves in a perfect horizontal line', observed Tom Abercrombie, who took this photograph when he was one of the first journalists to reach the South Pole in 1957.

wonderful place but there is a very real feeling of remoteness, of literally being at the end of the earth.

Cameras clicked as the irrepressible expedition cameraman George Lowe rushed around, wearing a straw aloha hat, wielding a large movie camera. 'There was a bizarre moment', Martin recalled, 'after the British party began opening the first mail they had received since leaving Shackleton Base two months earlier, George Lowe discovered he had received an income tax notice.' Later, the party were treated to a lunch of hamburgers, creamed corn and a large cake with red, white and blue icing. Bottles of bourbon were opened, but the British preferred a quick cup of tea, keen to get on their way. There was time to pause but no time to celebrate. Like shaking hands on the summit of a mountain, the job was only half done – the difficult descent was yet to come. However, Hillary had already laid the trail to Scott Base, and therefore Fuchs could race 'downhill' to complete the crossing.

By 2 March 1958 the first crossing of Antarctica had been accomplished. The journey of 2,158 miles (3,473 kilometres), from the Weddell Sea to McMurdo Sound, had taken just 99 days to complete. A welcoming committee had assembled in front of Scott Base as Fuchs arrived, along with throngs of photographers eager to capture the historic moment. After a cup of tea, Fuchs disappeared for a shave and a bath, during which he was given the news that Queen Elizabeth II had awarded him a knighthood for his achievement.

As with other great expeditions past, a resounding welcome was given to Sir Vivian and his team as their ship *Magga Dan* reached port. A great first in exploration had been attained, but it was the science that Fuchs wanted the Commonwealth Trans-Antarctic Expedition to be remembered for. The expedition's arrival in New Zealand was: '... the end of the expedition as the public saw it, but for us it is the beginning of a new endeavour – for now we must produce the results, which, we believe, will justify the early faith and vision of all those who supported us in the beginning, and sustained us to the end.' The public followed the new wave of expeditions eagerly, but it was not science that they wanted; it was stories of adventure that gripped the popular imagination and dominated the headlines, which is a craving that continues to this day.

The 'heroic age' was over, yet Antarctica could still be a place for drama as well as discovery. Although scientific endeavour would predominate in the decades that followed, the South Pole would continue to inspire men and women to acts of madness and brilliance.

Left: Lightweight aluminium bridging being used to provide traction to recover the sno-cat known as *Able* from its partial fall into a crevasse, in 1958 during the Commonwealth Trans-Antarctic expedition. This hugely successful undertaking attracted a global audience and Vivian Fuchs's team completed the first overland crossing of the continent. *Below:* Snow-goggles used by Sir Vivian Fuchs during this crossing of Antarctica.

The Future Past

FERGUS FLEMING, 2011.

The American explorer Vilhjalmur Stefansson made no bones about it: his profession was deluded. When people talked of discovering new places, of going where no man had gone before – it was rubbish. Why? Because at one time or other, during millennia of migration, almost every bit of land had already been trodden by human feet. Writing in 1947, he explained that, 'our very best stories are lucky when they are no worse than second-best'. There was only one spot on the planet he was willing to admit an explorer could call his own, and that was Antarctica.

It was a purist's point of view. But then purity was what Antarctica was about. When the first navigators reached its shores in the mid-nineteenth century they were awed by the gales and pack-ice they encountered, and even more so by the frigid vastness of the continent. It was pure in every sense of the word: a cartographical blank, a wilderness whose interior was so hostile as to preclude the existence of any life forms whatsoever. Here, humans were very much the interlopers – a fact not lost on the naturalist Joseph Hooker who accompanied James Clark Ross on his 1839–1843 voyage. 'There is a certain awe,' he wrote, as first Mount Erebus and then the Great Ice Barrier hove into view, 'that steals over us all in considering our own total insignificance and helplessness.'

The spiritual reverence in which these early explorers held Antarctica was matched by the cerebral nature of their purpose. They were scientists (more properly, 'Natural Philosophers') who had been dispatched by their governments to probe the arcane workings of the world. James Cook's first great voyage in 1768–1769, for example, was to observe the transit of Venus and thereby determine the Earth's distance from the sun. James Clark Ross was there to measure magnetism – as he described it, one of nature's 'great and dark powers'.

When news spread of their discoveries, it sparked an appropriately mystical reaction. Starting with the publication of Samuel Taylor Coleridge's *The Rime of the Ancient Mariner* – itself inspired by Cook's voyages – the themes of ice, darkness, death and divinity were adopted ardently by Romantic writers and poets. Of the many 'cold' narratives none was more telling than Edgar Allan Poe's *The Narrative of Arthur Gordon Pym of Nantucket*, in which the hero plunges into the world's southernmost axis to be greeted by a vast, white apparition that may or may not have been God.

For all its literary and scientific mystique, Antarctica remained a dangerous and expensive place to reach. By the late 1800s governments had abandoned the polar regions, leaving their exploration to whoever felt brave enough and could raise the necessary cash. The result was dubbed the 'heroic age', and nowhere did they congregate more dramatically than at the South Pole.

Polar heroism had its tawdry side. Everyone who led an expedition knew that he needed to return with either a dramatic conquest or a tale of great suffering – something, at any rate, to attract the public's attention. Most of the heroes hoped to recoup their costs by what they earned from journals, lectures and (in due course) films. As Ernest Shackleton wrote, the winnings could be great, 'particularly when you come home from an expedition with a big hurrah'. Roald Amundsen, who teetered forever on the verge of bankruptcy, stated explicitly that he had no interest in the South Pole save to bolster his reputation – and thereby make some money.

Yet beneath the commercialism lay a glittering truth: for the first time in history explorers were opening an undiscovered continent. Wherever they went and whatever their motives – sensationalism as with

Amundsen, or scientific inquiry as with others – they could be certain they were breaking new ground. This was what Stefansson was talking about; and it was this that made Antarctica, and the South Pole in particular, such an irresistible lure. Carsten Borchgrevink, who in 1898–1900 led the first expedition to winter on Antarctica, managed even to lend it a spurious, Nietzschean grandeur. 'Man's philosophy,' he declaimed, '[has] reached the glittering gates of the Poles where eternity rules in stern silence, awaiting the hour when time is ripe through the sacrifice of mortals, for man to be allowed to follow his philosophy and to enter the Polar crystal palaces, and to satisfy his thirst for certainty.'

The 'heroic age' was blown away by the First World War. When it came to heroism, how could the suffering of a few attention-seeking 'penguins', as Winston Churchill called them, compare to the thousands who died daily in the trenches? Besides, the capture of the South Pole in 1911 had removed both the thrill of the chase and the public enthusiasm that had financed it. From being an object of poetic inspiration and near-frantic fascination, Antarctica dropped rapidly from the popular gaze. Thereafter its exploration and study would proceed at a more measured pace.

There remained a legacy that few, perhaps, would have considered at the time. In an age of progress and expansion, when people spoke of new worlds, new horizons and new futures, Antarctica represented exactly the opposite. Despite being the newest of new worlds, nobody could make a future there: all they could do, as Stefansson intimated, was tell stories about it. And stories, in an undiscovered continent, were its history. In an inversion of the standard dynamic, the early explorers had not so much opened a future as created a past.

Above: 'Explorers', an acrylic on canvas by Susie Hamilton, 2003. 'For the last ten years', she explains, 'I have painted cowboys, explorers and criminals – men seeking liberation outside the laws and limits of society in dangerous, exhilarating places'.

CHAPTER 7
THE LAST DEGREE

South Pole Station sits on a bulge of ice two miles thick at the centre and thinning gradually toward the coasts. There is nothing around but ice under empty space. The place is a visual Alcatraz where the surrounding nothingness bends one's attention inward, back to the station.

NICHOLAS JOHNSON, FROM *BIG DEAD PLACE*, 2005.

Encircled by a ring of international flags, a polished globe sits atop a gaily painted, red-and-white-striped pole. Nearby, a permanent collection of state-of-the-art laboratories, supply depots and well-insulated living quarters stand out boldly against the vastness of the ice, stretching to the horizon and beyond. This is the modern South Pole; a surreal place inhabited by scientists and 'Polies' (the support staff, such as technicians, computer nerds, maintenance crew and cooks), some of whom have lived for several seasons at the remote Amundsen–Scott research station. It is a scene that would astonish, and probably dismay, the early explorers who risked their lives to reach this elusive spot. Yet, despite the glaring proximity of the scientific base, for modern-day adventurers and 'extreme tourists', the carnival-style marker of the Geographic South Pole remains an enduring goal.

In November 1956 a group of men stood at the South Pole – they were not explorers, neither were they scientists; instead, the team consisted of engineers who had been commissioned, as part of the United States Navy's Operation Deep Freeze, to build a permanent scientific base at the South Pole. In a scene that was far removed from Scott's experience 45 years earlier, the silence of the polar plateau was broken by the rumble of large aircraft overhead, which dropped hundreds of tons of equipment, supplies and prefabricated buildings by parachute onto the ice. The new base would forever change the image of the South Pole, and it is known today as the Amundsen–Scott South Pole Station.

By the mid-1950s, Antarctica had entered a vibrant new era. Admiral Byrd had pioneered many technical innovations in the far south, and these, together with radio equipment and gasoline generators to provide electric power, had made it all the more feasible to live in Antarctica. Bases began to be erected across the continent, with the British, Australians, Americans, French, Norwegians, Chileans, Argentinians and New Zealanders all laying formal territorial claims and acting out their own rituals of sovereignty. Deception Island became the most hotly contested of places, with the British, Argentinians and Chileans all establishing bases within shouting distance of one another, which caused tensions at government level. However, on the ground, sovereignty was decided with a far more light-hearted approach – the winners of games of football or darts would be the holders until the next match. As for the South Pole, the United States designated itself the guardian of this strategic place and has maintained a consistent line since the 1950s. 'If we weren't at the South Pole, there would be a mad scramble for territory', Tim Wirth, the Clinton administration's Under Secretary of State for Democracy and Global Affairs, said as recently as 1996: 'We're the only country that can manage the logistics in that extraordinary place ... we have to maintain this presence to maintain the continent's neutrality.'

The 'neutrality' of Antarctica was secured with a treaty designed to ensure the continent would be used only for peaceful purposes, and to preserve

Left: The flags of the Antarctic Treaty signatory countries encircle the ceremonial South Pole, January 2011.
Below: The geodesic dome of the second Amundsen–Scott South Pole Station, built in 1975 to house modular buildings, sleeping quarters and scientific laboratories. The base of the dome was originally at the surface level of the icecap but has been slowly buried by snow and ice year on year. The dome was officially decommissioned in 2008 and has now been completely dismantled.

Go Hard or Go Home

JEFF RUBIN, *THE POLAR TIMES*, 2006.

Polies, as they proudly call themselves, have their own lingo.

No one ever calls it 'the South Pole' or even 'the Pole.' It's just plain 'Pole,' as in, 'I got an offer to go to Pole and fell in love with the place.'

No one calls the station by its official name, Amundsen–Scott South Pole Station – that's used only in print. The new elevated station is just the 'El Station'.

Polies often shun their real names for nicknames. 'Nobody knows me as Carlton,' says construction project manager Carlton Walker, who started with the United States Antarctic Program in 1990 as a plumber/pipe-fitter and has spent half of the last 16 years living at Pole. Now, he oversees the construction crew of 120 workers, who call him 'C-Note,' or simply 'C.'

Recent Pole residents have included Slaughterballs, Slinky, Jake Speed, Long Break Bob, Tree Beard, Froggy, Cupcake, Princess, Hippie, P-Dog-E, Spermy and Nude.

Ain't That Tough

The workers – 25% of them are women – work a 9-hour day, six days a week. In the 24-hour summer daylight, three crews work shifts round the clock. 'It's a harsh continent,' they rib each other, then admit that things are really not too bad at all, what with abundant good food, expense-free living, and email and Iridium phones to break the isolation (for about 12 hours a day, when a satellite is in range).

'We say "It's a harsh continent,"' says Walker, 'but we say it tongue-in-cheek, because it's just not. When you look at the guys that built the original Pole station, or when you look at the living conditions that even some of the other stations have now, compared to what we have at Pole, it just ain't that tough. It just ain't.'

High and Dry

Pole sits at 9,300 feet, but low barometric pressure makes it feel more like 11,000. Just walking around – let alone doing heavy work – can be exhausting. Everybody sucks wind for the first few days in the oxygen-starved atmosphere. Headaches, weird dreams and poor sleep plague the beginning of the season for some.

With relative humidity just 3%, dehydration is a constant threat. To avoid ending up in Medical with an IV in your arm, Polie advice is 'pound the water, lay off alcohol, and cut back on caffeine.' To prevent nosebleeds, pack your nostrils with Vaseline. And when your fingertips crack in the dryness and won't heal, repair them with superglue.

Hangovers, thanks to the dryness, are especially wicked. 'You've never had a hangover at Pole?' asks Walker. 'Trust me, it's gonna suck.'

Above: Modern life in Antarctica. Polies relax in the library and recreation room of a research base at the South Pole, 1992. A photograph by Galen Rowell.

Antarctica as an international laboratory for scientific research. The Antarctic Treaty was signed on 1 December 1959 by the 12 nations with active interests in the Antarctic, coming into force in June 1961. With participating nations having to maintain a constant presence, new, permanent bases thereafter welcomed waves of enthusiastic young men who travelled in the footsteps of their polar heroes.

In 1962 the British Antarctic Survey (BAS) was formed out of the pre-existing Falkland Islands Dependencies Survey (FIDS), which was itself a renaming of the wartime expedition, Operation Tabarin, to establish permanently occupied sites in the Antarctic. Using teams of huskies shipped from Greenland, men from the BAS's 19 stations and three refuges charted great swathes of new territory and rediscovered some of the huts from historic expeditions.

Among the men was British explorer Wally Herbert, who in 1968–1969 would lead the first crossing of the Arctic Ocean via the North Pole – an epic 3,800-mile (6,100-kilometre), 16-month journey over the constantly moving, splitting pack-ice from Point Barrow, Alaska, to Spitsbergen, Norway. As a young surveyor and explorer-in-training, Herbert mapped an area of around 46,000 square miles (119,000 square kilometres) of previously unexplored country in the Antarctic throughout the 1950s and early 1960s as part of the FIDS programme. 'We were in fact almost a throwback to the days of Scott and Shackleton in terms of our equipment and experience', he recalled. Using dog-teams, Herbert and others set out into the unknown, with the pure and simple aim of laying down charts and recording valuable scientific data. The names he gave to the various obstacles he encountered were, he later wrote: '… an indication of the age we were at the time, and the virility of youth: the "Horrendous Drop", the "Deadly Traverse", and the "Crushing Cwm".' So vast was the continent, with so little yet charted, that a single sledge journey was a pioneering adventure. Nevertheless, the achievements of Shackleton, Scott and Amundsen were within easy memory, and there was an unmistakable sense of being connected to the past. On the fiftieth anniversary of Scott reaching the South Pole, Herbert and three companions made the first ascent of Mount Fridtjof Nansen. As Herbert later recalled:

> 'Great God! This is an awful place,' Scott wrote in his diary on 17 January 1912, 'and terrible enough for us to have laboured to it without the reward of priority.' Those immortal words were singing in my ears for the seventeen hours we were on that 13,330-foot mountain, cringing in a stabbing wind, struggling to do our survey, stopping every few minutes to blow into our gloved hands and massage our stiff bodies. The misery and exhaustion we suffered dug deeply into our reserves, and the long, long trudge back down to camp almost claimed the four of us. It was less windy down below and the sun was soothing, but in spite of the risks of resting we were compelled to lie down every few yards.

From the eastern side of Mount Fridtjof Nansen's massive dome the men had glimpsed part of Axel Heiberg Glacier, and Herbert and his compan-

WALLY HERBERT COLLECTION
photo- ANT 154

WALLY HERBERT COLLECTION
photo- ANT 94

WALLY HERBERT COLLECTION
photo- ANT 225

WALLY HERBERT COLLECTION
photo- ANT 92

WALLY HERBERT COLLECTION
photo- 'ANT 237

WALLY HERBERT COLLECTION
photo- ANT 207
MADE IN AUSTRALIA
61

WALLY HERBERT COLLECTION
photo- ANT 166

ANTARCTIC

USNAis support for field parties
WALLY HERBERT COLLECTION
photo- ANT 152 173/203
MADE IN AUSTRALIA Kodak

WALLY HERBERT COLLECTION
photo- ANT 185

WALLY HERBERT COLLECTION
photo- ANT 201

WALLY HERBERT COLLECTION
photo- ANT 203

5

WALLY HERBERT COLLECTION
photo- ANT 218

WALLY HERBERT COLLECTION
photo- ANT 179

WALLY HERBERT COLLECTION
photo- ANT 253

WALLY HERBERT COLLECTION

WALLY HERBERT COLLECTION
photo- ANT 182

WALLY HERBERT COLLECTION
photo- ANT 89

ANTARCTIC

WALLY HERBERT COLLECTION
photo- ANT 89

ion Vic McGregor decided that it would be fitting to attempt to retrace Amundsen's pioneering route through its crevasse fields and spectacular ice-falls. Herbert had reread Amundsen's account of his ascent and descent of the glacier until he knew each stage by heart, but he had found many ambiguities – unsurprising, perhaps, given that the narrative had not been intended as a route guide for future travellers. Amundsen had taken only two photographs and neither photograph showed the ice-falls; he had made no maps and had left no route sketches. 'We could only assume that the amount of ice flowing down the valley was the same as it was fifty years before, and we could only assume that his account was true until it was proved either grossly exaggerated or, what was more likely, very modest.' Amundsen's trek down the glacier on his return from the South Pole was apparently so uneventful that it was barely mentioned in his book, yet Herbert knew that the Norwegian explorer was a master of understatement, which soon became clear as they reached the head of the glacier:

It was an overcast day, oppressive with tension; shadowless; still. The brink of the first drop could not be seen, but we could feel it waiting to swallow us. Amundsen had called it the 'severe, steep slope'. We fastened the Norwegian flag I had made out of bits of bunting and torn handkerchief to the front of the leading sledge, prepared the rope brakes, called to the dogs and lurched forward.

We skied off the ledge and down a thousand-foot drop onto a smooth table of snow which reached out towards the icefalls. At the corner of the table the ground fell away in a gaping precipice. Before us was such a scene of turbulence and ice chaos that words were stifled by emotion – I had seen nothing to surpass the power, the beauty in that scene of turmoil. Into the cwm, walled by frowning rock and capped by mountains of sliding ice, fell thundering, grumbling avalanches, exploding snow in white cushions, curling, settling, staining the floor with debris. We stood transfixed and stared in horror at the lacerated wounds and torn white flesh of the glacier far below. The knives of nature had slashed that valley with such viciousness, that mere man – so insignificant – could surely not creep through it. But Amundsen and his men had done so fifty years before.

We swished over small ice-bridges with yawning crevasses on one side and chasms on the other. We descended like chainshot on truant skis, and in the cold grip of fear we hurtled towards the yawning mouth and came to a trembling stop on the tip of a chasm. We picked ourselves up and as we dusted off the snow we felt the leaping pride of having safely negotiated the crux of Amundsen's route.

Like Herbert, the expedition physician Hugh Simpson also enjoyed the strong link with historic explorers that their travels gave them. Several years earlier, in May 1957, after scaling part of the great spine summit of

Left: A selection of slides from the personal collection of the late Sir Wally Herbert, taken during his memorable expeditions to Antarctica as surveyor and explorer in the 1950s and 1960s.

Above: During his re-enactment of Mawson's epic trek, Tim Jarvis contemplates his makeshift replica crampons – created from old packing cases with the nails pushed through – before tackling the steep blue ice of the polar plateau as it descends to the sea. The photograph is by his expedition partner, John Stoukalo, 2006.

Graham Land, which runs from the Rockies through the Andes and into the Antarctic Peninsula, he and his companion Roger Tuft gazed out over a spectacular scene:

> Looking to the west was the Bellingshausen Sea and we could see the place where the American explorer Palmer thought he had discovered the Antarctic but, at the same time was beset in fog and suddenly he heard bells ringing, the ship's bells of the Russian explorer Bellingshausen who had also discovered it. Looking east into the Weddell Sea you can see Joinville and Vega Islands and beyond where Shackleton's *Endurance* had been crushed. We could see the route of Nordenskjold's explorers who were coming south to join their compatriots on Snow Hill Island and who were contemporaries of Scott on his first expedition. Their discoveries are their monument, fossilised remains of trees show that the Antarctic Peninsula had a forest and then in the far, far distance we could see the Orkney Islands situated on the end of the great Scotia tectonic plate discovered by the Scottish Expedition.
>
> We did not talk, we were mesmerised by the moment, we were conscious that all the snow around us was loose and the slightest wind would destroy the visibility. We turned our sledge around while our tracks were still visible and hurried back to our tent at 3,000 feet to brew a cup of cocoa.

To men such as Herbert and Simpson, although journeys of theirs that connected, accidentally or otherwise, with other moments in polar history were gratifying, particularly when it involved being the first to follow in the footprints of a great explorer such as Amundsen, they were just an element of a larger remit – the group was, after all, in Antarctica to map the white spaces.

CELEBRATING THE PIONEERS

In the years to come, others would also follow in the wake of their heroes, but for different reasons. In 2005 four amateur adventurers, and former members of the British Army, were taken to the South Pole by seasoned guide Geoff Somers. What set them apart from the hundreds of other similar short treks across the 'last degree', was that their kit replicated that of Scott's team. Wearing authentically reproduced period clothing, such as merino-wool balaclavas and undergarments and gabardine fine-weave cotton outer clothing, the men slept in pyramid tents with reindeer-skin sleeping bags and hauled sledges lashed together with flax, gut and leather. Although officially navigating by traditional theodolite and sextant, the team had a GPS and a satellite phone for emergencies. It was a stunt, but a worthwhile one – the expedition raised just under £900,000 for charity.

For entirely different reasons, Australian adventurer Tim Jarvis set out in 2006 to re-enact Mawson's extraordinary journey. Jarvis had already spent time in Antarctica, breaking the world record for the fastest unsupported journey to the South Pole (47 days) in 1999 with fellow Australian Peter Teseder. Jarvis found it confusing that this achievement was compared with those of his childhood heroes, such as Amundsen and Mawson:

> The obvious points of reference for my achievement sat uncomfortably with me – I wondered whether it was really comparable with the journeys of old where the boats were wooden but the men who travelled in them were iron through and through. I took a strange comfort in the notion that the bastion of 'doing things the old way' still existed even as I made plans to break it down. And so the notion of undertaking a journey not as a modern explorer with breathable synthetics, Kevlar and dehydrated meals but as authentically as possible, as an explorer of old with heavy wooden sled, animal pelts and heroic-era stoicism hooked me. If it could be achieved, then truly there would be no more to do. Perhaps then I could stand up and be counted.

Jarvis admitted that his re-enactment could never completely replicate the experience felt by Mawson. Doctors were checking his physical condition, a film crew was following him and he employed a number of other safety precautions – nevertheless, he believes the journey provided him with an insight into the explorer he would not have gained otherwise:

> I felt that putting on the woollens, mitts and Burberry clothing and assuming the outward appearance of those explorers of old strangely seemed to imbue you with some of their resolve. Purely psychological, but many aspects of expeditions of course are. What I did know for sure was that, despite pride at having completed my journey, I felt more than anything humbled by it. I had an even greater respect for what Mawson and Mertz achieved. Theirs was without doubt a terrible journey, and one that mine in the modern era could not claim to have replicated. I had got as close as I could and that was bad enough. By subjecting myself to a similar journey to that of Mawson and telling his story parallel with mine, I hoped it would help bring his ordeal to the attention of the larger audience I believed it deserved, shedding light on the events that unfolded down on the lonely Antarctic plateau – the 'home of the blizzard' – almost 100 years ago.

'These replays aren't simply a grasp at lost glory', says Jeff Blumenfeld, editor and publisher of the website ExpeditionNews.com. 'You can retrace a trip to see how things have changed or to verify an earlier expedition.' But most re-creators, he admits, simply yearn to celebrate a piece of hard-won history.

Experience on the ice often colours the way that men and women write about the South Pole, and those that went in search of it. For example, Sir Ranulph Fiennes, who has led a life of adventure, and was the first person to reach the South Pole twice overland, is certain that in recent years we have been unkind, perhaps uncharitable to the memory of men such as

Above: In 2005 a handful of amateur adventurers, led by veteran guide Geoff Somers, attempted to experience something of Scott's endeavours by trekking to the South Pole in quasi-replica clothing. Although the reasoning behind the expedition may have been questionable, the group raised a huge amount of money for charity.

*"Rations low. May
have to eat the
TV documentary crew."*

Above: As the centenary year approaches, this 2010 caricature by Steve Russell suggests that the story of Scott's South Pole endeavour remains well known and that public interest in it shows little sign of abating.

Right: Victor Boyarsky logs the progress of the 1989–1990 Trans-Antarctica expedition on the wall of his tent at the South Pole.

Scott, whose legacy has often been ignored or misinterpreted. As a biographer of Scott, Fiennes believes that he has a unique slant: 'I have put myself in the place of the British explorers and used logic based on personal experience to reconstruct the events. No previous Scott biographer has man-hauled a heavy sledgeload through the great crevasse fields of the Beardmore Glacier, explored ice-fields never seen by man or walked a thousand miles on poisoned feet. To write about Hell, it helps if you have been there.'

Modern polar travellers who are as attuned to history as they are to their own ambitions have found that looking to journeys past adds another dimension to their experiences. Among them is Norwegian ex-marine commando and accomplished explorer Børge Ousland. By the time he first arrived in Antarctica in 1995, Ousland had already skied across Greenland's icecap (a journey few had attempted since Nansen's crossing in 1888), completed the first unsupported ski-trek to the North Pole from Ellesmere Island, with Erling Kagge, and, in 1994, made his own solo trek to the North Pole. His next great adventure was to make a solo crossing of Antarctica, using just skis and sail. During his trek, the journeys of Scott and Amundsen frequently came to mind as his route crossed theirs. Like Wally Herbert, Ousland experienced renewed respect for Amundsen as he retraced the legendary explorer's route through the Axel Heiberg Glacier:

> Silence Valley was a real test of endurance. Many times I wondered if Amundsen really had faced the depth of loose snow with which I had to contend now. It was almost incomprehensible to me how anyone could have climbed here in such conditions. It was bad enough going down.
>
> … in order to keep moving at all, I soon had to revert to the counting technique. First I tried counting to a hundred before pausing, but even this proved too much. Soon I was down to fifty, leaning on my ski-sticks and gasping for breath after each pull …. It was almost funny. I who'd imagined the whole thing would be a piece of cake, all downhill slopes and good running, only to come up against this. It was a dreadful slog. Well, it must get better sometime, I thought, attempting to keep my spirits up. During the whole of that first day on the glacier I only covered six kilometres, my shortest distance so far. I couldn't remember facing such awful conditions before … I'd get there in the end, it was just a matter of time. There was nothing else for it. The most important thing was not to wear myself out completely, or overstrain tendons and muscles that had already taken a pounding.
>
> … After twelve terribly gruelling hours, I had got off the glacier. I was so exhausted by the time I pitched camp that I had problems keeping my balance. But, my heavens, how wonderful. Down at last, quite unbelievable. My respect for Amundsen has increased enormously today. I'd regarded his journey as a dawdle more or less, but I take my hat off to him for being the first man up this glacier. What slopes! And those poor dogs. I'm glad it wasn't me

that had to climb these slopes. The glacier fell three thousand
metres in just fifteen kilometres and that's some gradient.

In the last stages of his trek he would also find fresh admiration for Scott, as
he neared a crevasse field that had been described by both Scott and Shackleton as highly dangerous. He was thankful that he had advance weather
information through his radio, and that he was travelling during a relatively
benign time of the year, neither of which Scott had been able to benefit
from. He noted:

> At the South Pole it is supposed to start turning nasty from the
> middle of January onwards. Down where I was there should still
> have been plenty of time. As soon as the sun came out it was
> warm and pleasant, but when it clouded over, and especially when
> ice-mist descended, it was raw and cold. I was glad I wasn't going
> to be there in February, or March. Not many kilometres off, Scott
> and his men had fought their last desperate struggle to reach safety
> at 'One Ton Depot'. Scott must have known quite early on that it
> was very late in the year. In spite of this, they spent almost an
> entire day on the return journey collecting geological samples
> from the summit of the Beardmore Glacier. That really amazed
> me. The weight of 13–14 kilo rocks was bad enough, but time was
> critical, and was to prove more so. It was to be his downfall.

Having been beaten to the South Pole, Scott knew that the scientific side of his expedition would be all the more valuable, and the scientific material his team gathered during the expeditions has stood the test of time and is a vital part of his legacy. In his last journal entry, Scott had written, 'For God's sake look after our people' – and the British public rallied to do so. Such was the outpouring of sympathy that the memorial fund raised £75,000 (approximately £3.4 million in today's money), which helped to pay off the expedition's debts and left a surplus to be distributed between the families of the dead and to set up the Scott Polar Research Institute in Cambridge, which opened in 1920. The institute is now one of the foremost centres for polar history and scientific research.

THE ANTARCTIC LABORATORY

Almost a century later, science is still at the heart of most human activity in Antarctica – the continent now is effectively one vast scientific laboratory, with a huge infrastructure of many hundreds of personnel across the continent supporting a wide range of international meteorological, glaciological and geographical studies. The station at the South Pole is also of crucial strategic relevance – a symbol of a real American geopolitical presence, despite the internationality of the location and the useful science being undertaken there.

Those who live at the American outpost are a motley crew – some hoping for adventure, others signing up for a season out of idle curiosity. Although a posting at the Amundsen–Scott station is a unique experience, for many

of the workers the novelty soon wears off. Life in such a place is a challenge on many levels, not least because of the inescapable isolation, violent storms, temperatures that often dip below minus 73 degrees C (minus 100 degrees F) and the six months of polar night. For those coming to the South Pole to work there are a host of unimagined problems: anything made of plastic shatters, hammers crack and uninsulated power cords snap; exposed skin will freeze instantly to metal. As writer Jeff Rubin observed, it is a place where mistakes hurt. 'You quickly learn not to put a pencil in your mouth when marking measurements,' he remembers carpenter Kate Allen telling him. 'The lead sticks to your tongue.'

Perhaps less obvious are the challenges of day-to-day life within the confines of the station's well-equipped but impersonal atmosphere. As Anthony Brandt recalled:

> The isolation, the weather, and the cold drive people into themselves. Unless you are a scientist there is nothing to do in Antarctica except deal with its conditions. Inescapably it tests people, tests their spirit, their endurance, their courage. No one can survive there naked, yet, as the accounts of the explorers make clear, the place strips your soul. It has fascinated a great many people. Who are you? What are you made of? This is the place to find out.

Left: A US Air National Guard LC-130 Hercules sits on the snow-covered runway while supplies are unloaded and the plane is refuelled during a mission to the Amundsen–Scott South Pole Station in 2005. The aircraft is equipped with ski-landing gear that allows it to land on ice or snow while air-lifting supplies to remote locations and scientific camps throughout Antarctica.

Above: Scientists, technicians and managers of the United States Antarctic Program take up every available seat in the cargo bay of a United States Air Force C-17 Globemaster III on its regular flight from New Zealand to the American base at McMurdo. This flight was the first one of the spring 2005 season, when an intense schedule of flights raised the head-count at McMurdo from a few hundred to about 1,700 people for the scientific season.

What Castles One Builds

Will Steger and Jon Bowermaster, 2011.

'What castles one builds now hopefully that the Pole is ours.' Captain Scott's personal diary, 5 January 1912.

As we near the bottom of the Earth the sun is becoming more intense each day. I was in Jean-Louis's tent for the radio check in the early evening, and we unzipped the doors to let in the sun's rays. It was as if we'd clicked on a very bright 250-watt light bulb. The sun did seem to have regenerative powers, and in fact on Douglas Mawson's 1912 expedition – the time he lost both a sled and two teammates to crevasses and the conditions – he used the sun for just that purpose. He was in East Antarctica, at a slightly lower elevation than this, and during the day he would lie naked in the leeward side of his sled, on a piece of canvas, and soak in the rays of the sun for several hours. He insisted the sunlight renewed his strength, as powerful as if it were food or a vitamin.

As Jean-Louis and I sat, waiting to make contact with Patriot Hills, he talked about the day. 'Sometimes it is like Antarctica has no soul,' he said, 'like it is another planet, not a place for man. But other times, when you have a very nice sky like today, when you realize you really are on Earth, I feel like I am in a big, wondrous temple. Today when we saw triple halos I thanked the sky out loud.'

His birthday party turned into the usual logistical meeting but was a very warm, friendly affair. We talked about the area of inaccessibility resupplies, rehearsed the statement we planned to read at the South Pole, discussed the watch time that we would keep after the South Pole and the general schedule of events for our three days off. The magnetic spirit of the South Pole is drawing us now, and everyone has mellowed. Though the Pole is still a few days away, the past mornings have begun with a fresh feeling, a sense that this was not to be just another day of the same old grind but one that brought us closer to the Pole. It actually felt, for the first time since we'd arrived in Antarctica, as if there was an ending nearby, though we are well aware we're only halfway home.

Our arrival at the Pole does represent an ending of sorts. Prior to just ten days ago it seemed as if there would never be an end to this trip. My mind couldn't even consider the concept of 'ending.' But reaching the South Pole is as if we're walking through a gateway to the other side of Antarctica. Already I can feel the effect on my mind of passing that mark; I feel more positive, reinvigorated. It's funny how, after this arduous physical ordeal, it is our minds that need a break more than our bodies.

While I have tried to hold off getting too excited about our arrival, I have to admit that there is magic about the poles, a feeling engendered in us of being very young and excited. Now Jean-Louis and I – and only a few other men in history – have traveled overland to both, and the fascination continues. I think the others feel the same way, and as always Victor's excitement is the most intense. He told me today arriving at the South Pole would be 'like visiting Disneyland, Las Vegas and Mars simultaneously.'

11 December 1989, Day 138.

… Around noon the heavy skies lifted and we spotted a large Hercules LC-130 aircraft on the horizon ahead, making a low angled approach to what we assumed must be the Amundsen–Scott base. We couldn't hear the plane, yet we knew we were close to where it was landing. When we stopped for lunch we could just barely make out an antenna on the horizon.

As we traveled after lunch we were surprised at how fast the base appeared. By two-thirty we could see its well-known dome under which most of the base's

activity takes place, as well as plowing equipment, snowbanks and the end of the runway. By three o'clock we could make out the tent they'd set up for us on the far side of the runway and then a semicircle of flags flapping in the distance and what appeared to be a big row of red gasoline drums sitting beneath them.

The red barrels turned out to be the base personnel – sixty of the ninety currently stationed there – bunched around the ceremonial barber's pole that marks the geographic Pole. They were waiting for us with handmade signs and cheers. The dogs ran as a bunch rather than in a straight line when they saw the people, and as we drew near we could hear their clapping and I could read a sign that said 'Hello from Minnesota!' It was almost as if my dogs could make it out too, because they veered off ten degrees and crashed right into the crowd that held it, tails wagging. We wrestled the dogs to a halt, took off our skis, and were swallowed by the crowd of well-wishers.

… Before we left the Pole we posed for more pictures around the barber's pole, beneath the semicircle of

twelve flags representing the original signatories of the Antarctic Treaty. Forty people saw us off at 5:00 a.m. I had brought a flag with Peace written on it specifically for these pictures, hoping it would make for a powerful international statement, and when we raised it among the six of us the gathered crowd responded with applause and some tears. That was the most magical moment of our stay at the South Pole. Quickly, due to the cold, we packed the flag away and with little fanfare sledded off. After five miles the base disappeared behind us, masked from sight by the undulating terrain.

Above: From left to right, Keizo Funatsu, Jean-Louis Etienne and Victor Boyarsky sit behind their sledge to take shelter from the wind while they eat, during Will Steger's Trans-Antarctica expedition. Steger wrote: 'Given the cold conditions, lunch was often the cruellest part of the day, everything – nuts, chocolate, granola bars – had to be thawed in thermos cups of hot water to prevent teeth from cracking instantly.' On 11 December 1989 this team became the first since 1912 to dogsled to the South Pole, having covered nearly 2,000 miles (3,200 kilometres) in 138 days.

Although it is never less than dangerous, in some moods it is also beautiful …. but the beauty comes in tandem with terror, which even in the best of conditions stands off just to the side. Beauty and terror together constitute the sublime. Antarctica may be the most sublime of Earth's landscapes.

The frozen icescape of Antarctica may be spectacularly attractive, but the inhabitants of the South Pole may as well be living on a space station. Nicholas Johnson, a worker posted to 'Pole' in 2003, described the place as:

… an outpost with all-you-can-eat desserts and an endless procession of theme parties …. A small town … where everyone had frequent flyer miles and no one had wisdom teeth …. A town with disco clothes and high-power microscopes. A town into which people have smuggled goldfish and where a pet snail from a head of lettuce faces execution by government mandate. A town where going outside requires authorization. A town responsible for divorces. A town where corpses have reportedly been stored in the food freezer and where it is illegal to collect rocks. This was America, I realized, but all in a tight bundle.

The tourists and expeditioners who are flown in to 89°S and trek the last degree – about 69 miles (111 kilometres) – to the South Pole do little to impress the most seasoned 'Polies' who eat, work and sleep at the extremity of the Earth. Those who attempt more daring or absurd methods of reaching the South Pole are regarded with ambivalence or scorn, and the antics of some 'novelty' expeditions has over the years contributed to a tough attitude by those running the Amundsen–Scott station. 'The official cold shoulder is meant to discourage people from coming to Pole,' according to writer Nicholas Johnson. 'This means that if you rowed a boat down past 80 degrees south, crossed an ice shelf, climbed glaciers, crossed mountain ranges, avoided crevasses, didn't die of frostbite, hypothermia, infected wounds, starvation, or suicide, finally made it to approximately the coldest, most hellishly isolated spot on the globe, and asked for a dish of tater tots, you might be told "no" …. While tourists on plane flights are generally either ignored or treated to hair-trigger courtesy, Polies are more enthusiastic about cross-continent expeditioners who actually work for their glory.'

IN SEARCH OF ADVENTURE

Among these adventurers were the Norwegians Eirik Sønneland and Rolf Bae, who, in 2000, claimed what was, up to that time, the longest unsupported transcontinental trek (2,360 miles/3,800 kilometres) in Antarctic history, from Queen Maud Land to the station at McMurdo Sound, via the South Pole. Sønneland recalled feeling almost ecstatic as they neared the South Pole, although, after trekking across hundreds of miles of white nothingness, the 'roads' and traffic lights of the station's runway seemed quite incongruous. Nevertheless, their reception was not as cold as that experienced by some:

Closing in on the ceremony place and the South Pole, about twenty or thirty people were walking with us, asking all kinds of questions, many I don't remember. I was in some kind of trance, happy. One girl, from the gift shop I believe, asked me why my sledge was still so full when we arrived. I answered, 'Because we are going to McMurdo.' Some guy behind me said, 'Crazy Norwegians ....' People applauded as we closed in on the Pole. Rolf said to me, 'Slow down Eirik, you are walking like crazy.' My mind was another place, the South Pole was ours, and I wanted to be with my best friend when we touched the most southern point in the world. A lot of pictures and greetings. A girl came over and took my hand, 'I'm Jensen, the station manager ....' When I looked at her face I swear it must have been the most beautiful face I'd ever seen. (… I hadn't seen a girl for 13 months.) With all the wonderful people at the base I felt real warm for the first moment on the whole trip … seriously.

For Børge Ousland, the South Pole, just as it was for Sønneland and Bae, was only one element of his solo crossing of Antarctica. The value was far more than simply attaining the South Pole itself:

Doing a long solo trip in Antarctica does change you. On a trip like that there is no one else to relate to other than nature and yourself. So you have a deeper dialogue with nature and yourself. The trip is therefore not just a physical journey but very much a state of meditation where you reach levels inside you that you did not know existed … you touch some basic feelings that I believe have dwelled deep inside every human being since the Stone Age, which is the feeling of being at one with nature.

Cross-country skier Liv Arnesen experienced a similar feeling of connection to the wilderness on her solo journey to the South Pole in 1994. Having made a crossing of the Greenland icecap as part of an all-woman team in 1992, Arnesen wanted to test herself further and go it alone. She found the solitude of an Antarctic solo journey both challenging and uplifting. Experiencing near-perfect conditions, she became invigorated by the sense of endeavour as she neared her goal:

As the days passed on my way to the South Pole, I felt that I got more and more joy and energy. The undulating Antarctic landscape of white and blue and grey, the patterns in the snowdrifts and in the skies all mixed with the poetry I read at night   making it as much a mental expedition as a physical one. Even though I was pulling a sled weighing 220 lb (100 kg), the hard work is not what I remember. It was the feeling of being at one with nature – of knowing why I was there, what life is, who I am.

Such journeys, particularly the solo treks, become a very personal quest; a means of discovering one's strengths while overcoming weakness, fear and doubt. As Ousland mused light-heartedly: 'It's strange, all this slog, it's

become my method, my way of growing, conquering, becoming strong. And there's been quite a bit of slog too. Ten years as a diver in the North Sea, spending six of seven hours a day working 150 metres down, for three weeks at a stretch, leaves its mark. I'm glad I found myself a safer job and became a polar traveller instead.' But reaching the South Pole can be an anticlimax. During his journey, Ousland had dreamed of the South Pole being as it was when Amundsen and Scott had first arrived, 'so remote, harsh and beautiful'; instead, he found it to be 'like a big factory'. Jason Anthony remembers fuelling a flight for employees of Scott Base, near McMurdo Sound, who had won a lottery to go to the South Pole for an hour, and seeing the explorer in the final minutes of his transcontinental trek:

> Ousland, a lean bearded Norwegian, was calm but seemed as strange and wild as an electron. We had a quick conversation, but other trucks were pulling up with people who, like me, asked dull questions of a quiet man at the pointy end of history. I was still a relative novice on the ice, so being at the crossroads of history like this was simply extraordinary. The only thing I had in common with him, as it turned out, was the amount of time we spent at Pole. Ousland just stopped momentarily in his crossing, and it turned out that the pilots of our flight were also in a hurry, afraid that they'd miss dinner in McMurdo. We would be on the ground at Pole for only twenty minutes.

Adventurers such as Fiennes, Ousland and Kagge, as well as Will Steger, Alain Hubert and Victor Boyarsky, are all among the elite of our modern-day polar heroes. They are tough and inspirational characters and Antarctica is a suitable playground in which to test their skills. According to Belgian Alain Hubert, who has been to both poles and co-founded the International Polar Foundation:

> Antarctica is a challenge for any human being with an adventurous streak. In my case I was driven by a certain taste for freedom, for testing my limits for physical endurance in the face of excruciatingly difficult conditions, by the fascination for limitless horizons and by the threadbare nomadic existence. Each time I find myself in the raw untouched landscapes of Antarctica, I ask myself if there is not some other way, less tortuous and less ambitious, of achieving the same state of exhilaration and experiencing the same sensations of freedom.

Fiennes comments:

> When I am asked for my own life motives I openly admit that expedition leadership is quite simply my chosen way of making a living: and under 'occupation' in my passport the entry has always stated 'travel writer'. Mike Stroud, my team-mate in our endeavour to cross the Antarctic continent in the summer of 1992, always found my financial motivation upsetting and 'commercial'.

Above: In 1994 Norwegian Liv Arnesen became the first woman to ski alone to the South Pole.

Right: 'Anywhere else on Earth these peaks would be a national park', said photographer Gordon Wiltsie of the crags of Fenriskjeften, which means 'the jaw of Fenrir' in Norwegian. Evoking a row of flesh-tearing teeth, the telling name is derived from a fierce wolf in Norse myth. These extreme and remote pinnacles in Queen Maud Land now attract the attentions of the world's best mountaineers and big-wall climbers.

His own rationale was more romantic. He talked of stunning landscapes and equated his adventures with a more intense version of the pleasures he had found as a boy from mountaineering, hill-walking and rock-climbing. I am not introspective and find it awkward having to dig within myself to produce replies to journalistic questions about motivation. I like the response of Jean-Louis Etienne when asked why he went on polar expeditions. He replied: 'Because I like it. You never ask a basketball player why he plays: it is because he enjoys it. It is like asking someone why he likes chocolate.'

Antarctica still draws many adventurous spirits to it, and this no doubt is because of our innate curiosity – every generation needs some individuals to step beyond what is thought to be possible, to brave danger just to see what is beyond the next ridge of mountains, the next vast crevasse field or the next towering crest of pressured ice. 'The unknown has always fascinated humankind', comments Sønneland. 'We are born curious. Close contact with nature is important for us to be able to understand our surroundings, both physical and psychological.' Antarctica has become a symbol for challenge and adventure, he continues:

... a continent which offers many of the most important things in human life; hard work, responsibility, sorrow and happiness. People are different, complex. It is not always easy to understand yours or others' motivations for reaching a goal. Is it the goal in itself which appeals, or is it the long and demanding journey which leads you there? By exceeding our limitations we will find out – through good or bad – what it means to be a living being. All development occurs through stretching our limits.

Why Walk to the South Pole When You Can Fly? Erling Kagge, 2011.

I sailed to Antarctica on the sailboat *War Bay* from Bermuda in 1987. Antarctica became a love affair. As soon as the idea of becoming the first human to ski to the South Pole alone manifested itself some years later, I made the decision to do it, and stopped thinking about anything else. It is an absurd thing to do, but love makes you blind. I fell in love with the idea of skiing into a white nothingness, with everything I would need for an entire expedition on my sledge, and, as I wrote in my diary, to be able to feel that: 'Past and future are of no interest. I am living more and more in the present.'

When you begin, the sun's orbit is tilted; it is arched higher in the southern sky, and lower in the northern sky. The tilt of the sun's arc becomes less and less pronounced as you walk south in the midnight sun, the trip is one long day, and when you eventually get there, the sun has the same altitude above the horizon for twenty four hours. Antarctica has more hours of sun than Southern California and less precipitation than the Western Sahara. A desert made of water. On day 14

I wrote: 'I can hear and luxuriate in the stillness here. It feels good to be alone in the world.'

Seven days later I pencilled: 'At the beginning, everything appeared white and the beauty lay in the endless uniformity. Since then, my senses have developed and my experience of nuances in nature has become ever greater. Flat can also be beautiful.' When I began, everything was white all the way out to the horizon, but as the weeks passed by I began to see more colours; variations of white, some blue, red, green and yellow.

I developed a dialogue with the environment, threw some thoughts into nature, and got new ideas back. ... And I started to take pleasures from small things, or, as I mentioned in my diary Day 22: 'At home, I only seem to appreciate "big bites". Being down here teaches me to value small pleasures – a nuance in the colour of the snow, the wind as it lays itself to rest, a warm drink, the patterns of the cloud formations. The stillness.' My travel across a part of Antarctica became more

of a travel into myself, than to the pole itself.

'Many people will be jealous, but very few would have been in my place', I thought on one of the last days. After 50 days and nights with no radio contact I reached my goal and on day 49 the diary says: 'Just after midnight. 25 kilometres from the South Pole. It is so beautiful that I get a lump in my throat. I've felt lonelier at large parties and in big cities than I do here.'

A feeling and experiences you will never have in paradise or by flying to your goals, because you have to suffer on the way to make your love affair worthwhile.

I believe everyone should find their own south poles.

Below: Panorama of the modern South Pole – scientific base, living quarters, equipment stores, fuel dumps and a construction site for the new station – photographed by Joan Myers in 2002. 'Living at the South Pole', she relates, 'is like living in a space capsule or on another planet. It's disconcertingly unfamiliar'.

Sønneland believes that going on a long ski trip in Antarctica must be the closest one can get to approximating travel in space while remaining on Earth: '… cold and lifeless in all directions, with only the tent and your clothes as thin shells between you and eternity. Two beings, making their way through eternal wind, eternal snow, eternal cold. It can be called brainwashing, in a positive way. Instead of feeling bloated and lazy, you are hungry and sharp. You are balanced between things which strengthen and weaken you. But you have to stay focussed. If you sprain an ankle at the pole, the Red Cross will not come to the rescue. The South Pole can eat you alive.'

Erling Kagge, who was the first to accomplish the so-called 'three-pole challenge' (of reaching both North and South poles and the summit of Everest) and the first to walk to the South Pole solo, believes that most people primarily travel to Antarctica for everything that is *not* there, and only to a lesser degree for what's there: 'The lack of heat and other people, few disturbances, little shelter from the weather, hardly any safety nets if something were to go wrong. The minimalistic environment becomes a part of the enriched feeling of using your potential, being present in your own life, reaching for something which is beyond yourself and eventually to feel happy. If most people could do it, then you would have to find somewhere else to travel to.'

People are drawn to the South Pole and the challenge of Antarctica's wild places by all sorts of personal motivations and imagined glories. 'Where else but the South Pole can you feel exactly like a dab of paint on the Earth, a cold steel pin on a map of the Earth?' asks Jason Anthony. 'Where else can you feel so well the fragments of space and time wash through you? This hollow wind is cold, racing in from nowhere and continuing on to nowhere, convincing you that you are between Nowheres, physically and philosophically, making you feel both beautiful and afraid, even after you trudge back to the heat behind walls.'

An obsession with 'firsts', Anthony observes, has been a major Antarctic theme from the early examples of 'farthest south' and mid-century traverses through the South Pole to today's unsupported crossings and first climbs of unnamed peaks. We even treat the continent's geography as if it were some superlative Olympic champion; the highest, the driest, the coldest, the greatest:

> The Pole is the essence of first-ness. My favourite announcements are those that come at the height of tourist season: 'The first Canadian couple to ski to the Pole has arrived; the South Pole welcomes the youngest person to reach both Poles; Mass will be celebrated by the Pole's first visiting Russian Orthodox priest, etc.'

> I think that these 'firsts' are actually 'lasts', and that in part explains the fervour of one hundred summers of claim-staking. The South Pole was the last great race, the last Pole of new horizons. The Antarctic interior is the last open ground, and though it will remain open for some time, people want their name recorded before the record books are closed

Above: Dr Ibrahim Abdulhamid Alam, one of the first two Saudi Arabian tourists to visit the South Pole, both partial sponsors of Will Steger's 1989–1990 Trans-Antarctica Expedition.

Right: Renowned mountaineer and big-wall climber Conrad Anker ascends his rope near the summit of Queen Maud Land's Rakekniven spire, in a majestic photograph by Gordon Wiltsie, 1997.

Now, after decades of difficult travel, easy tourism has joined arduous endeavour at the Pole, bringing the long shadow of familiarity. Every year, private expeditions bring skiers, runners, and shoppers to our station to experience the last degree of latitude. As a result, and for the first time, Antarctica is running out of firsts.

Each year, hundreds of adventurers are drawn to the Antarctic on expeditions of varying difficulty, often with enthusiastic public relations' teams hired in the hope of establishing them as the most exciting 'explorer' of the moment. For example, on 13 January 2011, Norwegian 'extreme athlete' Christian Eide completed the fastest solo and 'unsupported' overland ski journey from the sea to the South Pole in just 24 days. Pulling a small sledge with all his supplies, he raced across the polar plateau in perfect weather conditions, averaging almost 30 miles (50 kilometres) a day. 'I didn't feel lonely once,' he says, 'I just thought, wow, I'm lucky to be here.' An impressive record, but an achievement that is only really possible because one does not need to conserve energy and supplies for the long haul home. Exhausted, he packed up his gear and was able to take a short flight back from the South Pole. Much has changed in the century since Scott's men trudged to this awful, and yet glorious, spot.

While these 'fast and furious' expeditions have their place, to some of the old guard the ego often outshines the achievement. Press releases that compare part-time enthusiasts to heroes such as Amundsen and Scott are an anathema. Edwin Mickelburgh is not alone when he despairs that history is: '... being taken for a ride in the guise of people passing themselves off as something they are not. Not only is that a lie, it is an unforgivable travesty of all that had once been; an insult to the memory of those who had suffered such privation and sometimes death in a time when the unknown was truly "unknown" and communication, let alone rescue, was not an option. We must not confuse the antics of adventurers, however skilful or ludicrous, with the pioneering journeys of the explorers who made the world known to us all.'

Ironically, there is a comparison that can be made between Scott and some of the 'extreme athletes', gritting their teeth and skiing furiously to better an existing world record. As Ranulph Fiennes points out: '... in the twenty-first century, modern expeditions vie with one another to complete journeys of physical toil. Journalists who castigate Scott for using men rather than dogs will in their very next article belittle a modern polar traveller for seeking any outside help beyond his or her own unaided manpower. Scott would either be amused or bemused.'

'Today's polar trophies go to those who reach their goals by the toughest means, unsupported by outside contrivances, be they dogs or snow-machines', he maintains, adding that Scott, on this basis, had achieved more than Amundsen. 'In the latter half of the twentieth century great geographical challenges were taken on, first by the "easy" way, using every means available, and then by the difficult purist route. Thus Everest, in the 1950s, was climbed by a mass assault with teams of Sherpas and oxygen cylinders and, in the 1980s, by that toughest of all climbers Reinhold Messner, alone and aided by nought but his own physical power and iron will.' Fiennes continues:

One of Amundsen's great Pole team, Helmer Hanssen, said: 'It is no disparagement of Amundsen and the rest of us when I say that Scott's achievement far exceeded ours .... Just imagine what it meant for Scott and the others to drag their sleds themselves, with all their equipment and provisions, to the Pole and back again. We started with 52 dogs and came back with 11, and many of these wore themselves out on the journey. What shall we say of Scott and his comrades, who were their own dogs? Anyone with any experience will take off his hat to Scott's achievement. I do not believe men ever have shown such endurance at any time, nor do I believe there ever will be men to equal it.

Nevertheless, there is still a natural urge among many to step where no one has stepped before, to experience something for the very first time and to enter the record books, by whatever means. This takes on ever more inventive – some may say ludicrous – forms (the first to bicycle across the polar plateau, the first to run naked, the first to be dragged by kite, the first to uni-

Above: The Silversea luxury tourist ship *Prince Albert II* cruises in the Lemaire Channel, shot by German photographer Thomas Haltner, 2008.

cycle, and so forth), possibly because there are few, if any, genuine new 'firsts' that can be achieved at the South Pole. Further afield, an industry flourishes around extreme activities, in particular mountaineering. Mount Vinson, the highest on the continent, has become the chief draw as part of the 'seven summits' challenge – to scale the highest peaks on each continent – and big-wall expedition climbers try to tackle the granite spires of Queen Maud Land, which protrude from the polar ice like the fangs of some giant wolf.

Then there are the 'extreme tourists' who are flown to within the 'last degree' of the South Pole so that they can trek the final stretch themselves. Some are guided, many blog about their experiences and a few make television programmes of their 'heroics'. All of them experience just enough of the plateau to feel the exhilaration of having reached this alluring spot. Full of visions of heroes of the past, they arrive at the South Pole for their photographs to find its flags, scientists, oil drums – and their return flights home. Tourism, 'extreme' or otherwise, is a multi-million dollar industry in the South. Cruise ships of all sizes work on a tight schedule, trying to avoid their passengers encountering those from a competitor's vessel as they spill out of their zodiac inflatables and swarm over the huts of Scott and Shackleton. For most of these visitors, a trip to Antarctica, or indeed to the South Pole, is a dream come true – a chance to experience one of the world's last great wildernesses and to connect in some way with the heroism of times past.

For these individuals, the South Pole is the ultimate objective, and from there they look forward to a warm flight home. For others, such as Fiennes, Kagge and Ousland, the culmination of their adventure is usually still a long hard trek away, and then the attainment of their goal runs far deeper. As Ousland neared the end of his solo transcontinental trek, all this came into clear focus. For more than two months, his world had been himself, his sledge and equipment, and the ice. Although he had regular radio contact with the outside world, his style of journey was perhaps the closest a modern explorer could get to experiencing the isolation of heroes in a previous age.

> Many thoughts filled my mind now that I'd soon be at my goal and my dream was about to be fulfilled. It would be strange meeting people again. I hoped it would be a gentle transition. To arrive at one's destination after a journey like this was almost too overwhelming. In a way one balks at it, perhaps it's a bit like being set free after a long prison sentence. All the desires, hopes and dreams, the unimaginable effort that's been put in, all build up great expectations. It can't be otherwise when such huge things are set in motion. A journey like this goes right to the core of your existence and shakes up your very being.

As Edwin Mickelburgh puts it, the experience: '... can play havoc with your life, too, forming unrealistic expectations that can detach you from the realities of the "normal" world. Some, literally, and in the most tragic sense, never get over the experience, especially if they have been involved in traumatic situations of life and death. There are many brave, unassuming men (and perhaps more recently women) in the annals of Antarctic exploration who

have failed, one way or another, to re-adapt to what they often regard as a lacklustre world after their return.' Perhaps the most famous example was Apsley Cherry-Garrard who, as one of the youngest members of Scott's *Terra Nova* expedition in 1910, was in the party that discovered the frozen bodies of Scott, Wilson and Bowers in the spring of 1912. 'He was haunted by the experience for the rest of his life,' Mickelburgh reflects, 'especially as he felt he might have saved them had he sledged further south the previous autumn to meet them on their return from the Pole. Cherry-Garrard, shy, sensitive, nervous, self-deprecating but extremely courageous went on to write *The Worst Journey in the World*, a searingly cathartic document that did much to save his fragile sanity in later years. Shackleton, too, a "hero's hero" if ever there was one, was never at ease back in civilization and admitted that apart from being an Antarctic explorer he wasn't much good at being anything else. Yes; however much, or however little, Antarctica will never let you go.'

Above: On a brief jolly from their cosy cruise ship in 2008, a group of tourists take a march, penguin-like, across the frozen ice of the Weddell Sea.

A FUTURE FOR ICE?

So, beyond the personal triumphs, the satisfaction of ambitions and the culmination of dreams, what value do Antarctica and the South Pole actually represent? Perhaps, as Mickelburgh suggests, the question should be turned the other way around – of what relevance would it be to anyone if Antarctica wasn't there?

> Historically, if Antarctica did not exist, the exploration of the world would have an enormous 'black hole' in it – the difference in how we have come to perceive our planet would be equally great. The ancient Greeks believed there must be a continent at the South Pole, if only to act as a counter-balance for the land they knew existed in the north. They were more correct than they

A Tunnel Runs Through It

DICK WOLAK, *THE POLAR TIMES*, 2002.

'We are living at the South Pole,' proclaimed the *National Geographic* magazine of July 1957. And so they were, at the new research station built for the start of the International Geophysical Year (IGY) of 1957–58. And though the station was intended for only a few years' use, we were still living there 18 years later, 20 to 30 feet below the snow surface, and always wary of the stresses and strains evident throughout. Those of us who had read Paul Siple's *90° South*, a narrative of that first winter at the South Pole, were thrilled at the opportunity to be a part of this historic facility, even if only for its last austral summer.

… The final wintering party at the original station in 1975 (soon to be referred to as 'Old Pole') was made up of 13 Navy men and 8 civilian scientists. Their winter routines, which had shaped their existence since February 17th, disappeared in the annual madness that is station turnover. Station population on that first night jumped to 49 (two winterovers had departed on the opening flight). The station would be 'left alone' by air operations for the next three days to allow the passing of as much operational fact and cultural lore as the two support crews could handle. Typically, by the afternoon of November 5, both groups were scanning the horizon for the second bird of summer and the liberation that it brought to all.

Once turnover was complete, November settled down some. Science personnel flooded in along with many more construction workers, materials, and equipment. The old station, no longer the object of structural or mechanical improvements, gamely carried on. It showed its years in the distortion of buildings, metal arches, and shoring timbers … at that point, our activities took on a very specific focus. Dedication of the new station was scheduled for January 9, and extensive preparations were needed. On January 4, we celebrated our 'last supper,' a gala occasion that marked the end of food service in the old station's galley.

Dedication Day was the last hurrah for Old Pole. All of the visiting party, including representatives of Congress, the National Science Board, SCAR and NSF [Scientific Committee on Antarctic Research and National Science Foundation] toured its tunnels. In my view, the most significant visit was that of Mrs Ruth Siple to her late husband's former workspace. Old Pole was, of course, 'old school' when it came to gender lines. It wasn't until 1969 that the station saw its first female visitors, and a number of other day visitors followed in subsequent summers. However, the total number of 'female/overnights' during the station's lifespan was probably no more than 60.

… When the core services of food and communications moved out of Old Pole, residents were free to relocate either to New Pole or the Construction Camp on a self-paced basis. As their work schedules allowed, individuals could stake out new living space and move their belongings piecemeal. The process would be complete when the mass of transported material favored residence in the new location, whereupon bedding and toothbrush sealed the deal.

On January 24, the population of Old Pole was still at 12, while 61 others at Pole lived at either the new station or the Construction Camp. A few days later, 3 of 17 men returning to McMurdo left from Old Pole, reducing the number of 'tunnel rats' to 9. On the evening of January 30, I finished my fire and generator rounds at Old Pole and was surprised by an unexpected observation. As I prepared for bed, I recounted in my journal that '… movement has started out of the old station … had 8 of 9 move today … actually, I'm the last and only person left living here.' I was briefly perplexed, and wondered if that was a good idea; but it was late, I was dog tired, and the mile-long trudge (with bedding) to the new station had no appeal whatever.

When I became the last one out, I guess I was responsible to get the lights. But that didn't happen for several days, as we were moving massive quantities of equipment and supplies from Old Pole, and the heat and power were great benefits. The lights finally did go out on February 3. By then, I had moved to the Dome, but was still doing generator watch at the old power plant. At ten that evening, it seemed the time had come. I took a last walk through, lowered the flag at the 'Holy Stairs' entrance – the rather twisted, wooden stairway that connected the tunnel adjacent to the medical and communications buildings to the snow surface near the aircraft taxiway and photographic pole – and pulled the fuel cutoff on the generator.

Back at the new station, I informed the others, and a nostalgia party was declared. In retrospect, perhaps more should have been done in ceremony.

But everyone was working at his limit preparing for station closing in less than ten days, and there seemed to be little energy for additional scheduled events. As it was, the original US Amundsen–Scott South Pole Station was toasted well into the night amidst music and movies of the 50s and 60s. It was a sincere and fitting tribute.

Below: Meteorologists in the original base at the South Pole, devoted to their work during the long polar winter, photographed by Tom Abercrombie on 4 April 1958.

realized, even if the notion of 'balance' means something critically different for us in a time of multiple threats to our planetary ecosystem. Physically, if Antarctica didn't exist, we would be living on a completely different planet. Such is the effect of that enormous chunk of ice at the bottom of the world in regulating that to which we scarcely give a moment's thought. The climate, oceans, the other continents, their flora and fauna, even our own species, would be radically different.

Not only is Antarctica a critical component in the puzzle of what makes our world the way it is, the sheer magnitude of its difference from anything else that exists on the planet has made it an evolutionary 'driver' across millions of years. The unsuspecting man in the street would certainly know about it if Antarctica, with 90 percent of all the world's ice, wasn't there – but then he, most probably, wouldn't be there either. In the case of Antarctica 'out of sight' means dangerously 'out of mind'. Lastly, and more difficult to define, is the psychological effect of the presence of Antarctica. Undoubtedly it provides a 'bolthole' for those who need, and respond to, what its icy wastes have to offer. More tellingly, perhaps, I have heard it said by people who have never seen it and will never go there, that it is 'enough to know that it is there'. For them it is a kind of archetypal, natural symbol, whose largely unviolated snows give reassurance and hope in a world of ugly uncertainties.

The value of Antarctica as a scientific laboratory cannot be underestimated. It allows subtle changes in our planet's climate and evolution to be tracked, which is of more importance now than ever. But the future for science at the South Pole, or at least the Amundsen–Scott South Pole Station, may be in the balance.

With snow accumulating around any structures on the polar plateau to a depth of around 4 feet (1.2 metres) per year, the original South Pole station, known as Old Pole, soon became snowbound and was eventually abandoned in 1975 in favour of a series of new bases, each more modern than the last. As the stations have been built on a moving glacier – moving towards the South Pole at a rate of about 33 feet (10 metres) per year – the central berthing, galley and communications units have been constructed and relocated several times.

The most recent incarnation replaced the base housed within a geodesic dome. Raised up on stilts and known by staff as El Station, the base is the most modern facility in Antarctica and boasts features that were unimagined just a couple of generations ago. 'Some people say it's progress, and in a way it is', a thoughtful Polie had mused to Jeff Rubin as it was being built. 'I mean, it will be a station that is state-of-the-art in a lot of ways. But there are people who will show up at Pole, and basically never walk outside, unless to go back to the plane. Is it progress when there are people who will come here and never go outside? Not in my mind.'

Right: A scientist trudges back to his base at the South Pole, a moment captured by Tom Abercrombie in October 1957 during the International Geophysical Year. Humans have continuously inhabited this special place at the bottom of the world ever since. Although a hundred winters have now passed since the first men stepped foot here in 1911 it remains a fascinating, haunting and inspiring landscape.

Overleaf: A team of Chilean scientists traversing the polar plateau in 2006 to survey Lake Ellsworth, one of more than 150 subglacial lakes on this continent. A Camoplast tracked snow vehicle is pulling a convoy of modular units, including a living quarters and a mobile scientific base. Once the lake has been surveyed scientists hope to build a probe and drill down to the lake to explore its sediments and obtain water samples, which may unlock the secrets to the unknown past of these parts of Antarctica.

Meanwhile, Old Pole has now completely disappeared. When recently a tractor crashed through the roof of the base, its structure having weakened under the pressure of accumulated ice, it became clear that the area posed a serious hazard. In December 2010, 54 years after its construction, a demolition crew drilled a warren of holes into the ice, packed the old wooden roof with dynamite and blew it sky-high. 'It was a little sad,' John Rand, the consultant engineer for the US Army was quoted as saying, 'but the day goes on.'

And so life at the South Pole continues. The well-insulated research base becomes ever more like a space station during the long polar winter, with only its most intrepid inhabitants able, or willing, to venture outside. Come the summer, light returns and the science resumes. The South Pole remains an alluring prize for dreamers and the foolhardy alike, a ceremonial stage for exhausted expeditioners, foreign dignitaries and the more extreme breed of fortunate tourist. Yet without the Amundsen–Scott station, without humankind's footprints in the snow, the South Pole remains merely ice and horizon – a geographical point on our planet that, like a magnet, still draws a new generation to the wild, white spaces of the South.

EPILOGUE
ON POLAR JUNKIES
LESLIE CAROL ROBERTS

I spend much time seated at a table in the Southern Hemisphere, not far from a man sneaking lemon drops in this candy-forbidden zone called the 'Archive'. It strikes me as a funny place for handwriting, journals and letters to live – stories so alive and rich with a place unknown to most, but now carefully held hostage in glassine folders, filed by alphabetical order and chronology. Like bodies bound in ice, left to move ever so slowly with glacial rivers to the sea. Can't you hear the writers moan? 'Set them free.'

Reading the personal papers of visitors to Antarctica from those early days, talking with today's polar explorers, there is a unifying undercurrent to their stories – what you could call a *pleasing crudeness* to Antarctic endeavours. When ships were stuck in the ice, the crew got out and dynamited the floes. If they had no dynamite, they used picks. Scott almost lost *Discovery* to the ice and James Paton's diary in New Zealand's Canterbury Museum talks about offloading all the ship's supplies and the endless digging of ice. I reckon it was a good thing those men had no aerial view of what they were up against. Could you imagine that? I can hear them now: 'I'm not digging that fucking ice.' For entertainment, they printed newspapers and wrote poetry and painted watercolours of the sunsets. It all seems rather folksy, in their rustic bunkhouse, lined with men in thick sweaters, smoking pipes; like an extreme summer camp for people with the polar bug.

We all dream of it – the landscape rises like a vapour, whirls around in the clouds, goes looking for receptive minds. It seeped into Frank Worsley's head one night as he slumbered. He dreamt of walking down Burlington Street in London, navigating a street filled with ice-blocks. He noted what a curious dream it was, yet felt strangely compelled to retrace the path, so in the morning he wandered down Burlington Street, looked up and saw a sign, 'Imperial Trans-Antarctic Expedition', climbed the stairs, presented himself to Shackleton and Frank Wild and told them how he had been lured to their doorstep by a dream. Mariners are superstitious. Wild and Shackleton saw this able man having been sent to them as an act of grace. It was his fate. Little did they know this act of grace would be of the most extraordinary kind: Worsley was the man who would save their lives. Here was their saviour.

Then this story: A small plane flying Edmund Hillary from here to there during the often-overlooked Commonwealth Trans-Antarctic Expedition. The pilot, a young Kiwi, decides to heave some treats down to the lads laying the camps for Hillary's trek to the South Pole. 'What's this?', Hillary asks, holding what looks like a doorstopper. 'Fruitcake, home-baked in Christchurch', comes the reply. 'They'll love that one', says the pilot. Pitched out the window, cake becomes concrete, iced, weighted, a death-bomb of flour and candied fruit soaring down at the unsuspecting men, cheering below. Everyone runs as the cake smashes onto the ice. It's not in any books, that story. It's one that is told by polar junkies over a quiet ale, filed under real tales of real times on the real ice.

What is a polar junkie? My friend the great historian Baden Norris has told the stories of Antarctic exploration for well over 40 years. He is a polar explorer – he has been there a dozen times. I know polar junkies well: all Antarctica, all the time. Fragments of news like the drowning of a marine biologist by a leopard seal; Russians drilling into never-touched Lake Vostok; glacial ice moving with the cycle of the moon; a seal-tooth bracelet for sale at auction, then who sold it, who bought it, and for how much. Polar junkies love rosters, line-ups, *Who's Who* style recountings of the minutiae of expeditions: names and birthplaces of bygone explorers, what they did in the world wars, where they are buried, whether their descendants are polar junkies too.

You hear it in stories of South Pole workers forming a peace sign with their bodies on the ice, and in tales of traversing glaciers, told by tough scientists as tears well in their eyes. 'We did not think we were going to make it.' So. This is beginning and leitmotif. Always the idea that Antarctica triumphs, plays its steady game of cold, wind, crevasse. Always the idea it will be there for us, guarded by fierce seas, shrouded in cold, hard ice.

San Francisco, 2011.

A SOUTH POLE TIMELINE

An eclectic and unashamedly subjective timeline of Antarctic firsts, lasts, major (and minor) milestones, triumphs and tragedies.

1588 • 9 SEPTEMBER Explorer and privateer Sir Thomas Cavendish returns to England having completed his circumnavigation of the globe via the Strait of Magellan in his ship *Desire*. The word 'penguin' is used for the first time, describing the southern bird in his journal. On a later voyage in 1592 he dies in the South Atlantic, but the navigator John Davis continues and discovers the Falkland Islands.

1770 • 1 FEBRUARY The earliest known drawings of Antarctic tabular icebergs, floating north from this mysterious region to beckon the brave, appear in the logbook of Edmund Halley's *Paramore*. 'Flatt on the top and covered with Snow … these mountains of ice in the Fogg.'

1773 • 17 JANUARY Captain James Cook and the crews of *Resolution* and *Adventure*, on Cook's second major voyage of discovery, become the first men to sail within the Antarctic Circle. They would cross the Antarctic Circle three times in various parts of the Southern Ocean during this voyage, and in doing so they also became the first to circumnavigate Antarctica, although they would never see this great southern continent.

1790 The sealing industry's first exploratory season on South Georgia. The men are primarily Americans from the ports of New England, as much of Europe is still embroiled in war.

1810 • 11 JULY Australian Frederick Hasselborough discovers Macquarie Island while searching for new sealing grounds.

1819 • 19 FEBRUARY Englishman William Smith is blown to the south while rounding Cape Horn and spots the South Shetland Islands, although he does not land. Authorities at home do not believe his discovery, so he returns that October to step ashore and claim them for Britain.

1820 • 28 JANUARY Russian explorer Thaddeus von Bellingshausen is within the Antarctic Circle in Vostok and Mirnyi at 69° 21′S, and on this day many believe he is the first to sight the fabled Terra Australis, describing 'an icefield covered with small hillocks'. He also returns to Antarctic waters the following year, discovering the Alexander Islands. He also completes a circumnavigation, the first since Cook to do so.

1820 • 30 JANUARY The Royal Navy sends Edward Bransfield, with William Smith as his pilot, to search the waters to the south of the South Shetlands. It is claimed they are the first to sight the Antarctic Peninsula and to accurately chart any part of the Antarctic continent.

1820 • 17 NOVEMBER As a member of a sealing fleet from New England, American Nathaniel Palmer on the sloop *Hero* claims to see the peninsula while attempting to search for new breeding grounds and it is possible that they also made a landing.

1821 • 7 FEBRUARY American sealer John Davis, in the *Cecilia*, is also searching the waters beyond the South Shetlands and likely becomes the first person to land on the continent, stepping ashore at Hughes Bay on the Antarctic Peninsula.

1821 Eleven men from the sealer Lord Melville spend the first recorded Antarctic winter on land, on King George Island in the South Shetlands.

1823 • 20 FEBRUARY Englishman James Weddell sails to 74°S, the farthest south yet reached, in a sea that now bears his name. Icebergs were spotted, but no land was in sight. Few are able to penetrate this vast, ice-chocked region again for almost 80 years.

1829 • 9 JANUARY Likely the first scientific work in Antarctica, William Webster reaches Deception Island in the South Shetlands aboard the *Chanticleer*, and makes a series of pendulum and magnetic observations.

1831 • 24 FEBRUARY English navigator John Biscoe in the *Tula* and *Lively*, working for a British sealing business (the Enderby Brothers), discovers land and names it after his employers. It is the first sighting of Antarctica in the zone south of the Indian Ocean. He is also the first to confirm that a great mass of land could exist, rather than scattered islands.

1839 • 9 FEBRUARY English sealer John Balleny, another Enderby employee, sails from New Zealand in the *Eliza Scott* and the *Sabrina*, searching for new land. He discovers an island group, which he names for himself – the Balleny Islands. He makes the first landing south of the Antarctic Circle there.

1840 • 19 JANUARY American naval officer Charles Wilkes reports his first sighting of the Antarctic landmass, an area now known as Wilkes Land, although he later changes his log to 16 January in hope of precedence. It is the first American expedition to specifically aim for Antarctica. Many of his other discoveries are later called into question; some of his coastlines are quickly erased from the chart as subsequent navigators sail cleanly through them.

1840 • 19 JANUARY Charismatic French explorer Jules-Sébastien Dumont d'Urville crosses the Antarctic Circle with his ships *Astrolabe* and the *Zélée*. They sail slowly to the west, skirting walls of ice, before some members of his crew disembark on a rocky island to drink claret and raise the French tricolour. He names and claims the land beyond, Terre Adélie, in honour of his wife.

1841 • 9 JANUARY British naval expedition led by Sir James Clark Ross with *Erebus* and *Terror*, in search of the Magnetic South Pole, makes the first entry into the sea that now bears his name. He discovers Victoria Land, the Ross Ice Shelf, a grand mountain range and active volcanoes. Less important, but interesting to some, later that year (on New Year's Eve, in fact) the expedition also holds the first ever fancy dress ball in Antarctica.

1874 • 16 FEBRUARY Sir George Nares's *Challenger* is the first steam driven ship to cross the Antarctic Circle. Sponsored by the Royal Society, this grand oceanographic voyage is also the first Antarctic foray whose aims were solely scientific. Chief among other reputable, and some forgettable, firsts on this voyage are the first photographs of Antarctic icebergs. Early camera equipment had been taken south before on other ships, but as yet no pictures survive. It is hard to prove that images were made prior to this.

1892 • 4 DECEMBER Norwegian Carl Anton Larsen of the *Jason* lands near the Antarctic Peninsula on Seymour Island, discovering fossils of extinct species and providing the first reliable clues to the continent's previously warm climate.

1895 • 18 JANUARY During Henryk Bull's voyage in the Antarctic, Cartsen Borchgrevink, a member of the party, finds lichens on an island nearby, the first signs of plant life. On 24 January Borchgrevink and two others rush to jump ashore at Cape Adare, claiming the first substantiated landing on the Antarctic continent proper.

1898 Adrien de Gerlache and the crew of *Belgica* are trapped in the pack-ice off the Antarctic Peninsula and are forced to spend the winter locked into a floe, drifting with the currents. They are the first to survive an Antarctic winter so far south and the first scientific vessel to reach the continent itself. On 26 January, on the snowy slopes of Two Hummock Island, expedition member Roald Amundsen is likely the first man to ski in Antarctica. A few days later, Gerlache, Amund-

sen, physician Frederick Cook and other companions go sledging on Brabant Island, again the first to try this technique of overland travel in the far south.

1899 Carsten Borchgrevink is back, this time leading a multinational crew of Australian, Norwegian and British mariners on *Southern Cross*. They land at Cape Adare, build huts and become the first party to deliberately winter on the continent and to use the latest new-fangled gadgets: a Primus stove and a 'cinematograph' movie camera. It is also the first time dogs were used on the continent.

1900 • 16 FEBRUARY A party from Borchgrevink's *Southern Cross* make the first sledge journey across the Ross Ice Shelf, attaining a new farthest south.

1902 Swedish geologist Otto Nordenskjöld and five companions spend two winters on Snow Hill Island and make a number of pioneering sledge journeys. Their ship *Antarctic* is caught in the pack-ice and crushed. Miraculously its crew manage to survive the winter and make their way back to the island, where the whole party is rescued in 1903 by an Argentinian relief ship.

1902 • 4 FEBRUARY Captain Robert Falcon Scott makes a balloon ascent (in *Eva*) during the *Discovery* expedition. Ernest Shackleton goes up armed with a camera and takes the first aerial photographs of the polar ice.

1902 • 21 FEBRUARY German explorer Erich von Drygalski and his crew on *Gauss* become trapped between the floes. They discover and map Kaiser Wilhelm II Land and, although stuck in the ice for a year, they undertake a valuable programme of scientific research.

1902 • 2 NOVEMBER Scott, Shackleton and Edward Wilson begin their overland journey towards the South Pole across the Ross Ice Shelf. After two months of toil they reach a new farthest south of 82° 17′S, although suffering from snowblindness, exhaustion and the beginnings of scurvy, they are forced to turn their sledge northwards once more in a struggle to return to base. *Discovery* is caught in the ice, but with the assistance of *Morning* and *Terra Nova*, the ocean swell and well-directed explosives, she is finally free and they head for New Zealand.

1904 • 1 FEBRUARY French explorer Jean-Baptiste Charcot, expeditioning in the *Français*, begins his survey of the western coast of the Antarctic Peninsula and they put the ship into the ice to overwinter. The following summer they discover a number of new islands and chart new coastlines, extending the work of Gerlache. Charcot returns south in 1908 in the *Pourquoi-Pas?* continuing to better delimit the nature of the continent.

1904 • 12 MARCH William Speirs Bruce and the members of his Scottish National Antarctic Expedition on the *Scotia* are locked in the ice, having discovered Coats Land, the first true sighting of land to the southerly extremities of the Weddell Sea. The wind suddenly comes up from the southwest and the ship is released. It's an expedition full of eventful firsts: perhaps the first surviving moving pictures taken and, no less important, the first Antarctic bagpipe concert. Gilbert Kerr dons his kilt to play to the emperor penguins.

1904 • 16 NOVEMBER Carl Larsen builds the first permanent whaling station at Grytviken on South Georgia. Within ten years, more than 20 other bases and factory ships are operating in these waters.

1908 • 21 JULY Britain initiates its first formal claim to Antarctic territory, encompassing all areas and islands to the south, between 20 and 80°W. In 1917 the claim is delimited, in an effort to help regulate whaling activities in the Southern Ocean. The claim was originally called the Falkland Islands Dependencies, but in 1962, following the successful Antarctic Treaty negotiations, the British Antarctic Territory is created.

1909 • 9 JANUARY Shackleton, Frank Wild, Eric Marshall and Jameson Adams surpass Scott's efforts in 1903 to reach a new farthest south of 88° 23′S, just 97 miles (156 kilometres) short of the South Pole. The group is exhausted and severely undernourished, and Shackleton makes the brave decision to turn back and fight another day, rather than push on into the unknown. 'Better a live donkey than a dead lion', he would later remark.

1909 • 16 JANUARY Other members of Shackleton's *Nimrod* voyage, Edgeworth David, Douglas Mawson and Alistair McKay become the first men to reach the South Magnetic Pole. On this voyage a car is used for the first time (although not with much success) and the overwintering party also produces *Aurora Australis*, the first polar book – written, edited, illustrated, printed and bound in Antarctica – and now, understandably, highly desirable among collectors.

1911 • 19 OCTOBER After one abortive attempt, which had led to a near-mutiny, Roald Amundsen sets off from his base at Framheim in the Bay of Whales, some 60 miles (96 kilometres) closer to the Pole than Scott's hut at Cape Evans. With Amundsen are four companions, four sledges and 52 dogs.

1911 • 1 NOVEMBER Forced to delay his departure, fearing the intense cold of the Great Ice Barrier would hamper his ponies, Scott's party finally sets out from the security of the hut. At this stage the party is 15 men in all,

separated into teams for laying depots and other support. 'Bowers was the last to leave', recalled one expedition member. 'I ran to the end of the Cape and watched the little cavalcade – already strung out into remote units – rapidly fade into the lonely white waste to southward.'

1911 • 14 DECEMBER Norwegian victory for Amundsen. His team reach the South Pole, taking observations and calculating their position as exactly as possible. All five men sign their names and letters are left for their king, and for Captain Scott, in a tent surmounted by the Norwegian flag. Olav Bjaaland, Oskar Wisting, Sverre Hassel and Helmer Hanssen were all crucial to this success. The 'race' is won but the journey is far from over. 'A cigar at the Pole', Amundsen writes in his diary with characteristic understatement.

1912 • 17 JANUARY Despair and bitter disappointment for Scott and his team as they reach the South Pole but discover sledge-tracks and the crushing truth that the Norwegians have beaten them to it. The following day they come upon the tent. 'Great God! This is an awful place', Scott wrote in his journal. 'Now for the run home and a desperate struggle. I wonder if we can do it.'

1912 • 25 JANUARY Amundsen and his team reach the safety of Framheim after 99 days out on the ice. On 7 March Fram sails into Hobart, but Amundsen does not immediately shout about his successes. In London the *Daily Chronicle* carries the scoop the following day. Amundsen's silence is rewarded; the newspaper paid him the equivalent of £150,000 for exclusive world rights. That night in Hobart he is besieged by journalists who try to break down the door of his bedroom. For the next few weeks the headlines are all his.

1912 • 29 MARCH Journey's end for Scott. Eleven miles short of their stash of supplies. 'I do not think we can hope for any better things now', he wrote, after severe frostbite, exhaustion and a raging blizzard had confined him to his tent for over a week. Evans had collapsed on the return march; Oates had headed out into the teeth of the storm, walking to his death. Bowers, Wilson and Scott leave their last letters, which are found with their frozen bodies by a search party the following November. 'We shall stick it out to the end, but we are getting weaker, of course, and the end cannot be far', Scott scrawls in his diary. 'It seems a pity, but I do not think I can write more. For God's sake look after our people.'

1913 • 9 JANUARY Far from this scene another drama unfolds. After the death of his companion Mertz, Douglas Mawson begins his lone trek across George V Land to his base at Commonwealth Bay and against all odds he manages to reach safety. During this expedition, radio is used for the first time in Antarctica, and the first radio contact with another continent is made, although the explorers could only transmit a message. Two-way communication is established later that year. Mawson was also the first to bring an aircraft on expedition here, though it never flew because it crashed before leaving. Its wings were removed and it was used as an 'aero-tractor'.

1913 • 10 FEBRUARY *Terra Nova* reaches New Zealand and news of the Antarctic disaster is cabled around the world. The true horrors of the tragedy are revealed in London as the news of the deaths of Captain Scott and his companions makes the late editions of the evening papers. A national memorial service is held in St. Paul's Cathedral on Valentine's Day. In July the *Strand Magazine* begins a best-selling serialization of Scott's journals.

1914 • 18 JANUARY Scott's original sledging journals are placed on display in the Manuscripts Saloon of the British Museum.

1915 • 27 OCTOBER Shackleton gives the order to abandon ship. He had returned south with the dream of crossing the continent, but his Imperial Trans-Antarctic Expedition is abandoned as *Endurance* is crushed in the ice of the Weddell Sea after drifting for nine months. The expedition turns into an epic of survival as his party take to the ship's boats to eventually make landfall at Elephant Island in the South Shetlands. Meanwhile, members of Shackleton's Ross Sea party lay depots on the other side of the continent in anticipation of his progress to the South Pole and beyond. Three members of this party die, although the rest are rescued in 1917.

1916 • 24 APRIL The *James Caird* is launched with Shackleton and his five companions beginning a perilous voyage through monstrous seas to reach South Georgia, and thence to cross the island's mountainous interior to reach the whaling station of Stromness. On his fourth attempt Shackleton finally returns to Elephant Island to rescue his crew; not a single man is lost.

1915 • 5 NOVEMBER The Admiralty unveils Kathleen Scott's memorial statue of her late husband in Waterloo Place, London. 'In times of war', a newspaper reported, 'it is good to remember the Navy's unwarlike yet dangerous work, in which Captain Scott showed all the great qualities of the sailor, the explorer, and the man of science'. Herbert Ponting's films are shown to rally the troops on the Western Front.

1920 • 26 NOVEMBER Cambridge University approves the foundation of the Scott Polar Research Institute, a permanent scientific legacy to Scott and his companions. It is inaugurated in 1926 and its building is opened in 1934.

Above: Aurora Australis, the first book created and printed in Antarctica, during Shackleton's *Nimrod* expedition in 1909.

1922 • 5 JANUARY In the early hours, Shackleton suffers a fatal heart attack aboard *Quest*. He is buried in the cemetery among the whalers of Grytviken, South Georgia.

1923 • 6 SEPTEMBER The first 'one-volume' cheap edition of Scott's journals published by John Murray as a special 'school reader'. In various forms, it would sell almost 100,000 copies by the end of the decade.

1924 • 5 MARCH Ponting releases a feature-length version of his Scott film, *The Great White Silence*. His film is later purchased for the nation by the British Empire Film Institute. In 1933 he releases the first sound version of his film as *Ninety Degrees South*.

1928 • 16 NOVEMBER Hubert Wilkins completes the first flight in the Antarctic at the Deception Islands in the South Shetlands. He was in the sky for some 20 minutes in the *Los Angeles*, a Lockheed Vega monoplane. Later in December a longer flight is made over Graham Land.

1929 • 29 NOVEMBER After a ten hour flight in the *Floyd Bennett* from their Little America base near the Bay of Whales on the Ross Ice Shelf, American Richard Evelyn Byrd and three companions become the first to fly over the South Pole.

1934 Byrd makes his second expedition and chooses to winter alone, becoming the first man to dare such challenging isolation. It made for a gripping tale and, ever the showman, he also makes the first human voice radio broadcast from Antarctica.

1935 • 20 FEBRUARY Accompanied by her Norwegian sea-captain husband, Danish-born Caroline Mikkelsen steps ashore at the Vestfold Hills, becoming the first woman to set foot on the Antarctic mainland.

1935 • 23 NOVEMBER American aviators Lincoln Ellsworth and Herbert Hollick-Kenyon depart from Dundee Island for Little America. Over the course of some 2,300 miles (3,700 kilometres), in six stages over two weeks, they complete the first flight across the continent.

1943 Argentina stakes its territorial claims (after Britain, New Zealand, France, Australia, Norway and Chile), which overlap with existing British and Chilean claims in the Antarctic Peninsula region and the three countries become locked in a dispute that is not resolved until the late 1950s, and then only partially.

1943 Britain's secret Operation Tabarin is launched to strengthen its presence in the region, as well as to deter German U-boat activity in the Southern Ocean, establishing bases on the Antarctic Peninsula at Port Lockroy, Hope Bay and Deception Island. After the end of the war, the Falkland Islands Dependencies Survey (FIDS) is created to continue British activities in the region.

1946 US Navy Operation Highjump, easily the largest Antarctic expedition yet undertaken, heads south with a total of 4,700 men, 13 ships and more than 20 aircraft. A base is again established at Little America. Coastal surveys and cartographical advances are considerable, aided by icebreakers, an array of overland vehicles and more than 70,000 aerial photographs. Large swathes of the continent finally take a detailed form. Operation Windmill continues this work in the 1947 season, with tracked vehicles and helicopters used with some success.

1948 Finn Ronne's Antarctic Research expedition is the first to include women. Jennie Darlington and Edith 'Jackie' Ronne are also the first women to overwinter, hunkering down with the men in a small station on Stonington Island. Jackie, Antarctica's so-called First Lady, would later return there many times as a fêted lecturer on the cruise ships and as a special guest of the US for its flight in 1971 to commemorate the 60th anniversary of Amundsen's successful expedition.

1948 • 1 NOVEMBER Ealing Studios releases *Scott of the Antarctic* with John Mills in the title role. The film garners mixed reviews but receives a Royal Command Performance and boosts sales of Scott's journals.

1956 • 31 OCTOBER Humans once again set foot at the South Pole when a party led by Admiral George Dufek of the US Navy lands there for the first time. The aircraft, an R4D named *Que Sera Sera*, is piloted by Conrad Shinn. Over the course of the summer a base is constructed at the South Pole as the focus of the US Navy's military-scientific Operation Deep Freeze. Under the leadership of Paul Siple and naval officer John Tuck, 18 men become the first to overwinter at the South Pole. Since the winter conditions there had never been measured, the station is built partially underground to protect it from the worst imaginable weather.

1957 • 23 JANUARY An official dedication ceremony for the South Pole is held at McMurdo with speeches and a radio broadcast from President Eisenhower. The Amundsen–Scott South Pole Station – as it would be named in honour of the pioneers – has now been rebuilt, demolished, expanded and upgraded over the years. Despite the difficulties of life at the South Pole the station has been continuously staffed by research and support personnel since 1956.

1957 The International Council of Scientific Unions begins a series of global activities from July 1957 to December 1958, named the International Geophysical Year (IGY). In Antarctica, 12 nations, including the USA, the Soviet Union and Britain, conduct major investigations into the polar ice sheet and the upper atmosphere. In all, scientists from nearly 70 countries are involved. The Soviet Union begins construction of Vostok Station, and other bases are established on the continent's inhospitable coasts. The success of IGY persuades all parties that territorial conflicts have to be resolved in favour of international collaboration and that scientific work should continue.

1957 • 18 SEPTEMBER In the depths of the austral winter, temperatures at the South Pole drop to minus 77.2 degrees C, the coldest ever recorded on Earth up to then. Siple and his men become the first people in history to witness sunset and sunrise at the South Pole, events that are separated in Antarctica by six months of darkness and this unrelenting, unimaginable cold.

1957 • 15 OCTOBER The first commercial flight is made to the Antarctic continent. The two hostesses, Ruth Kelley and Pat Heppinstall, become the first women to visit an American Antarctic base.

1958 • 4 JANUARY The hero of Everest, Sir Edmund Hillary, becomes the first since the Amundsen and Scott teams to reach the South Pole overland. He makes his dash there at the head of a convoy of converted tractors, having laid a series of supply depots for the Commonwealth Trans-Antarctic Expedition. Vivian Fuchs, its redoubtable leader, arrives at the South Pole on 20 January, having made a pioneering journey by sno-cats from the shores of the Weddell Sea. Fuchs's team would continue and complete the first overland crossing of the continent by reaching the Ross Sea on 2 March, thus achieving Shackleton's dream.

1959 • 1 DECEMBER Following weeks of intensive negotiation the Antarctic Treaty is formally signed by the 12 leading nations that had participated in the IGY, and it comes into force in June 1961. The treaty is framed as an agreement so the continent 'shall continue forever to be used exclusively for peaceful purposes'. Key provisions include: the importance of scientific research, the need for international cooperation, the banning of all forms of military activity and nuclear testing, and the suspension of all sovereignty disputes for the duration of the treaty.

1961 • 14 MARCH The first recorded birth at the South Pole: Pandora the hamster produces twins.

1969 • 12 NOVEMBER Women are included for the first time in the United States Antarctic Program's field research and, accompanied by Rear Admiral Welch, they arrive by aircraft at the South Pole for a photo opportunity. Six women were bundled onto the flight amid some not inconsiderable media hype, including geologist Lois Jones, biologist Pam Young, and a reporter for a Detroit newspaper, Jean Pearson. Arms linked together, they all jumped off the aircraft cargo ramp at the same time, walked round the South Pole and posed for pictures. After a spot of lunch with the men stationed there, and a few more shots before the cameras, they promptly flew back to McMurdo.

1975 • 9 JANUARY After many seasons of construction, politicians, scientists and support crews gather at the South Pole as the American National Science Foundation opens its new Amundsen–Scott Station: a novel geodesic steel-arched dome built on the surface of the ice sheet, within which a clutch of prefabricated buildings and scientific laboratories shelter.

1979 A challenging book that changed everything in the narrative history of the South Pole – Roland Huntford's biography *Scott and Amundsen* unglamorously debunks the British hero. It is a good novel, in parts beautifully written; yet it is a poor history. In 1985 the work is adapted for television by Trevor Griffiths as *The Last Place on Earth* and Captain Scott's reputation takes a further nosedive.

1980 • 20 MAY The Antarctic Treaty parties sign the Convention for the Conservation of Antarctic Marine Living Resources, the first time that fishing activities have been brought under regulation, although attempts flounder in the first few years amid disagreements. In 1986 the International Whaling Commission agree a moratorium on commercial hunting in the Southern Ocean, but Japan continues to hunt and other pro-whaling nations try to overturn the legislation.

In recent years pressure groups such as Greenpeace and Sea Shepherd have entered the fray. The political and resource management of the Antarctic has become a global issue.

1980 • 15 DECEMBER British adventurer Sir Ranulph Fiennes, with companions Charlie Burton and Oliver Shepard, reach the South Pole using motorized skidoos. After staying a while there, and enjoying an impromptu game of cricket, they continue their journey. They successfully descend the Scott Glacier and arrive at Scott Base on 11 January, completing a traverse of the continent. This is just one part of the legendary Transglobe Expedition, the first circumnavigation of the Earth from North Pole to South Pole.

1985 British Antarctic Survey scientists at Halley and Rothera bases publish research that details the depletion of the ozone layer (which helps filter the Sun's ultra-violet radiation). Later, NASA scientists confirm that the whole of the Antarctic is affected by pollution from the industrialized countries, particular those in the northern hemisphere. The discovery of this 'ozone hole' leads to a new view of Antarctica, as a place where, despite its remoteness, human activity elsewhere threatens its existence.

1987 The runway at Patriot Hills is opened for the use of private flights. It soon becomes a major logistical hub for air travel in Antarctica.

1989 • 17 JANUARY As part of an intrepid skidoo cavalcade, Shirley Metz and Victoria Murden become the first women to reach the South Pole travelling overland.

1989 • 11 DECEMBER An international party led by American Will Steger arrives at the South Pole having travelled overland with dogs from the Larsen Ice Shelf. The party continues on to Russian research base Mirnyy, to complete a full crossing of the continent, a journey of some 3,741 miles (6,020 kilometres).

1989 • 31 DECEMBER Although they do not begin their journey from the coast, Arved Fuchs and Reinhold Messner are the first to reach the South Pole overland without animal or motorized assistance, relying only on skis, the wind and a winning combination of skill and brute strength. They continue on to Scott Base to complete an impressive crossing.

1991 The Protocol on Environmental Protection finally leads to the banning of mining for at least 50 years. Signatories agree to commit themselves to the environmental protection of the Antarctic through comprehensive impact assessments on their activities, including scientific bases and operations. The recognition is explicit – that we all have a duty, on behalf of a global community, to ensure that activities here do not harm the Antarctic.

Above: The New Fortuna Glacier on South Georgia, taken by Frank Hurley during Shackleton's *Endurance* voyage.

1993 • 7 JANUARY Norwegian extreme adventurer Erling Kagge reaches the South Pole having made the first solo and unsupported journey from Berkner Island. He chooses to have no radio contact to the outside world for the duration of his expedition.

1993 • 16 JANUARY Sir Ranulph Fiennes and Michael Stroud arrive at the South Pole during the course of their epic adventure to cross to the Ross Ice Shelf. Fiennes becomes the first man to have travelled overland to the South Pole twice.

1994 • 8 FEBRUARY The first Internet connection is established at the South Pole, via satellite link. The first message to the outside world is a simple one: 'Hello There!!'

1994 • 22 FEBRUARY Fearing the impact of dogs on the wildlife native to Antarctic coasts, a new clause is inserted in the Antarctic Treaty outlawing these animals. Ninety-six years after they were first used here, on the *Southern Cross* expedition, the last dogs finally leave Scott Base. Bjorn, Herbie, Monty, Footrots and Nimrod board a plane bound for New Zealand.

1994 • 24 DECEMBER Impressive Norwegian Liv Arnesen becomes the first woman to ski to the South Pole alone.

1996 • 19 DECEMBER Norwegian extreme adventurer veteran Børge Ousland reaches the South Pole overland from Berkner Island. He continues on to McMurdo, to achieve the first solo complete unsupported crossing of the continent.

1999 More than 150,000 visitors attend the brilliant polar exhibition at the New York Natural History Museum, spark-

ing a revival of interest in the 'heroic age' of Antarctic exploration, and in the adventures of Shackleton in particular.

2001 Polar scientists show that Scott's team faced unusually bad weather on their return from the South Pole, as Scott himself had argued in his last message.

2004 • 23 DECEMBER American guide Matty McNair becomes the first woman to reach the South Pole and then complete a return journey overland. Taking her children with her, she uses parasail kites to drag them all back across the ice.

2006 Adventurer Bruce Parry recreates the Scott and Amundsen race in a six-part series for the BBC. His British team are soundly beaten by their Norwegian counterparts in a trek across the Greenland icecap. A number of English adventure tourists continue to undertake last-degree treks to the South Pole itself, making grand claims about their experiences in the process, yet they are almost always bested by the Scandinavians.

2008 • 12 JANUARY Dignitaries and government officials are specially flown in to the South Pole for the official dedication ceremony of the new elevated station. It is a huge two-storey building, raised up on adjustable columns to prevent it from being buried by the drifting snows.

2010 Last days of the Old Pole, the first station of 1957. Long abandoned and surrendered to winter blizzards, it lies buried under 100 feet (30 metres) of snow, presenting a danger to vehicles moving about the extended South Pole site. Over three days in early December holes are drilled down to its wooden roof and it is packed with dynamite. With the press of a button a relic of the past is demolished, blasting a shower of snow sky-high. Now both earlier stations are gone and only the elevated station remains. During the summer season the population here swells to more than 200, reflecting the logistical support needed for the ever-increasing range and diversity of research taking place there. In the winter just a few dozen overwinterers are left to keep the station functional through the long months of Antarctic night. Rising up from the polar plateau, these industrial space-cabins are a radical departure from Amundsen's pyramidal tent, the first manmade structure erected here one hundred winters ago.

SOURCES

Roald Amundsen, *The South Pole* (London: John Murray, 1912)

Liv Arnesen and Ann Bancroft, *No Horizon is so Far: Two Women and their Extraordinary Journey Across Antarctica* (Cambridge: Da Capo Press, 2003)

Louis Bernacci, *To the South Polar Regions* (London: Hurst, 1901)

Tor Bomann-Larsen, *Roald Amundsen* (Stroud: Sutton Publishing, 2006)

Anthony Brandt, *The South Pole: A Historical Reader* (Washington: National Geographic Adventure Classics, 2004)

Rudmose Brown and William Spiers Bruce, *The Voyage of the Scotia* (Edinburgh: Blackwood, 1906)

Richard Byrd, *Little America: Aerial Exploration in the Antarctic, The Flight to the South Pole* (New York: Putnam's, 1930)

Apsley Cherry-Garrard, *The Worst Journey in the World* (London: Constable, 1922)

Frederick Cook, *Through the First Antarctic Night 1898–1899* (London: William Heinemann, 1900)

James Cook, *Three Voyages of Captain James Cook* (London: William Smith, 1842)

David Crane, *Scott of the Antarctic* (London: Harper Collins, 2005)

Erich von Drygalski, *The Southern Ice-Continent. The German South Polar Expedition* (Cambridge: Bluntisham Books, 1989)

Jules D'Urville, *An Account in Two Volumes of Two Voyages to the South Seas by Captain (later Rear-Admiral) Jules S-C Dumont D'Urville* (Melbourne: Melbourne University Press, 1987)

Ranulph Fiennes, *Captain Scott* (London: Hodder and Stoughton, 2003)

Ranulph Fiennes, *Mind over Matter: The Epic Crossing of the Antarctic Continent* (London: Sinclair-Stevenson, 1993)

James and Margery Fisher, *Shackleton* (London: Barrie Books, 1957)

Vivian Fuchs and Edmund Hillary, *The Crossing of Antarctica: The Commonwealth Trans-Antarctic Expedition 1955–58* (London: Cassell, 1958)

John Giaever, *The White Desert* (London: Chatto and Windus, 1954)

Hermann Gran, *The Norwegian with Scott: Tryggve Gran's Antarctic Diary 1910–1913* (London: National Maritime Museum, 1984)

Tom Griffiths, *Slicing the Silence* (Sydney: University of New South Wales Press, 2007)

Alan Gurney, *Below the Convergence: Voyages towards Antarctica 1699–1839* (London: Pimlico, 1998)

Alan Gurney, *The Race to the White Continent: Voyages to the Antarctic* (New York: Norton, 2000)

Edmond Halley, *The Three Voyages of Edmond Halley in the Paramore* (London: Hakluyt Society, 1981)

Wally Herbert, *A World of Men: Exploration in Antarctica* (London: Eyre and Spottiswoode, 1968)

Wally Herbert, *The Polar World* (London: Polarworld, 2007)

Meredith Hooper, *The Longest Winter: Scott's Other Heroes* (London: John Murray, 2010)

Roland Huntford, *The Last Place on Earth* (London: Abacus, 2000)

Nicholas Johnson, *Big Dead Place: Inside the Strange and Menacing World of Antarctica* (Los Angeles: Feral House, 2005)

Max Jones, ed., *Robert Falcon Scott Journals: Scott's Last Expedition* (Oxford: Oxford University Press, 2005)

Max Jones, *The Last Great Quest: Captain Scott's Antarctic Sacrifice* (Oxford: Oxford University Press, 2003)

Erling Kagge, *Alene til Sydpolen* (Oslo: Cappelen, 1993)

Harry King, *The Antarctic* (London: Blandford Press, 1969)

Geir O. Klover, ed., *The Roald Amundsen Diaries: The South Pole Expedition 1910–12* (Oslo: The Fram Museum, 2010)

John Langone, *Life at the Bottom: The People of Antarctica* (Boston: Brown, 1977)

Huw Lewis-Jones, *Face to Face: Polar Portraits* (London: Conway and Polarworld, 2009)

George Lowe, *Because It Is There* (London: Cassell, 1959)

Bill Manhire, *The Wide White Page: Writers Imagine Antarctica* (Wellington: Victoria University Press, 2004)

Douglas Mawson, *The Home of the Blizzard* (London: William Heinemann, 1915)

Douglas McKenzie, *Opposite Poles* (London: Hale, 1963)

Edwin Mickleburgh, *Beyond the Frozen Sea: Visions of Antarctica* (London: Bodley Head, 1987)

Hugh Robert Mill, *The Life of Sir Ernest Shackleton* (London: William Heinemann, 1933)

Benjamin Morrell, *A Narrative of Four Voyages* (New York: Harper, 1832)

Joan Myers, *Wondrous Cold: An Antarctic Journey* (Washington: Smithsonian Books, 2006)

Otto Nordenskjold, *Antarctica: Two Years Amongst the Ice of the South Pole* (London: Hurst and Blackett, 1905)

Børge Ousland, *Alone Across Antarctica* (Oslo: Boksenteret, 1997)

James Croxall Palmer, *Thulia: A Tale of the Antarctic* (New York: Colman, 1843)

Herbert Ponting, *The Great White South*
(London: Duckworth, 1921)

Stephen J. Pyne, *The Ice: A Journey to Antarctica* (Washington: University of Washington Press, 1998)

Beau Riffenburgh, *Nimrod* (London: Bloomsbury, 2004)

Lesley Carol Roberts, *The Entire Earth and Sky: Views on Antarctica* (Lincoln: University of Nebraska Press, 2008)

James Clark Ross, *A Voyage of Discovery and Research in the Southern and Antarctic Regions* (London: John Murray, 1847)

Jeff Rubin, *Antarctica* (Melbourne: Lonely Planet Publications, 2000)

Robert Falcon Scott, *The Voyage of the Discovery* (London: Smith, Elder, 1905)

Robert Falcon Scott, *Scott's Last Expedition* (London: John Murray, 1923)

George Seaver, *Edward Wilson of the Antarctic* (London: John Murray, 1935)

Ernest Shackleton, *The Heart of the Antarctic* (London: William Heinemann, 1909)

Ernest Shackleton, *South: The Story of Shackleton's 1914–1917 Expedition* (London: Heinemann, 1919)

Nobu Shirase, tr. Hilary Shibata, *Nankyokuki* (Tokyo: Tanken Koenkai, 1913)

Susan Soloman, *The Coldest March: Scott's Fatal Antarctic Expedition* (Carlton: Melbourne University Press, 2001)

Francis Spufford, *I May be Some Time* (London: Faber and Faber, 1996)

Will Steger and Jon Bowermaster, *Crossing Antarctica*, (London: Bantam Press, 1992)

James Weddell, *A Voyage towards the South Pole* (London: Longman, 1825)

Edward Wilson, *Diary of the Discovery Expedition to the Antarctic 1901–1904* (London: Blandford Press, 1966)

Edward Wilson, *Diary of the Terra Nova Expedition to the Antarctic 1910–1912* (London: Blandford Press, 1972)

Frank Worsley, *Endurance: An Epic of Polar Adventure* (London: Allan, 1931)

ARCHIVAL COLLECTIONS

National Archives, Kew; National Library of Australia; National Library of Norway; Royal Geographical Society; State Library of Victoria; Scott Polar Research Institute; University of Cambridge Library

CONTRIBUTORS

AUTHOR BIOGRAPHIES

DR HUW LEWIS-JONES is a historian and editor from the University of Cambridge, formerly Curator at the Scott Polar Research Institute and the National Maritime Museum. Huw writes and lectures widely about exploration and the visual arts. The first book in his acclaimed *Face to Face* photography series, *Polar Portraits*, was released in 2009 and has been published in numerous foreign languages. He recently completed *Arctic*, which he wrote with adventurer Bruce Parry, to accompany the popular BBC television series.

KARI HERBERT is an author and photographer, the daughter of the renowned polar explorer Sir Wally Herbert. Kari's most recent book *Heart of the Hero*, describes the remarkable lives of the wives of the famous polar travellers. Kari and Huw now run the indie publisher Polarworld. They live close to the sea in Cornwall.

OUR MODERN CONTRIBUTORS

JASON ANTHONY worked in Antarctica from 1994 to 2004. An award-winning author, his Antarctic essays have been published in *Orion*, *VQR* and *The Best American Travel Writing*, among others, and commended as one of *The Best American Essays* in 2006. His first book, *Hoosh: Roast Penguin, Scurvy Day and Other Stories of Antarctic Cuisine*, is due out soon from University of Nebraska Press.

LIV ARNESEN is a Norwegian skier, adventurer and motivational speaker. In 1994 she made international headlines by becoming the first woman to ski solo and unsupported to the South Pole, travelling some 745 miles (1,200 kilometres) over 50 days on the ice. In 2001, with fellow explorer Ann Bancroft, they became the first women in history to cross Antarctica's landmass.

JON BOWERMASTER is a six-time grantee of the National Geographic Expeditions Council and an award-winning writer and filmmaker. His adventures and reporting have taken him around the world several times, including more than 20 visits to Antarctica. He co-authored *Crossing Antarctica* with polar explorer Will Steger in 1990, and in 2009 he produced 'Terra Antarctica', a documentary film about the Antarctic Peninsula, which his team travelled by sailboat, foot, small plane and sea kayak. For the past decade his focus has been on the health of the world's oceans and man's relationship with them.

SIR RANULPH FIENNES is described as 'the world's greatest living explorer' by the *Guinness Book of Records*, and his achievements prove this is no exaggeration. He was the first man to reach both poles by surface travel and to cross the Antarctic continent unsupported. He is the only person yet to have been awarded two clasps to the Polar Medal for both the Antarctic and the Arctic Regions. Fiennes has led more than 30 expeditions, including the first polar circumnavigation of the Earth, and in May 2009 he successfully reached the summit of Mount Everest.

FERGUS FLEMING was educated at Oxford University and trained as a barrister before working as a furniture-maker and editor. He is one of Britain's leading popular historians and the author of six acclaimed histories of exploration: *Barrow's Boys*, *Killing Dragons*, *Ninety Degrees North*, *The Sword and the Cross*, *Cassell's Tales of Endurance*, and most recently *The Explorer's Eye*. He is a Fellow of the Royal Geographical Society and lives near Gloucester.

PROFESSOR TOM GRIFFITHS teaches history and the environment at the Australian National University, Canberra. Tom's books and essays have won prizes in history, science, literature, politics and journalism. His most recent monograph, *Slicing the Silence: Voyaging to Antarctica* won the 2007 Queensland Premier's and the 2008 NSW Premier's awards for non-fiction and was the joint winner of the Prime Minister's Prize for Australian History in 2008.

SIR WALLY HERBERT was a pioneering explorer and an award-winning writer and artist. During the course of his polar career, Sir Wally travelled with dog teams and open boats well over 25,000 miles (40,000 kilometres) – more than half of that distance through previously unexplored areas. During his five years in the Antarctic he mapped on foot some 45,000 square miles (116,000 square kilometres) of new country, and is most famously remembered as the leader of the first expedition to cross the Arctic Ocean from Alaska to Spitsbergen via the North Pole.

TIM JARVIS is an environmental scientist, author and adventurer. He has undertaken unsupported expeditions in both polar regions. He is the author of two books, *The Unforgiving Minute* and *Mawson: Life and Death in Antarctica*, the latter based on the award-winning international documentary film of the same name, supported by the United Nations Environment Programme in 2009. His most recent expedition involved a successful retracing of Douglas Mawson's survival journey using the same clothing, equipment and starvation rations as the famous explorer. Tim's next expedition will be to retrace Ernest Shackleton's 'double' – sailing a replica *James Caird* boat across the Southern Ocean from Elephant Island to South Georgia and then climbing over South Georgia's mountains.

NICHOLAS JOHNSON has worked as a fish-cannery cleaner in the Aleutian Islands, an office manager at a software company, a sales clerk at Banana Republic, a taxi driver in Seattle, an English teacher in South Korea, a valet at the International House of Pancakes, a warehouseman in Iraq, a contract manager in Afghanistan, and as a celebrity gossip columnist for a porn mogul. He has also worked six summers and three winters in Antarctica, including a year at the South Pole. He is the author of the book *Big Dead Place: Inside the Strange and Menacing World of Antarctica* and editor of the website bigdeadplace.com.

ERLING KAGGE was the first in history to walk alone to the South Pole, and the first to reach the North Pole, the South Pole and the summit of Everest. He has sailed across the Atlantic, around Cape Horn, to the Antarctic and the Galapagos Islands. Most recently Kagge crossed New York City via its train, subway, water and sewage tunnels, living underground and only getting to the surface to change tunnels. Kagge has a law degree from the University of Oslo and has studied philosophy at the University of Cambridge.

EDWIN MICKLEBURGH studied painting before becoming a film-maker and photographer. He has travelled widely in Africa, South American, the Himalayas, Greenland and the Canadian Arctic, but it is Antarctica that has exercised a special attraction for him for over 40 years. A member of the British Antarctic Survey, his award-winning book *Beyond the Frozen Sea* detailed some of his experiences on this remarkable continent.

JOAN MYERS has spent a lifetime exploring and photographing. From her early work with a view camera in black and white, printed in platinum, through her recent colour digital work in Antarctica, she has concentrated on human interaction with the landscape. Her book *Wondrous Cold: An Antarctic Journey* was published by Smithsonian Press in 2006, and a travelling exhibition opened at the Natural History Museum in Washington, DC, the same year, which toured for four years.

BØRGE OUSLAND is a renowned explorer, writer and film-maker, and perhaps the world's leading polar traveller. A national hero in Norway, he is widely admired not only for his achievements in exploration but also for the core values he promotes: humility, meticulous planning, self reliance and an appreciation of the natural world. After working as a North Sea diver and training with the Norwegian special naval forces, Ousland's first major polar adventure was a crossing of Greenland in 1986. He made the first unsupported trek to the North Pole in 1990, doing it again solo and unsupported in 1994 in just 52 days. In 1997 he completed the first unsupported solo crossing of Antarctica, an epic journey of 1,768 miles (2,845 kilometres) in 64 days, experiencing temperatures as low as minus 56 degrees C (minus 69 degrees F). In 2001 Ousland made the first solo crossing of the Arctic Ocean, from Siberia to Canada via the North Pole and in 2006 he reached the North Pole with fellow epic adventurer Mike Horn, this time becoming the first to dare the trek solely in the 24-hour darkness and intense cold of the polar night.

PROFESSOR STEPHEN PYNE teaches at Arizona State University and is the author of numerous books about fire and on exploration as a cultural activity. A National Endowment for the Humanities fellowship sent him south for the 1981–1982 field season, which resulted in the best-seller *The Ice: A Journey to Antarctica*.

LESLIE CAROL ROBERTS is the author of *The Entire Earth and Sky: Views on Antarctica*. She first went to Antarctica with Greenpeace and has spent more than four months there. As a Fulbright Fellow, she has researched the lives of the polar explorers, combing archives in four countries. She is writing a play about Frank Worsley's life and a novel based in Antarctica.

JEFF RUBIN is author of Lonely Planet's best-selling guidebook to Antarctica, first published in 1996 and now in its fourth edition. He first visited Antarctica in 1987 and has returned dozens of times as a journalist and as a lecturer and guide. He served for more than a decade as the Antarctic editor of *The Polar Times*, the magazine of the American Polar Society, originating its 'Due South' column. One of his primary research interests now is early Antarctic history.

EIRIK SØNNELAND was the expedition leader of the first wintering at the Norwegian Antarctic research station Troll in Queen Maud Land, from 1999 to 2001, which was the first Norwegian wintering on the continent in 40 years. He was just 24 years old. During the winter, Sønneland and his three teammates Rolf Bae (expert expeditioner), Frode Nedrebø (technician) and Gunnar Børre Thoresen (medical doctor) prepared the station for the next year's research expedition by installing water-treatment systems and communications, as well as contributing to medical and group psychology research. At the end of October 2000, Bae and Sønneland skied unsupported from Queen Maud Land via the South Pole to McMurdo Sound, some 2,360 miles (3,800 kilometres) over 105 days, performing what was then the longest unsupported ski trek in history.

WILL STEGER has been adventuring since he was 15, including first ascents in the Peruvian Andes, and dog-sledding more than 15,000 miles (24,000 kilometres) in the Arctic. In 1986 the American led an expedition to the North Pole without resupply, and later made a historic south-north journey across Greenland. In 1990 his team completed a 3,471-mile (5,586-kilometre) traverse of Antarctica, the first crossing of the continent by foot. He has written many books, including *North to the Pole* and *Saving the Earth*. In 1995, he was awarded the National Geographic Society's John Oliver La Gorce Medal for 'accomplishments in geographic exploration, in the sciences, and for public service to advance international understanding', and in 2007 he received the Lowell Thomas Award from the Explorers Club for his ongoing work on raising awareness of global warming.

DICK WOLAK has been part of a broad range of Antarctic operations since 1972 supporting field research at all the American stations, aboard the wooden research vessel *Hero*, in the McMurdo Dry Valleys, and as far afield as the Russian research station Vostok. He was the last leader of the original station at the South Pole, and after closing the base he stayed on to oversee the first winter in the newly completed geodesic dome. In recognition of his contribution to Antarctic exploration Wolak Peak was named for him in the Transantarctic Mountains.

Text copyright resides either with the writer or the estate of each extract. The editors and publishers acknowledge permission to reprint copyright material in this book and are grateful for the willingness of many people to contribute to this project. Every effort has been made to trace or contact all copyright holders. The publishers would be pleased to rectify any omissions brought to their notice at the earliest opportunity.

The book has benefited hugely from the kind support and expertise of many individuals. From archivists, private collectors and librarians through to veteran explorers and field scientists, all have generously shared their experiences. They are too numerous to list, but our thanks will be shown in other ways in the future. Closer to home, our particular gratitude to our mothers, Di Hilary Boyle, for her love and continual encouragement, and Lady Marie Herbert, polar traveller, author and teacher; both now super grandmothers. To little Nell, this one's for you.

PICTURE CREDITS

INDEX